T0363574

Justyn Walsh is a former corporate lawyer, investment banker and asset manager, and has worked in Africa, Asia, Australia, Europe and the Middle East. He is currently the chair of a financial technology company and sits on the advisory board of a venture capital firm, and is the author of *Investing with Keynes* (Black Inc., 2021). Now Sydney-based, he holds degrees in Law and Economics.

For Ada, Dan, Tom & Joe

EATING THE EARTH

Why we need
to change
the way we
do business
with nature

THE

EARTH

JUSTYN WALSH

UQP

First published 2023 by University of Queensland Press
PO Box 6042, St Lucia, Queensland 4067 Australia

University of Queensland Press (UQP) acknowledges the Traditional Owners and
their custodianship of the lands on which UQP operates. We pay our respects to their
Ancestors and their descendants, who continue cultural and spiritual connections to
Country. We recognise their valuable contributions to Australian and global society.

uqp.com.au
reception@uqp.com.au

Cover design by Christabella Designs
Cover image by Olekcii Mach / Alamy Stock Photo
Author photograph of Justyn Walsh by Jom Spencer
Typeset in 11.5/16 pt Adobe Garamond Pro Regular by Post Pre-press Group, Brisbane
Printed in Australia by McPherson's Printing Group

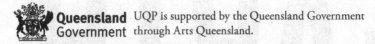 UQP is supported by the Queensland Government
through Arts Queensland.

 UQP is assisted by the Australian Government
through the Australia Council, its arts funding
and advisory body.

A catalogue record for this book is available from the National Library of Australia.

ISBN 978 0 7022 6613 3 (pbk)
ISBN 978 0 7022 6775 8 (epdf)
ISBN 978 0 7022 6776 5 (epub)

UQP uses papers that are natural, renewable and recyclable products made from
wood grown in well-managed forests and other controlled sources. The logging and
manufacturing processes conform to the environmental regulations of the country
of origin.

MIX
Paper | Supporting
responsible forestry
FSC® C001695

CONTENTS

EARTH

THE ELEMENTS

I meant no harm. I most truly did not.
But I had to grow bigger. So bigger I got.

Dr Seuss, *The Lorax*

PREFACE

In late July 2019 I flew into Paris Charles de Gaulle after a couple of days of business in the Middle East. The plane touched down in the early afternoon, and, on leaving the airconditioned decompression chamber that is the modern airport, it felt like I was still in mid-summer Dubai. The mercury had climbed to 37 degrees Celsius, just shy of 100 degrees Fahrenheit, the start of a three-day heatwave that climaxed with a record-breaking temperature of 42 degrees Celsius in the centre of Paris. Later that first afternoon, as I walked from my hotel to a meeting on the other side of the Seine, the ground shimmered like a desert mirage and those who had not already sought respite under a tree or by a fountain trudged along like sleepwalkers, visibly slowed by the clotted air. I met with executives from a French fashion house to discuss a possible supply partnership, and amid the ostentatious simplicity of their office, hung with the coming season's scarves and coats, I dripped beads of sweat, for this building was constructed for another time and another climate.

My journey to this place had been a roundabout one. I grew up in a one-pub town on the east coast of Australia, formerly a fishing and mining settlement that was on its way to becoming an Insta-worthy tourist destination. During school holidays I worked as a deckhand on a professional fishing boat and picked vegetables on the properties that studded the red volcanic soil of the hinterland. I was the first of my family to go to university, and after briefly flirting with marine biology as a possible vocation, I instead heeded the sober counsel of my elders and opted for law and economics. I was a corporate lawyer for a short period, but figured that if I was going to be working 15-hour days then I may as well become an investment banker, where at the very least I would be at the pointy end of deals. Leading the itinerant life of an international banker I saw much of the world – including time spent in the frontier economies of East Asia, sub-Saharan Africa and the former Soviet Union – and witnessed firsthand the impact of globalisation on our planet, marvelling at the transformative power of free markets but viewing other developments with an increasing sense of unease.

In the first decade of our new century I took some time off as a salaryman and wrote a book on John Maynard Keynes. Keynes had been the one glamorous figure in an otherwise arid university economics curriculum – he was a Cambridge don, key member of the Bloomsbury set, bestselling author, husband of a world-famous ballerina, valued government adviser, ennobled member of the House of Lords, midwife to the IMF and the World Bank, and the father of modern macroeconomics. Keynes delighted in assaulting conventional wisdom, deploying pungent prose as his weapon of choice, and in the depths of the 1930s Depression he argued that markets were not always the miraculously efficient and self-adjusting system venerated by classical economics. Orthodox economic thought, Keynes maintained, 'has ruled over us rather by hereditary right than by personal merit', and its policy prescriptions often confounded common sense. Rather than reprimand reality for failing to live up to the exacting standards of theory, Keynes instead developed an economic model that embraced, explained and attempted to remedy real-world imperfections.

Having written the book, and no longer with any other plausible alibi, I re-entered the world of suits. For a couple of years I shuttled between London and Moscow, helping to establish Russia's first large-scale private sector infrastructure fund. It was a time of buoyancy and hope in Russia, the country denounced less than two decades earlier as the epicentre of an Evil Empire and the mortal enemy of the West. I saw capitalism in its most brutal Darwinian incarnation, all red in tooth and claw – as I was advised early on, 'Never ask an oligarch how they made their first million'. These latter-day Robber Barons were being smoothed out and legitimised by us Westerners, butlers with briefcases, and had become increasingly fluent in the corporate language of shareholder value creation, social licence and win-win outcomes. The global financial crisis of 2008 hit Russia late, but hard – the stock market held up for a few weeks after the Lehman Brothers collapse in September, but by the end of the year the main index had fallen by around 70 per cent from levels only six months before. At the end of that year, with things looking shaky in Russia and our first child on the way, I decided that it was time to go home.

We returned to near where I had spent my high school years, living on a former dairy farm on what prior to European settlement had been part of 'the Big Scrub', a misleading and careless description, for this was once Australia's largest expanse of subtropical rainforest. White arrivals had only reached this part of the country in the 1880s, but by the turn of the twentieth century just 1 per cent of the original forest remained, pillaged first by cedar-getters and later cleared for farming. There was some remnant rainforest on our small piece of land – towering trees above a tangled understorey of plants and fallen wood, and from this patch would emerge trundling echidnas, huge carpet snakes and the occasional lolloping koala. Each morning a butcher bird would wake us with the same seven-note melody, and most evenings a mob of wallabies would come to graze on the pickings in front of the house. Although I never saw one, lyrebirds – shy, almost mythical, birds famed for their mimicry – were also reputed to be in the area. The troubadour songs of the male lyrebird, broadcast over the winter courtship months, sample the sounds of the forest around them – not only other birds and mammals, but more recent human intrusions such as chainsaws and even mobile phone ring tones, and I sometimes wondered if they also kept alive the calls of species now long gone from the region.

Family matters then obliged us to return to Sydney, and I became an investment banker once again. This time I focused on the food and agriculture sector, which suited me fine – up until I was at university, my grandparents had what I think of as the Platonic ideal of a farm, a mixed enterprise of livestock, crops, fruit trees, a vegetable garden, even a creek with rainbow trout and busy platypuses, and for me it was the most beautiful place on Earth. My new job entailed a move to the Middle East, that hydrocarbon-rich but carbohydrate-poor part of the world, where I talked to sovereign wealth funds and other large institutions about investing in Australian farmland and food businesses. Interest was strong – the Arab Spring, triggered in part by rapidly escalating food prices, was still fresh in the minds of these parties, and they were looking for alternative ways to improve food security and price stability for their fellow citizens. Armed with capital, I then searched for companies in Australia that might have an appetite for external investment, and came across an organic food company that had a problem most businesses would kill for – not enough supply to meet ballooning consumer demand.

I liked the company and the management so much that I joined them. Australia has more organically certified land than any other country, and this company was one of the world's largest organic protein suppliers. While there I learned about alternative land management techniques, low-input practices for which consumers were increasingly willing to pay a premium – a somewhat more attractive hybrid model that melded the older ways of farming with the larger-scale methods that had spread across much of the globe. I spoke to people on the ground about soil health and its connection to animal health and human health, and started reading about climate change and other manmade impacts on the natural world. Up until that point, I sheepishly admit that climate change was for me what it is for many people – little more than background noise, a confusing arena of conflicting opinions and sometimes competing facts. I had compared it in my mind to the Y2K bug, that millennial panic when some predicted that planes would fall from the sky and critical infrastructure buckle as computers clicked over from 1999 to 2000 – a space seemingly inhabited by Doomsday preppers and boffins fixated on their own narrow area of interest. But as I reviewed the dispassionate scientific articles, increasingly reading like obituaries foretold as the grey areas of uncertainty evaporated, it was clear to me that this thing was real.

Informed by what I had learned at the organic food company, I then founded a regenerative farmland fund in partnership with the scion of one of Australia's leading farming families. He shared my conviction that food and fibre could be produced in a sustainable way, and that farms did not have to kill everything other than the particular monocultured crop or animal in order to prosper. In 2018, in the early stages of the fund, I was invited along with a number of others to join some of the world's pre-eminent marine and climate scientists for a few days at the Heron Island Research Station, located on a coral cay at the southern end of the Great Barrier Reef. Although Heron had escaped the worst of the mass bleaching events over the preceding two years, patches of skeletal white scarred the surrounding waters, and our hosts explained that due to human-caused factors most of the reef was expected to be barren within 30 years. The realisation that this sprawling natural wonder, reliably pulsing with life and colour for many thousands of years, now had an expected end date far less than an average human lifespan was for me a monumental wake-up call.

Just over a year after the Heron Island trip, the Great Pandemic of 2020 – ironically, perhaps caused in part by the land-clearing and intensive farming practices that we sought to challenge – cruelled the fund, as our offshore backers could not travel to the hermit kingdom that was Australia over those Plague Years. During this fallow period, and spurred on by what had been brought home to me at Heron, I started working on what would become *Eating the Earth*, but its genesis goes all the way back to my time in Byron Bay when I was a new dad. The initial working title was *Seven Billion Astronauts* – in galling testimony to my leisurely writing pace, a net one billion or so individuals have peopled the planet since I first started working on the manuscript – and for the last decade I have been thinking about how we got to this place of tremendous material abundance but plummeting natural wealth, and how a new path forward might be charted.

Working on this book, I came to the conclusion that pretty much everything is story, and that the dominant story of our modern age – industrial capitalism – is in many respects a self-serving one, enriching a select cohort of the world's community while impoverishing those at the base of the global socioeconomic pyramid, future generations, and the natural world. As Karl Marx noted in the early days of the Industrial Revolution, 'the ideas of the ruling class in every epoch are the ruling ideas', and our storytellers-in-chief are those who benefit most from the current system. The form capitalism takes depends on what we define as 'capital', and to date the focus has been on manufactured capital – which together with human labour produces goods and services, typically using inputs prised from the Earth at no recorded cost other than the expense of extraction – rather than natural capital. In consequence, there is a nature-sized hole at the heart of mainstream economic theory – one that fails to properly value the natural world and account for its life-giving benefits, let alone its sheer grandeur.

Economics is, at its simplest, the study of limits, and at the time of capitalism's birth manmade capital was the constraining factor, with the gifts of nature assumed to be boundless. But the explosive, superhuman energy bestowed by fossil fuels – powering bulldozers, excavators, industrial fishing boats and the like, and silting our atmosphere and oceans with greenhouse gases and other forms of pollution – has flipped these relative scarcities. At an ever-accelerating pace since the Industrial Revolution, Western lifestyles have been underwritten by a type of planetary Ponzi scheme – one in which the withdrawals from the natural world are not supported by underlying capital replenishment. In what amounts to the global equivalent of selling the furniture to pay the rent, we are destroying our natural capital and calling it 'income' while failing to account for the corresponding decline in underlying wealth. We have been consuming as if, quite literally, there's no tomorrow, and many of Earth's life support systems now themselves need to be placed on life support.

Our overexploitation of the natural world is altering the climate, but this may not even be the biggest problem confronting twenty-first century society. Other roadkill from the capitalist locomotive – such as biodiversity loss and ocean acidification – is equally troubling, although the smoking gun of greenhouse gas emissions is usually somewhere in the background. Just as everything is story, so too everything is connected, and to navigate a possible way out of this predicament we must first understand the complex and interlinked territory to be traversed. A systems view that considers both the parts and how they interact is required, and to reflect these interdependencies I have structured the book in five sections, as follows:

Fire examines the rise of industrial capitalism from the late eighteenth century to its position today as the world's dominant faith. Powered by fossil fuels, capitalism has transformed immensely over this period, but it is still anchored to a past in which human-made capital was scarce and natural capital plentiful. The result of this outdated legacy is an economic system in which exponentially increasing production and consumption remains the chief metric of success while the damage inflicted on the natural world is largely uncounted, giving the appearance of wealth being created when in fact much of it is being destroyed.

Air looks at the phenomenon of global heating, caused by the transfer of astounding quantities of carbon from the Earth's crust to the atmosphere over the last two centuries, with scientists issuing increasingly urgent warnings about the intensifying climate crisis. Imposing a tax on greenhouse gas emissions to reflect the social costs of pollution is an obvious first fix, but this move has been vigorously repulsed by powerful entities acting in their own interests – initially through campaigns of outright denial, and more recently by subtler stratagems. Instead, other 'carbon market' mechanisms – which give the illusion of progress without always making real progress – have been proffered as an alternative.

Water considers the impacts of human activity on the Earth's aquatic environments, with a focus on the ocean – the true lungs of the world and a vital climate regulator. I examine biodiversity loss arising from both climate change and excessive resource exploitation, and suggest that the destruction of living carbon in the form of organisms may be an even greater problem than the burning of dead carbon in the form of fossil fuels. I also argue that the intricacies of some natural systems may defeat market-based solutions, and that other forms of governance can often better address certain collective action problems.

Earth focuses on agriculture, humankind's first Anthropocene endeavour, the founding revolution that spun us to where we are now. Although fossil fuelled intensive agriculture has delivered huge productivity improvements over the last century, food and fibre production is one of the main contributors to climate change and biodiversity loss, and will also be one of the principal casualties of a heating world. Uniquely, however, agriculture can also be part of the solution by helping to rebalance our lopsided carbon ledger through land management techniques that not only recarbonise the soil but also improve planetary health and ultimately human health.

Lastly, in *The Elements* I venture an argument for a 'Capitalism 2.0' – a new story that perhaps can steer us away from an economic system that manufactures a multitude of wants only to satisfy them by incurring huge ecological debt. Because some of the flaws in our consumption-driven modern global economy are more than just glitches in the system, but in fact *is* the system, I suggest that to produce game-changing shifts we must first change the rules of the game. Not only would this involve top-down modifications – such as adjusting economic incentives so that private advantage better aligns with the public good – but it will also require behavioural changes in societies that have been conditioned to focus more on short-term value rather than longer-term values.

I still believe that capitalism – that perverse doctrine asserting that self-interested behaviour can produce benefits for society as a whole – is the best economic system yet devised for the crooked timber of humanity. At its best, it fosters co-operation rather than coercion, trading rather than raiding, and encourages innovation and technological advance. But our current economic model is no longer fit for purpose – and if we are to stop this asset-stripping of the natural world then we must reconsider how we do business with nature. I like to think that I'm as clear-eyed and realistic as anyone – the initial optimism kindled by the Paris meeting, for example, was ultimately thwarted by the profit-maximising pragmatism of the sustainability team's more commercially focused colleagues – but I have faith that a better system can evolve.

Humans cannot resist framing everything into a story, and there is a temptation to invoke ideas of blame and sin and retribution when we consider what has been wrought on Mother Nature during this Anthropocene age. But our story is far more nuanced than a simple morality tale about the hubris of humanity, and our globalised world has achieved amazing feats in the modern era – things that would have been considered magical only a century or two before. It has been my privilege to meet and work with some of the world's leading voices in areas such as climate change, ocean ecology and sustainable agriculture, and to learn from them that this is our tale, and that it's not too late for a plot twist. To honour our self-styled appellation of Homo sapiens we need to marshal our collective wisdom and invent a new ruling story – one that acknowledges that humankind is a part of nature rather than apart from nature, that measures how life is enriched rather than destroyed, and that lives off nature's dividends rather than eating into its capital.

FIRE

1

THE BIRTH OF EGO-NOMICS

Igniting fossil fuelled industrial capitalism

Independence Day

Humans are story-making animals. Our waking lives and our night-time dreams, our religion or our adamant atheism, the nation in which we live and the anthems sung in its name – all nothing but fables agreed upon, as Napoleon once described the victors' versions of history. Stories impose the illusion of order upon the chaos around, spinning a yarn through the bewildering labyrinth of life. They teach us lessons about how to behave now while allowing us to exercise our unique powers of imagination to confect a shining new future. Stories have incited armies to the battlefield, abetted the colonisation of distant lands, and inspired Herculean collective feats. And our stories become true in the telling, whether it be JFK standing before Congress with a vision to land a man on the Moon before the decade is out, or the more mundane example of money, pieces of paper or disembodied digits which only have value because we choose to believe that they have value.

One of our most pervasive and powerful stories, that of modern capitalism, can be dated quite precisely. The year 1776 is best known for that fateful morning on the fourth of July when the thirteen United States of America formally cut the colonial apron strings with their Declaration of Independence, citing man's 'unalienable Rights [to] Life, Liberty and the pursuit of Happiness' as grounds for divorce. But back over in Mother Britain an even more world-shaking text, written by an eccentric Scottish philosopher, was still warm from the printing presses. Adam Smith's *An Inquiry into the Nature and Causes of the Wealth of Nations*, published in London in March 1776, upended conventional morality by asserting that selfish private actions can lead to society-wide benefits. In Smith's paradoxical formulation, the road to worldly heaven was paved with less-than-noble intentions – the myriad manoeuvrings of self-interested individuals exercising their free will in free markets would generate a 'universal opulence which extends itself to the lowest ranks of people'.

Smith explained that this miracle was due to another of humanity's unique attributes – the 'propensity to truck, barter, and exchange'. As he quirkily commented in *The Wealth of Nations*, 'nobody ever saw a dog make a fair and deliberate exchange of one bone for another with another dog'. Only humans, Smith argued, enlist their fellow creatures' self-interest to strike a mutually advantageous bargain. 'It is not from the benevolence of the butcher, the brewer, or the baker that we expect our dinner,' he observed,

> but from their regard to their own interest. We address ourselves, not
> to their humanity, but to their self-love, and never talk to them of our
> own necessities, but of their advantages.

A corollary of this deal-making drive is specialisation, which 'encourages every man to apply himself to a particular occupation, and to cultivate and bring to perfection whatever talent or genius he may possess for that particular species of business'. Smith asserted that by focusing on a specific line of work, and then trading the surplus of production with others if there is a net benefit in so doing, a person will be 'led by an invisible hand to promote an end which was no part of his intention' – the enrichment of society overall.

By suggesting that free markets were some sort of philosopher's stone transmuting the base metal of 'self-love' into the gold of public virtues, *The Wealth of Nations* provided intellectual ballast to the loftier ideals floating in from across the Atlantic. Armed with Smith's arguments, liberty and the pursuit of happiness were not just worthy political lodestars for citizens of the new American republic – conveniently, letting each person follow their own particular compass in the quest for fulfilment would ultimately deliver improved living standards to the community as a whole. Independence and individual freedom of action were not only self-evident truths, as codified in Philadelphia on the fourth of July, but they would also lead all of us to the economic Promised Land.

But perhaps the real Independence Day, for the wider world at least, occurred a few months before the declaration by the American Founding Fathers. On 8 March 1776, just a day ahead of the publication of *The Wealth of Nations*, the inventor James Watt commercialised the world's first industrial steam engine, a machine designed to draw water from an underground coal mine in the English midlands. Prior to the Watt engine, power came almost entirely from renewable sources – water, wind, or the sun. Water drove the mills of river-huddled cotton 'manufactories'; wind turned blades and pushed ships across seas; and, most importantly, plant photosynthesis converted sunlight, water and air into food, which in turn fuelled both workers and beasts of burden. Watt's steam engine broke open the piggy bank of photosynthesis by using coal, mostly fossilised plant matter, as its energy source – and, for the first time in history, power was untethered from the whims of nature. Humankind, it seemed, had at last obtained independence from the natural world.

Stitched up

This Holy Trinity of 1776 – the elevation of individual sovereignty as a transcendent truth in the Declaration of Independence, the sanctification of selfishness in *The Wealth of Nations*, and the tremendous mechanical power unleashed by fossil fuels – would give us the foundation for the great story of our modern age. It is the tale of a continuous increase in material abundance for the majority of the planet's population, vastly longer lifespans and higher literacy rates, and a steady progression towards democratic rule. Over the near quarter of a millennium since that revolutionary year, the world's population has increased 10-fold while average living standards per person are estimated to have multiplied by the same order of magnitude. Put together, the total annual amount of goods and services produced now is more than one hundred times greater than in Adam Smith's day, and a chart of historical annual world economic output describes a rocket-like trajectory, inching away from the ground in the late eighteenth century, with the booster engines kicking in around 1950.

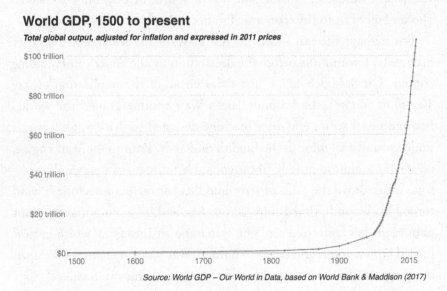

World GDP, 1500 to present

Total global output, adjusted for inflation and expressed in 2011 prices

Source: World GDP – Our World in Data, based on World Bank & Maddison (2017)

The period since the mid-twentieth century has been dubbed 'the Great Acceleration', a time during which huge swathes of the planet, especially in Asia, were dragged from subsistence or worse. Paralleling and propelling this lift-off has been the rise of capitalism as the world's dominant creed. Other than a few hold-outs like North Korea, every country has now embraced some permutation of 'capitalism' – which can be defined as an economic system in which the means of production are privately owned and individuals are guided by market signals in their search for profit. Even China – a Communist Party dictatorship and the best known standard-bearer, in name at least, for an alternative ideology – practises a form of 'state capitalism' in which almost two-thirds of all economic output is generated by the country's private sector. Seduced by the promise of material riches, these latecomers to the free enterprise party seem to have adopted the same pragmatic attitude to capitalism as Churchill's to democracy – that is, the worst system ever invented, except for all the others.

Capitalism, in its original incarnation as a double act inseparable from individual liberty, certainly delivers incontrovertible benefits. In addition to its matchless productivity, capitalism encourages decentralised decision-making and personal agency, efficiently winnows good business ideas from bad, and, in theory at least, promotes co-operation rather than compulsion. Although other fictions bolstering collaboration – such as granting corporations limited liability status and legal rights akin to humans – have been formally introduced from above from time to time, capitalism is essentially a bottom-up, self-organised network of billions of actors exchanging goods and services and information. And just as individuals specialise in a capitalist system, so too do nations – natural resources are distributed unevenly, climates differ, labour costs diverge, and each state will tend to focus on what it can most efficiently produce given these constraints. Countries have been successively annexed to the capitalist cause and, as a result of specialisation and exchange, supply webs of colossal productive power now cross borders and enmesh the entire world.

However as Adam Smith realised, an economic system predicated on self-interest needs to be restrained by countervailing forces if it is to beget a wide-ranging 'universal opulence' over the long run. The man press-ganged into the role of Father of Capitalism had no great fondness for what would later be called the capitalist class, noting that:

> People of the same trade seldom meet together, even for merriment and diversion, but the conversation ends in a conspiracy against the public, or in some contrivance to raise prices.

Only widespread competition – or the threat of competition – would, Smith argued, rein in Big Business, 'who have generally an interest to deceive and even to oppress the public' by 'raising their profits above what they naturally would be'. And an ecosystem of vigorously competing enterprises not only keeps prices and profits in check, but, as later economists would note, the contest of ideas and products in a free market also acts as a giant flywheel to the capitalist engine by driving innovation and incremental efficiencies.

Declaration of interdependence

Smith's celebration of competition also inaugurated the enduring tradition of economics and science trading stories. Charles Darwin's epiphany in the 1830s regarding evolution by natural selection – nature's own version of the invisible hand – was sparked by the economist Thomas Robert Malthus's *An Essay on the Principle of Population*, a grim book which asserted that demand from a rapidly growing human population would eventually exceed total food supply, resulting in a struggle for existence in which only the strongest and best adapted individuals would survive. In turn, Establishment interests later cherry-picked Darwin's insights and applied them in a crude form to the human sphere, arguing that a mercilessly competitive capitalist system simply reflected the natural state of things. Adam Smith's message had been comprehensively hijacked – competition switched from being a necessary counterweight to self-interest, and instead became an alibi for all manner of evils, from wealth inequality to racism to imperialism. In this brave new world of Social Darwinism, market economies increasingly mutated into market societies, accounting profit became the chief metric of success, and we moved from virtue being its own reward to reward being its own virtue.

In contrast to the bleak worldview later propounded by some of his disciples, Adam Smith's perspective was far more nuanced and uplifting. In *The Theory of Moral Sentiments* – Smith's first and, during his lifetime, more commercially successful book – he focused on another form of exchange within society, that of empathy and regard between fellow citizens. In the book's opening sentence, Smith observed that:

> How selfish soever man may be supposed, there are evidently some principles in his nature, which interest him in the fortune of others, and render their happiness necessary to him, though he derives nothing from it except the pleasure of seeing it.

Expressly rejecting the notion that humans are atomistic competitors driven by purely selfish desires, Smith recognised that we are fundamentally social creatures, that markets are a mere subset of society, and that their effective functioning depends on what we now call 'social capital' – that is, a shared sense of identity, norms and trust within a given community.

In broad terms, Smith argued that the exchange of goods and services within impersonal markets is motivated by self-interest, but in the wider social realm there were more altruistic factors at play. However, by formally validating selfishness as an operating principle in one part of society, Smith let the genie out of the bottle. The fellow-feeling identified in *The Theory of Moral Sentiments* is essentially an act of imagination, with Smith likening individual conscience to an 'impartial spectator' judging our actions in line with the views and opinions of others, which in turn influences and moderates our behaviour. But when the story we tell ourselves as a community shifts to the practical value of self-centredness and profit maximisation – when self-interest flips from sin to seemliness, when we can rationalise selfishness over group welfare – then we are liberated from the shackles of duty and expectation. Stories, when accepted, become future truths – and in consequence capitalism has become both a bridge and a barrier, uniting us in intricate networks spanning the globe while simultaneously fractioning humanity.

Adam Smith understood that a finely balanced interplay of self-interest and 'other-interest', of the individual and society, was essential for the creation of widespread wealth. Free markets work best when embedded in strong communities, but perversely the central tenet of modern capitalism – the clinical efficiency of masses of individuals following their own interests – erodes social capital over time. And capitalism also hollows out another important contributor to its success – the deferral of gratification, the ability to resist an immediately available reward in anticipation of obtaining something more valuable in the future. As some have noted, there is an inherent contradiction at the heart of the capitalist system – as producers, we are told stories about the value of hard work and self-restraint, but as consumers, we are urged to absorb the profusion of goods and services unspooling from the capitalist production line. The second narrative has ultimately triumphed, and we have become zealous converts to consumerism, shrugging off the Puritan peccadillos of thrift and temperance. The opium of the people, it sometimes seems, is no longer religion but shopping.

Capitalism's greatest strengths, then, are at the same time its most profound flaws. 'Allowing every man to pursue his interest in his own way', as Adam Smith put it, generates material plenty but has also frayed the social web, while this abundance has set aflame a wildfire of consumption. Our focus has shrunk from the community to the individual, our time horizons have contracted to the very near term, and our instinct to save for a rainy day has been defeated by a compulsion to spend. But the greatest failure of capitalism, exacerbated by these other faults, is its inability to properly value nature. Our prevailing economic model is now colliding with, and often eclipsing, the finite boundaries of the natural world. Freed from the old morality by the half-digested teachings of Adam Smith, and powered by fossil fuels, we are now undermining the very foundations of our wealth. Ultimately it is from the natural world that we draw our prosperity, and it is from the natural world that we must also find a new story.

2

REVOLUTIONARY ROADS

Humanity's fracture with the natural world

Overlords

Humankind's first rupture with the natural world occurred almost 12,000 years ago, at the dawn of the Holocene epoch, a Goldilocks period in which things were neither too hot nor too cold. In what may have been a response to changed climatic conditions, previously wandering bands of hunters and gatherers began farming in various places around the world – first in what has been called 'the Fertile Crescent', a wide stretch of land arching up from the Nile Valley into the Levant and down into the rich river plains of Mesopotamia, and soon after in locations as disparate as the Americas and East Asia. Agriculture domesticated humans as much as certain plants and animals, leading ultimately to what we call 'civilisation', replete with specialisations including a ruling class – initially priests and nobility, these days economists and businesspeople – telling their own self-justifying stories.

Many pre-agrarian communities had managed their landscapes through small-scale practices such as the controlled burning of grasslands and forest, but it was the Agricultural Revolution a dozen millennia ago that saw humankind's relationship with the natural world decisively pivot from one of co-operation to one of control. Rather than being constrained by the dictates of nature, settlers began to radically alter the non-human world to suit their needs, with huge projects such as land-clearing and the digging of irrigation channels set in train. Collaboration of this magnitude required not only decision-making hierarchies and sharply defined roles, but also increasingly sophisticated methods of state-based crowd control – laws, standing armies and fierce new patriarchal religions – to marshal and subdue manpower. The pyramids and ziggurats of the Fertile Crescent and the Americas, built to honour deities and despots, were only possible because of an underlying pyramid of power – one in which the labouring masses were squeezed from above by a parasitic elite, with wealth inequality widening as property ownership narrowed.

One of the defining features of these new agricultural societies was walls – to keep people and animals out or in, depending on their identity. The sedentary nature of farming communities, and their ability to store grain and corral livestock, allowed for the first time the accumulation of substantial quantities of goods. Not only did this lead to inequalities in material riches as property was appropriated and held by the proto–one percenters, but penned animals and silos fat with grain became tempting targets for nomadic raiders, and barricades were invariably built to repel the barbarians' periodic harvest of urban spoils. And, just as importantly, walls also kept flocks of people hemmed in place to be shorn by the stationary bandits of the overclass, with their commandments and taxes and power to compel labour. Islanded off from the rest of the world, 'nature' for these urban dwellers was an increasingly theoretical concept, separated by fences both visible and of the mind.

In these agricultural societies food production became the province of only a portion of the community, while a fortunate few sitting under the ruling class might work as bureaucrats, merchants or scribes. Mathematics and writing developed to record goods stored and their trade – the earliest written name identified so far was not a god or a great leader, but possibly a Sumerian beer baron dealing in barley around 5,000 years ago – and to facilitate this exchange money, and its shadow-partner debt, came into being. Humans increasingly trafficked in stories and abstractions – foundation myths, religious creeds, ideologies – while marks imprinted on to wet clay tablets gradually resolved into number systems and alphabets. The complexity of life was domesticated and distilled into symbols that confused models of reality for reality itself, and only labourers in the field tended to retain an unmediated connection with the natural world. Agrarian communities focused on just a handful of crops or animals, and became far less attentive to the eternal rhythms of the wider environment – the flow of animal migrations, the ripening of wild fruits, and the infinite interconnectedness of nature.

Despite markedly poorer and less diverse diets than free-range humans – and regular flare-ups of disease from high density co-living with fellow settlers, animals and opportunistic pests – farming populations grew rapidly. The ability to store food paved the way for wealth inequality and taxation, but it also provided valuable back-up supplies in lean years; like their captive livestock, women's value was increasingly based on their fertility, and birthrates exploded; and because intensive agriculture tended to exhaust the soil, there was a constant quest to exploit new territory and seize more manpower to work the fields. In the time since humanity's first revolution, the biblical command to subdue the Earth and exercise dominion over its creatures has been enthusiastically prosecuted by settled agrarian societies. As a result, agriculture has changed the face of the planet more than any other undertaking – so much so that today farmland occupies around half the planet's habitable area, with humans and their subject animals comprising an estimated 96 per cent of the world's total mass of mammals.

Unweaving the rainbow

Humanity's shifting relationship with the natural world – from one of partnership to one of dominance – was taken a step further with the Scientific Revolution, generally agreed to have begun in the mid-1500s with the publication of Nicolaus Copernicus's *On the Revolutions of the Heavenly Spheres*. Despite overturning the literally self-centred notion that the cosmos spun around Earth, Copernicus's heliocentric model heralded a new era of human hubris. Francis Bacon, the Saint Paul of the Scientific Age, declared half a century after Copernicus that *Scientia potentia est* – knowledge is power – and prophesied that the 'Empire of

Man over creation' would be secured through the application of reason and experimentation, which he likened to an Inquisition on the natural world. By drawing Mother Nature apart upon the Inquisitor's table of 'experimental philosophy' we could thereby control her, he claimed, and gain 'the power to conquer and subdue her, to shake her to her foundations', ultimately rendering the natural world the 'slave of mankind'.

In this ferment of rationalism and inquiry, in which stories now vigorously jousted in the arena of ideas, handed-down truths that had been jealously monopolised by royalty and religion began to be usurped. The Scientific Revolution was an almost entirely European phenomenon, fired by competition between warring countries on the fragmented continent, and often catalysed by dissident emigres who had challenged the received wisdom in their own countries. The Royal Society, based in London and the world's oldest existent academy of science, captured the spirit of the age with its motto *Nullius in verba* – take no-one's word for it. Scepticism was institutionalised, moving from heresy to orthodoxy, and ideas were subject to their own evolutionary forces – intermingling and adapting, exposed to empirical scrutiny, with only the fittest surviving. One belief system, that of the inviolable word of God filtered down to the unquestioning masses via His chosen representatives on Earth, was gradually thrown off and replaced by another religion – that of continuous material and intellectual progress arising from human ingenuity.

With the advent of the Scientific Revolution some Westerners moved from obeying God to playing God, and Isaac Newton – celebrated as the discoverer of 'the grand secret of the whole Machine' – was the culminating prophet of this new movement. In an astonishing burst of intellectual fertility, Newton cracked open many of nature's secrets by examining the smallest components in a system in order to understand the whole. His *Principia* became the new bible for the Age of Enlightenment, as world-changing for physics as *The Wealth of Nations* would be for economics just under a century later. Although the Law of Universal Gravitation set out in the *Principia* asserted that each particle of matter attracts every other particle in proportion to its mass and proximity – that, in effect, everything was connected and entwined, from celestial bodies spinning at unfathomable distances to a humble apple drawn to the ground – Newton ushered in a new reductionist worldview, one that broke down complex processes into simpler parts, in which humans could pull apart the clockwork universe and comprehend all.

The conviction that we could dissect the natural world into its component parts and thereby gain mastery over it was also applied to the practical matter of farming. Nature was seen as a machine, capable of further fine-tuning by humans, and innovations such as the selective breeding of higher-yielding plants and animals resulted in agricultural output outpacing population growth across much of the Western world. Improvements in agricultural productivity not only meant that progressively fewer farmhands were required to till fields and tend to livestock, but the drive for greater efficiency also led to the appropriation of pastures and forests formerly available to the wider community for grazing, cropping and wood-gathering. This process of 'enclosure' – the fencing and consolidation of communal land into privately held estates – overturned centuries-old rights of access for commoners, resulting in the centralisation of land ownership into relatively few hands. What had been freely available was now captured by an early version of Big Agriculture, and many villagers, previously self-sufficient but now part of the precariat, were obliged to become pawns in this new order or instead take their chances and join the exodus to the cities.

Adam Smith, always sharp-eyed when it came to the motivations of the Establishment, noted that 'civil government, so far as it is instituted for the security of property, is in reality instituted for the defence of the rich against the poor'. This dynamic was pithily summed up in an English folk song from Smith's time:

> They hang the man and flog the woman
> Who steals the goose from off the common,
> But leave the greater villain loose
> That steals the common from off the goose.

Smith realised that the legal system and its apparatus of enforcement were in some respects nothing more than a giant protection racket – the pomp and ceremony of 'justice' seeking to cover up, justify and entrench prior injustices. The ruling class made the rules, building walls around things of value – not only in relation to property rights, but through other means such as tariffs on imported food that increased profits for landowners and costs for everyone else. And where it suited them, the rulers tore down walls too, opening portals for the burgeoning market economy. Turned off the land and forced to live in what was becoming a monoculture of money, rural refugees fled the countryside and were obliged to become tradeable commodities themselves in order to buy the commodities of subsistence.

The death of dearth

The mass migration of workers into cities was perfectly timed for the next turn of the revolutionary carousel. The Industrial Revolution – beginning in earnest in the early nineteenth century – was an age marked by mechanisation, steam power, and, for the first time in history, steady and broad-based increases in material wealth in some parts of the world. Adam Smith, writing in the very early days of this period, marvelled at the productivity of the factory system by citing the 'very trifling manufacture' of pin-making in which

> ten persons [assigned specific tasks] could make among them upwards of forty-eight thousand pins in a day … But if they had all wrought separately and independently … they certainly could not each of them have made twenty, perhaps not one pin in a day.

Just as reductionist science had reduced complex problems into their constituent parts in order to solve them, the process of industrialisation carried this atomising impulse to the production of goods. Factory workers became cogs in the machine – specialising in just one function, forced to synchronise their movements to the relentless tempo of the mechanised production line – and a rising tide of goods was disgorged out of the industrial West.

In Adam Smith's home nation the industrialisation of production was attributable to many factors – increasing urbanisation, growing food surpluses, scientific breakthroughs, and a flow of raw material from the colonies – but it was the readily accessible seams of coal threaded underneath the land that sealed Britain's position as workshop of the world. Coal, the original black gold, was the perfect ally for early industrialists – although it was geographically concentrated in certain areas, once dug up it was portable and could be easily transported to cities where labour was plentiful and bargaining leverage lay very much with factory owners. And unlike wind or water power, steam power was not dependent on the vagaries of the natural world – it was the capitalist tool *in excelsis*, a biddable and obedient servant, a reliable platform upon which to build complex and precisely measured production processes. Coal delivered 'power' to the new capitalist class in both senses of the word – it was an easily tapped and explosive form of energy, and it also gave industrial magnates absolute control over both men and machines.

Fuelled by coal, the Western world commenced a renewed assault on nature. Humankind had been reshaping the planet for millennia, and modern humans were by no means the first of their species to unsustainably exploit the world around them – Homo sapiens' prehistoric procession out of Africa, for example, was followed by suspiciously timed megafauna die-offs in newly inhabited continents. But stories – in the form of knowledge accrued and passed on, and the accompanying belief that human resourcefulness could extract ever-growing material plenty from its surrounds – became a potent evolutionary adaptation. The cultural and technological leaps spurred by the Scientific and Industrial Revolutions increasingly overran the stately and incremental adjustments of the natural world, seemingly fulfilling Francis Bacon's prediction that, subjected to the trials of reason, Mother Nature would be compelled to give up her secrets and bend to Man's will.

Adam Smith then supplied the modern era's overarching story to this broader tale of human potential and progress – the proposition that the 'natural effort of every individual to better his own condition' will have the effect of 'carrying on the society to wealth and prosperity'. His thesis provided support not only to an infant republic proclaiming the right to liberty and the pursuit of happiness, for some of its citizens at least, but also to free market proponents who believed that a system driven by rational agents acting in their own interests would maximise overall human wellbeing. But this Adam committed another original sin, this time in the nascent field of economics. Although he recognised nature's vital contribution to the economy – in particular, the role of agriculture in providing a surplus that could feed and clothe workers in other sectors – Smith treated the natural world and its benefits as essentially a free gift. Nature's bounty was assumed by Smith to be a costless resource, only accruing economic value when it has been extracted and fed into the industrial machine. As a result, one of Adam Smith's enduring legacies has been economics' fixation on human capital and human-produced capital – skilled labour, accumulated knowledge, machinery and infrastructure – at the expense of natural assets.

This failure to account for the natural world, and instead focus almost entirely on the human realm, was an excusable oversight on Smith's part, for in his day the gifts of nature seemed limitless. Only a trickle of European pioneers in the newly independent United States had pushed west beyond the Mississippi, and whole continents awaited the civilising caress of the plough. Since the publication of *The Wealth of Nations*, however, the previously untouched world has unfurled before the advance of industrial capitalism – initially within national borders, later via colonialism, and more recently under the banner of 'free trade'. Now, in today's world of global markets and global resources, where almost every part of the planet has been mapped and mined and milked, there are vanishingly few new frontiers left. Ignited by fossil fuels, Smith's 'obvious and simple system of natural liberty' has metastasised into something far removed from the homespun rural idyll of the butcher, the brewer and the baker pursuing their own happiness by making others happy.

3

DAS JUGGERNAUT

Industrial capitalism's global advance

Let us prey

Perhaps better than anyone, it was a German firebrand exiled to Victorian-era London who grasped the world-engulfing potential of the new industrial order. Karl Marx was a frenemy of capitalism, simultaneously awed and appalled by its relentless drive and sheer fecundity. He noted with sneaking admiration that the capitalist class had 'during its rule of scarce one hundred years ... created more massive and more colossal productive forces than have all preceding generations together'. The bourgeoisie, as he called the owners of capital, had

> accomplished wonders far surpassing Egyptian pyramids, Roman aqueducts, and Gothic cathedrals; it has conducted expeditions that put in the shade all former Exoduses of nations and crusades.

But these prizes, Marx argued, had been won at a punishingly high cost. In typically muscular language, he contended that 'capital comes dripping from head to toe, from every pore, with blood and dirt' and required the 'subjection of Nature's forces to man [and] machinery ... [and the] clearing of whole continents for cultivation'.

Marx conceded that industrial capitalism had delivered riches to a select cohort of humanity, but at incalculable expense to those at the bottom of the social pyramid, to future generations, and to the natural world. Marx himself was not unfamiliar with grinding poverty – he was perpetually broke and once lamented that 'I don't suppose anyone has ever written about "money" when so short of the stuff', while his mother gently suggested to her wayward son that he should consider making some capital instead of just writing about it. Practising the communist mantra of 'from each according to his ability, to each according to his needs' on a personal level, Marx was bankrolled by his wealthy comrade and compatriot Friedrich Engels, heir to an Anglo-German cotton milling business. Manchester-based Engels was a double agent for the communist cause, dressing in a frock-coat and hat for his day job at the family firm Ermen & Engels while at night consorting with the downtrodden and dreaming of the people's paradise to come.

In addition to regular stipends to his London-based friend, Engels also provided Marx with a ringside seat at the Industrial Revolution. By the 1840s Manchester was the greatest industrial city in the world – the textile sector was an early adopter of steam power and Manchester was the epicentre of mass production, for a while processing around a third of the global cotton crop. The French sociologist Alexis de Tocqueville, writing in 1835, conjured a hellish vision of 'Cottonopolis' and its forest of belching chimneys:

A sort of black smoke covers the city. The sun seen through it is a disc without rays. Under this half daylight 300,000 human beings are ceaselessly at work. A thousand noises disturb this damp, dark labyrinth ... Here humanity attains its most complete development and its most brutish; here civilisation works its miracles, and civilised man is turned back almost into a savage.

Engels's own book – *The Condition of the Working Class in England*, a forensically documented charge sheet published in 1845 – damned living conditions in English industrial cities as 'the highest and most unconcealed pinnacle of social misery existing in our day'.

Engels's dispatches from the frontline of the industrial advance were avidly consumed by London-based Marx, and complemented by Marx's feverish note-taking in the Reading Room of the British Museum. Marx saw himself as both analyst and catalyst – he would 'lay bare the economic law of motion of modern society', and consciousness of these laws of economic evolution would pave the way for the eventual overthrow of the prevailing system. Marx argued that capitalism never catches its breath – it 'must nestle everywhere, settle everywhere, establish connections everywhere' – and that in this perpetual growth imperative and interconnectivity lay the seeds of its own destruction. He reasoned that the 'immiseration' of workers, whose destiny was 'reduction to a machine ... [and] enslavement to capital', would foment an uprising by the working class, united and readymade for revolt 'by the very mechanism of the process of capitalist production itself'. Among its many other manufactures, Marx declared that capitalism also produces its own gravediggers, and he predicted that once the oppressed realised that they had nothing to lose but their chains they would at last mutiny against 'the Juggernaut of capital'.

Marx was like an Old Testament prophet, bushy-bearded and raging against the established regime, brandishing his own Hegelian trinity of thesis, antithesis and synthesis to justify his predictions of the imminent collapse of capitalism due to its inherent contradictions. But the apocalypse never came in his lifetime, nor since – although, like many other cults, there are still faithful disciples who maintain that the End of Days, for capitalism at least, is nigh. Instead, capitalism has colonised countless other markets since Marx's time. Partly this was due to the existence of an 'industrial reserve army' of surplus labour – as the English economist Joan Robinson would hard-headedly remark a century later, in a market economy the only thing worse than being exploited by capitalism is not being exploited by capitalism – but also because agitators like Marx provoked a type of immune response in the body politic, spooking governments into moderating capitalism's most objectionable aspects.

But perhaps the main reason that the expropriators were never expropriated, in the West at least, is that the Dickensian horrors of Marx's day were increasingly offshored to other lands. The globalised supply networks of industrial capitalism supplied not only products but also plausible deniability – while sometimes loosening the chains on workers in the Western world, they conveniently drew a veil over capitalism's worst excesses further afield. Although Friedrich Engels decried the squalor and exploitation in English factory towns, conditions there were mild compared with many other parts of the world subject to capitalism's embrace. The mills that enriched the Engels family, for example, were largely reliant on raw cotton imported from American slave plantations – estates on which humans were treated as personal property, and self-interest was barbarously bought at the expense of others' interests. Auctioned in markets to the highest bidder, manacled and whipped and chained in the service of profit, humans were enslaved and driven in the same way that Francis Bacon had sought to subjugate nature.

Mind the gap

Although reports of its demise turned out to be greatly exaggerated by Marx, he accurately diagnosed capitalism's insatiable nature, its 'need of a constantly expanding market for its products ... over the entire surface of the globe'. In this 'world market', as he described it,

> industries ... no longer work up indigenous raw material, but raw material drawn from the remotest zones; industries whose products are consumed, not only at home, but in every quarter of the globe. In place of the old wants, satisfied by the productions of the country, we find new wants, requiring for their satisfaction the products of distant lands and climes.

Unlike most other classical economists, including Adam Smith, Marx did not believe that, after some early labour pains, capitalism would eventually find easy repose in a 'stationary state'. Rather, it was more akin to some sinister self-replicating virus, its appetite increasing by what it fed on – constantly confecting new desires for ever-expanding markets and then ransacking new lands to satisfy this proliferation of wants.

The perpetual motion machine that is industrial capitalism not only led to 'intercourse in every direction [and the] universal interdependence of nations', Marx asserted, but it also acted as a giant wrecking ball through traditional economic and social relationships. Capitalism was both dislocating and dis-locating – 'All old-established national industries have been destroyed or are daily being destroyed … [and] are dislodged by new industries', he observed in *The Communist Manifesto*, co-written with his inside man Engels in the revolutionary year of 1848, while raw materials and finished goods flowed in from every corner of the world. Marx lamented that:

All that is solid melts into air, all that is holy is profaned, and man is at last compelled to face with sober senses his real conditions of life and his relations with his kind.

This new reality was the corruption of all relationships to base monetary exchange, a 'callous "cash payment"' formulated 'in the icy water of egotistical calculation'. The 'cash nexus' – the commodification of almost everything as the planet was transformed into a giant marketplace – had, Marx argued, 'deprived the whole world, both the human world and nature, of their own proper value'.

Marx saw himself as a modern-day Moses leading the workers to a new Promised Land – 'Philosophers have previously only interpreted the world; the real task is to change it', he thundered – and by that measure he largely failed. He viewed capitalism as part of an inevitable evolutionary process, an intermediate step on a path that would ultimately result in the socialisation of the means of production and the dawning of a classless society. But the communist coup did not take place in advanced economies such as Britain and Germany as he had anticipated, but rather in industrial backwaters such as Russia and later China. Appropriately for the pre-eminent poet of globalisation, Marx's communist creed was more successfully exported to other continents and, by the mid-twentieth century, on the cusp of the Great Acceleration, countries comprising around half of humanity invoked Karl Marx as their ideological founding father.

For many decades, communism was a success when measured by sheer weight of numbers, but as Voltaire observed, God is not on the side of the heaviest battalions, but of the best shots. The story of Korea – a culturally and ethnically homogenous people who became proxies for ideological combatants the Soviet Union and the United States – provides two nation-sized petri dishes to assess the relative merits of communism and capitalism. Following the partition of the country in 1945, North Korea, which before the war was richer and more industrialised than the south, became a command economy in which the state owned all means of production and pulled all economic levers. In contrast, South Korea followed the capitalist road and, after a flirtation with authoritarianism, emerged as a vibrant democracy and one of the world's richest nations. Almost eight decades after the country was split in two, satellite photographs from the night sky starkly illustrate the divergence between the countries – in the south of the peninsula there is an archipelago of lights, while in the north there is unremitting darkness.

The spectre of worldwide communism summoned by Marx in *The Communist Manifesto* turned out to be just that – a phantom, a fleeting incarnation, with some remnant ghosts rattling away in a far-off attic. Partly this was because Marx's thinking also succumbed to its own internal contradictions. The English economist John Maynard Keynes reflected the views of the majority of his peers when he dismissed communism as 'complicated hocus-pocus', more Groucho Marx than Karl Marx, remarking to his students that he had read *Das Kapital* 'as if it were a detective story, trying to find some clue to an idea in it and never succeeding'. Perhaps inevitably for someone who saw the human construct of society as a face-off between monolithic classes rather than as a constellation of largely self-seeking individuals, Marx did not really understand complex systems. He sought to distil the vast sprawl of modern society into a simple morality play – a tribal fight between the bourgeoisie and the proletariat, the oppressors and the oppressed. Marx thought he was documenting the dying convulsions of industrial capitalism, but in fact he was witnessing its tempestuous birth.

E pluribus, unum

By ignoring the messy, entangled reality of the modern economy Marx completely underplayed its 'emergent properties' – complex, often unpredictable, collective behaviour in a system, arising out of the multiplicity of interactions between its individual constituents. Maynard Keynes summarised this dynamic perfectly:

> We are faced at every turn with the problems of organic unity, of discreteness, of discontinuity – the whole is not equal to the sum of the parts, comparisons of quantity fail us, small changes produce large effects, the assumptions of a uniform and homogeneous continuum are not satisfied.

The globalised economy, as Keynes implied, is a superorganism – an almost infinite network of knock-on and feedback effects and unintended consequences, a pulsating web of interactions in which small shifts in component parts can exert large effects on the whole. It is more akin to the biological systems seen in the living world than the mechanistic, linear models beloved by the hard sciences – and accordingly it is beyond the power of any single entity or individual to effectively steer such an unruly creation.

Adam Smith, however, had beaten Keynes to the punch in noting the unmanageable complexity of modern human society. A true systems thinker, Smith was sceptical of the ability of centrally planned economies to successfully impose an inflexible, top-down mechanism on its citizens. He expressed a barely disguised contempt for the 'man of system' who

> seems to imagine that he can arrange the different members of a great society with as much ease as the hand arranges the different pieces upon a chess-board. He does not consider that ... in the great chess-board of human society, every single piece has a principle of motion of its own, altogether different from that which the legislature might chuse to impress upon it.

Smith recognised that complex systems such as markets are 'adaptive' – comprising elements that are not just acted on, but that also react. More than just an assembly of inert objects, they comprise individual agents constantly changing tack in response to external factors, with these see-sawing feedback loops tending to reinforce stability across the system as a whole.

Rather than fantasising about systems concocted and controlled by some omniscient overseer, Smith instead celebrated the self-organising potential of human society which required no central co-ordinator. Spontaneous order, Smith argued, could be secured through the actions of highly motivated actors – as the French writer Mirabeau noted in an early nod to the Invisible Hand, 'The whole magic of a well-ordered society is that each man works for others, while believing that he is working for himself'. Capitalism, at its best, is the Golden Rule – 'do unto others as you would have them do unto you' – in motion. We are obliged to stand in another's shoes, trying to fathom what they want, to second-guess and satisfy their needs and desires. And in this idealised world there is no 'man of system' issuing diktats from above – in theory at least, we are, in the words of capitalist icon Milton Friedman, 'free to choose'.

Although Adam Smith never used the word 'capitalism' in any of his works, he supported 'the obvious and simple system of natural liberty' characterised by private ownership of property and the freedom to trade – what are considered to be the fundamentals of a capitalist economy. His vision was a hymn to co-operation, a decentralised process that productively channels the widely distributed energies of billions of individuals. As the Canadian-American economist John Kenneth Galbraith observed almost two centuries after *The Wealth of Nations*, in a capitalist system

> the important social decisions would be taken, not by fallible, cruel, and egotistical men but by a wholly impersonal mechanism. Anything that so effectively excluded a cult of personality was obviously an instrument of freedom.

Capitalism's cheerleaders argue that something so apparently democratic, that obviated the very visible hand of an authoritarian clique, must be a force for good – as Keynes, master of the economic soundbite, reasoned, 'It is better that a man should tyrannise over his bank balance than over his fellow-citizens'.

However, Adam Smith's Panglossian view that two people will only trade if it makes them both better off relies on a version of the world that exists mainly in textbooks. Marx noted presciently that industrial capitalism 'creates a world after its own image', and faithful to its Darwinian foundation myth it has mutated into something far different than in Smith's time. Marx co-wrote *The Communist Manifesto* in the aftermath of the 'Railway Mania' of the 1840s – a decade in which the British rail network spread across the country, with buildings and city centres razed to allow the passage of coal-fed steam trains ferrying people and products. Like these locomotives, Marx saw industrial capitalism as an enormously powerful machine, ruthlessly rolling forward to new frontiers and demolishing any obstacles in its path, but also increasingly unstable as it picked up momentum. The Railway Mania was followed by a spectacular financial crash in 1847, the year prior to the publication of the *Manifesto*, and highlighted one of the biggest flaws of capitalism – reinforcing feedback loops in the human-created world of finance that lead to cycles of boom and bust, in which capitalism's 'perennial gale of creative destruction' can become straightforward destructive destruction.

4

THE RECKONING

The capitalist locomotive derails

Booms go boom

It is an incontrovertible fact that fossil fuelled capitalism has lifted billions from abject poverty while at the same time boosting the material wealth of the already affluent. The World Bank estimates that the proportion of the global population living in extreme poverty, broadly defined as a daily income of around $2 or less, has fallen from almost 40 per cent to just under 10 per cent over the last three decades, with Asian countries the biggest beneficiary of this trend. Half a century ago Western nations accounted for over 50 per cent of global economic output and Asia only around 20 per cent, but Asia has now overtaken the Western world and today produces more than 40 per cent of the world's goods, with the uplift in production most pronounced in former command economies such as China and Vietnam. Cross-border trade comprises more than half of everything consumed in the world, and Adam Smith's vision of universal opulence due to specialisation and exchange has, on the face of it, been largely vindicated in the laboratory of life.

In addition to these material boons, capitalism's defenders also argue that it delivers other, less tangible, benefits. John Stuart Mill, writing in the same year that *The Communist Manifesto* was published, approvingly cited the civilising power of free exchange and individual agency:

> It is hardly possible to overrate the value, in the present low state of human improvement, of placing human beings in contact with persons dissimilar to themselves, and with modes of thought and action unlike those with which they are familiar ... commerce first taught nations to see with good will the wealth and prosperity of one another.

The bold claim that trade not only promotes prosocial behaviour at an individual level but can also deliver peace among nations was also made by the French philosopher Montesquieu a few decades before the publication of *The Wealth of Nations*. He reasoned that 'two nations that negotiate between themselves become reciprocally dependent', and that, because of this mutuality, the promise of material growth should trump dreams of martial glory. Montesquieu's thesis was seemingly borne out by events in industrialising Europe, which – other than the Crimean War in the mid-1850s and some more localised engagements – enjoyed a near century-long oasis of peace after the Battle of Waterloo in 1815.

Writing with a certain retrospective wistfulness about the closing years of this long peace, Maynard Keynes evoked a golden image of society in the first part of the twentieth century, just prior to the First World War, in which:

> The inhabitant of London could order by telephone, sipping his morning tea in bed, the various products of the whole earth, in such quantity as he might see fit, and reasonably expect their early delivery upon his doorstep.

The world at this point in time was cresting on the first great wave of globalisation – it would not be until the late 1970s that trade as a proportion of global output reached the same levels as recorded in 1914 – but as Keynes cautioned, civilisation is 'a thin and precarious crust' and the wealth of nations sits on relatively fragile foundations. Notwithstanding Montesquieu's sunny optimism, the First World War demonstrated that tribalism could in fact outweigh economic interests and degenerate into irrationality, violence and the catastrophic destruction of material wealth. The Great War obliterated Keynes's vision of interdependence and abundance, with millions of lives lost in the four-year conflagration, vanquished nations left destitute by what Keynes called the 'Carthaginian peace' of punitive reparations, and even the nominal victors labouring under huge debts.

This 'European blood feud', as Keynes termed it, hastened the power shift from the Old World to the New, and Uncle Sam grew fat on the remains of a continent still recovering, dazed and haltingly, from the conflict. America became the world's undisputed economic superpower, but paradoxically it turned inward, shaken by its brief, bloody excursion to Europe. Fuelled by cheap money and reduced tax rates for high earners, the country instead sought consolation in a massive binge of retail therapy. The techniques of mass production, honed during the war, were now applied to the civilian sphere, and radios, automobiles, and myriad domestic appliances spilled off America's assembly lines. A 'high tide of prosperity', as Keynes termed it, washed the shores of the United States, and the richest society ever known to the world embarked on what F Scott Fitzgerald later described as 'the most expensive orgy in history'. Seemingly defying gravity and the tenets of common sense, the US stock market – that seismograph of business and investor confidence – traced an almost vertical ascent in the last years of the 1920s.

Charles Mitchell, chairman of the National City Bank of New York and a noted stock market bull, typified the exuberant optimism of the time. He asserted in September 1929 that the market was 'like a weather-vane pointing into a gale of prosperity'. Unfortunately, Mitchell's meteorological metaphor was only half-right. Rather than a gale of prosperity, a perfect storm of financial destruction was bearing down on Wall Street. On the morning of 24 October 1929 – 'Black Thursday', as it later became known – the Wall Street bubble was pricked. Panic selling gripped the exchange in the morning, the financial haemorrhaging staunched only when a cabal of influential bankers stepped on to the trading floor, brandishing a pocketful of buy orders. In the last week of October, however, the financial bloodbath resumed, and stock ticker machines – overwhelmed by the unprecedented trading volume and spluttering tape long after the market had closed – tapped out a staccato requiem for the Jazz Age. The Great Crash was punctuated by occasional suckers' rallies, but by 1932 the Dow Jones index had fallen almost 90 per cent from its September 1929 peak.

Prophet warning

The events of October 1929 were in fact an early symptom, rather than the cause, of a far more malignant malady. The Wall Street sideshow had diverted attention away from unsustainable imbalances within the wider community – as the economic historian Robert Heilbroner noted, just prior to the Crash 'some twenty-four thousand families at the apex of the social pyramid received a stream of income three times as large as six million families squashed at the bottom'. Credit had largely been channelled away from the real economy and into financial speculation and consumption, and while easy money stoked the speculative inferno of the late 1920s, farmers and other primary producers struggled with poor prices and mounting debts. The gaudy mansion of American prosperity was top-heavy and teetering, perilously perched on the sandy foundations of instalment credit and margin loans, and the tremors on Wall Street had finally brought it down. There were foreclosures, runs on banks, and, ultimately, masses of workers laid off. By 1933, a quarter of the US workforce was unemployed, industrial production was only half that of 1929, and real income per capita had fallen to levels not seen since the start of the century. Over 5,000 banks had gone to the wall and 'Hoovervilles' – shanty towns of the dispossessed, named in honour of the incumbent President – scarred the country, like open sores on the great republic.

The Wall Street contagion quickly spread beyond American frontiers, the web of international relationships entangling nations and frustrating their best efforts to quarantine the growing financial pandemic. Worse still, in a Canute-like effort to hold back the deadening tide, Western governments sought refuge behind ever-higher trade barriers. In dismantling the structure of free trade, the developed world was slowly dismembering its golden goose – this protectionist race to the bottom halved the volume of international exchange in the four years following the Crash. Deprived of the oxygen of commerce, the world swooned into a state of near paralysis. Many orthodox economists welcomed this downturn as a type of Darwinian spring cleaning, in which underperforming enterprises would be jettisoned in the name of economic efficiency. These hardliners argued that the slump was no more than a rather spectacular manifestation of the 'business cycle' which coursed through all developed economies, and that, ultimately, the Western world would right itself and full employment be restored.

But as the 1930s stuttered on, there was scant evidence that the developed world was returning to health. Economies wallowed, unemployment levels remained stubbornly high, rumblings of discontent grew bolder, and citizens became restive. In 1932 US Army units – commanded by Douglas MacArthur and George Patton, and assisted by Dwight Eisenhower in his first taste of armed conflict – brutally cleared with bayonets and tanks and tear gas the makeshift camps of thousands of war veterans who had marched on the Capitol demanding government aid. That same year in Britain – where official unemployment levels averaged 20 per cent nationally, and up to 70 per cent in some regions – Sir Oswald Mosley, a former government minister, seeded the British Union of Fascists in the fertile ground of discontent and despair. And on Continental Europe, the Great Depression acted as a kind of giant centrifuge – hurling men and women away from the political centre, towards the extremes of socialism and fascism. But despite the ferocity of the Great Depression, orthodoxy's faith in the efficacy of markets remained largely intact, seemingly unperturbed by the millions of unemployed, the destitution of families, and the unravelling of nations.

Maynard Keynes deplored the equanimity of those who believed that markets would self-correct, and their serene assurances to the masses that society would eventually emerge from the Great Slump. In a stark rejoinder to those selling scorched earth policies of austerity, Keynes reminded them that 'in the long run we are all dead'. In the time of its greatest crisis, Keynes warned, capitalism simply did not have the luxury of waiting for the economy to heal itself. He observed that capitalism's chief virtue, and saving grace, had been its efficacy. If the free market system relinquished its claim to unparalleled productivity there was a danger that other, ostensibly less morally repugnant, social models would be preferred. As Keynes commented:

> Modern capitalism is absolutely irreligious, without internal union, without much public spirit, often, though not always, a mere congeries of possessors and pursuers. Such a system has to be immensely, not merely moderately, successful to survive.

The apparent failure of the free market system to 'deliver the goods', Keynes noted in 1933, meant that Western nations were increasingly willing to abandon their Faustian bargain with capitalism and instead embark 'on a variety of politico-economic experiments'. For a while in the mid-1930s, it looked like Marx's grim prognosis of the in-built obsolescence of capitalism may have been correct after all.

The Western world was becoming increasingly desperate – the capitalist system that had served it so well now seemed irremediably broken, and only extreme measures appeared capable of tearing it from its torpor. But despite his own antipathy to many aspects of the system, Keynes did not believe that capitalism was fatally flawed. The profound problems of chronic unemployment and economic stagnation had a simple cause, he asserted, and were amenable to a simple cure. In Keynes's opinion, the most serious threat to capitalism came not from the aspiring revolutionaries peddling their 'quack remedies', but rather from those who most strenuously proclaimed their fealty to the existing order. Keynes rejected the notion of free markets as infallible, and accordingly his policy prescription did not abdicate responsibility for economic welfare to an all-powerful market. Rather, the West's economic destiny was firmly in its own hands – governments could actively intervene to smooth the business cycle by increasing government spending to offset lower business and consumer activity. The celebrated Invisible Hand, Keynes implied, sometimes just needed a helping hand.

The mark of Keynes

Keynes's *The General Theory of Employment, Interest and Money*, published in 1936, disputed the orthodox doctrine that free markets always produce optimal results. Like its namesake, Einstein's General Theory of Relativity, Keynes's magnum opus overthrew the accepted theoretical structure, showing that markets were not necessarily analogous to the clockwork precision of Newtonian physics. Keynes likened classical economists to 'Euclidean geometers in a non-Euclidean world who, discovering that in experience straight lines apparently parallel often meet, rebuke the lines for not keeping straight'. In his opinion, parts of the classical doctrine, although theoretically elegant, were based on flawed assumptions and deduced outcomes clearly diverging from those in the real world. Keynes set himself the task of overturning the redundant truths of his predecessors – as he prophesied to the playwright George Bernard Shaw in 1935, *The General Theory* would 'largely revolutionise ... the way the world thinks about economic problems'.

The General Theory was written at a time when most of the developed world had already endured years of unemployment and stagnation – a situation that orthodox economic doctrine deemed impossible, as theory dictated that markets were self-correcting and naturally worked towards full employment. Keynes contested this view, recognising that just as an economy is an emergent system, a type of superorganism, so too are the financial markets nestled within, and that what is true for the parts is not always true for the whole. Keynes's most famous example of a 'fallacy of composition' was what later became known as 'the Paradox of Thrift' – which notes that while saving is good for the individual, if all individuals increase their savings then total spending will fall, leading to lower economic activity, and eventually resulting in lower savings for the population as a whole. Keynes challenged the prescriptions of his orthodox brethren – who asserted that just as in hard times a household should exercise strict financial discipline, so too should slump-afflicted governments practise financial sobriety – and argued that mainstream economics ignored the complexity of the economy and its capacity to generate destabilising feedback loops.

Keynes's warning that behaviour in the atomistic world of microeconomics cannot always be extrapolated to the sphere of macroeconomics – the study of aggregates – was informed by his own misadventures on the stock market. He learned the hard way that financial markets are sometimes buffeted by unpredictable squalls of 'whim or sentiment or chance' due to unavoidable uncertainty, cycling from irrational exuberance to catatonic despair, and that these pendulum swings in 'animal spirits' could in turn result in bouts of overinvestment or underinvestment. He noted that 'liquidity preference' – the desire to hold cash or near-cash – is a gauge of individuals' wariness about the future, and when individuals hoard their savings because of fears for the future, or when investors lack confidence to embark on new projects, the daisy chain of prosperity breaks and 'enterprise will fade and die'. When markets were languishing because of business and consumer pessimism, and Adam Smith's Invisible Hand becomes atrophied through inaction, Keynes advocated an external stimulus – 'an impulse, a jolt, an acceleration', as he put it. Once the economic engine had been reignited then, he commented, 'the classical theory comes into its own again from this point onwards'.

Despite the shrill alarmism of his critics, Keynes's intent was to save capitalism rather than depose it. Although he viewed the modern economy as far too complex to be steered by a single entity, Keynes asserted that on occasions it needed an external agent to act as a countervailing force against market failure. Keynes rejected the conventional wisdom, and instead counselled that governments should 'spend against the wind' in straitened times. Considering that Keynes's theory told many politicians exactly what they wanted to hear – that the path to recovery lay not in austerity but in higher spending and lower taxes for the voting public – it is surprising that his ideas took so long to be accepted by policymakers. It would not be until that period of sustained global public expenditure otherwise known as the Second World War that 'Keynesianism' – the belief that government expenditure should be used to fine-tune an economy's aggregate spending – usurped the theories of the classical school almost as comprehensively as Darwin's narrative had displaced that of Genesis.

Peacetime Keynesianism then slipstreamed behind a socioeconomic structure that had previously been mobilised for war purposes. High tax rates imposed as a 'conscription on wealth' during the Second World War were largely maintained, with the tax burden on the developed world's richest citizens often exceeding 90 per cent in the immediate post-war years; governments remained a key player in the real economy, spending heavily on public infrastructure such as highways and universities; and new multinational alliances, such as the Marshall Plan and what would eventually become the European Union, were forged. The Bretton Woods system, an international initiative inspired in large part by Keynes, established a cross-border monetary regime, set fixed exchange rates and restrained the ability of quicksilver capital to freely move across borders, with these controls nudging companies towards a focus on domestic investment opportunities. Under this new order the developed world saw wealth inequalities narrow, productivity rates increase, and enjoyed near-full employment. For almost three decades much of the world basked in conditions of 'permanent boom', with even Keynes's most vehement ideological adversaries reluctantly conceding that 'we are all Keynesians now'.

But although Keynes's heretical doctrine was instrumental in launching the Great Acceleration after the Second World War, he also bequeathed a less benign legacy to the modern world. In challenging the paradoxical doctrine of the Invisible Hand, Keynes proposed an equally counterintuitive proposal – that at certain times, profligacy could be the most responsible policy. Practitioners of 'sound finance', who clung rigidly to balanced budgets and the principle that expenses should not outrun revenue, were overthrown by Keynesians who embraced managed capitalism and the 'pump-priming' of economies. But this new guard tended to ignore Keynes's cautionary note that his policy prescription was only intended as a form of economic triage – that government spending should retreat to more neutral settings once employment and output returned to normal conditions, or be subject to belt-tightening if the economy was overheating. Rather than the Keynesian conception of the government as spender and saver of last resort, moderating not only the troughs but also the peaks of the business cycle, cafeteria Keynesians instead selected only the most palatable morsels from Keynes's canon.

In *The General Theory* Keynes observed that:

> Practical men, who believe themselves to be quite exempt from any intellectual influences, are usually the slaves of some defunct economist. Madmen in authority, who hear voices in the air, are distilling their frenzy from some academic scribbler of a few years back.

Although the Keynesian prescription of managed capitalism to counter destabilising feedback loops in markets was eventually overthrown by the neoliberal counter-revolution in the late 1970s, the voice of Keynes can still be heard whispering in the background through to this day. Keynes's academic scribblings, sometimes distorted by his followers, served to entrench the idea that increased spending was the go-to solution for most economic problems. In challenging the default policy of financial rectitude and caution Maynard Keynes inadvertently became an enabler for a capitalist machine that, having mastered mass production, now needed to encourage mass consumption.

5

THE SORCERER'S APPRENTICE

Capitalism conjuring gluts, and gluttons

Frankenmarket

In 1930, in the early stages of the Great Depression – when stock markets had crashed, dole queues were lengthening, and dark clouds of despair shadowed the Western world – Maynard Keynes, in a characteristically contrarian mood, proffered a vision of civilisation one hundred years hence. He imagined a world where, due to the supreme efficiency of the capitalist system, the 'struggle for subsistence' has been overcome and humankind has at last been led 'out of the tunnel of economic necessity into daylight'. Although Keynes thought that the cult of capitalism sanctified some of our least attractive tendencies into a credo for society, he maintained that it was a necessary crutch until we finally reached the sunlit uplands of abundance – 'wisely managed', he reasoned, 'it can probably be made more efficient for attaining economic ends than any alternative system yet in sight'.

Keynes himself exhibited an intensely ambivalent attitude to the accumulation of wealth. The patrician Englishman thought that, like economics itself, money was a mere expedient, nothing other than 'a means to the enjoyment and realities of life', and the pursuit of wealth little more than an 'amusement'. But, he reasoned, if we must let the 'strenuous purposeful money-makers' lead in order to enter an economic Eden then, on balance, this was an acceptable compromise. Those touched with 'the money-making passion' were, Keynes conceded, a necessary evil – for it would be in the wake of these individuals, impelled by their striving after profit, that the rest of humankind would be transported to a state of 'economic bliss'. Once this state of plenty had finally been achieved, Keynes predicted that people would seek 'to live wisely and agreeably and well', and economists would at last be relegated to their proper place in society – 'as humble, competent people, on a level with dentists', mere technocrats piloting with a delicate touch the ship of state.

Keynes was perhaps indulging in some wishful thinking when he conjured a vision of an enlightened time 'when the accumulation of wealth is no longer of high social importance'. But Adam Smith seemed to contemplate a similar outcome almost two centuries earlier when he predicted that an economy would settle into a steady state once it had acquired its 'full complement of riches'. In *The Theory of Moral Sentiments*, Smith shook his head at the man who:

> Through the whole of his life … pursues the idea of a certain artificial and elegant repose which he may never arrive at, for which he sacrifices a real tranquillity that is at all times in his power, and which, if in the extremity of old age he should at last attain to it, he will find to be in no respect preferable to that humble security and contentment which he had abandoned for it.

Sounding like an eighteenth-century hippie, Smith counselled that 'wealth and greatness are mere trinkets of frivolous utility, no more adapted for procuring ease of body or tranquillity of mind than the tweezer-cases of the lover of toys'. The hamster wheel of getting and spending, Smith seemed to be saying, would eventually be abandoned in favour of cultivating the art of living well.

However, for quite some time the transition from labourers to lotus-eaters proved stubbornly elusive – largely because some of the very attributes that helped vault Western citizens to material abundance also prevented them from sitting back and enjoying their good fortune. The German sociologist Max Weber had argued in the early twentieth century that 'the spirit of capitalism' arose in part because of a 'Protestant ethic' in north European countries and their offshoots which

> works with all its force against the uninhibited enjoyment of possessions; it discourages consumption, especially the consumption of luxuries ... And if that restraint on consumption is combined with the freedom to strive for profit, the result produced will inevitably be the creation of capital through the ascetic compulsion to save.

For a while, this dour dynamic worked well – the West prized the creation of wealth but was uncomfortable spending it, and the resulting tension tightened the bow string of early capitalist countries, propelling them to further prosperity by encouraging the accumulation of income-producing capital.

The 'industrious revolution' in the West contributed significantly to the prodigious productive power of capitalism, but in order to soak up the products generated by the capitalist Juggernaut the self-denying masses had to somehow be persuaded to abandon Calvinism for carpe diem. Accordingly, capitalism evolved from a machine for producing goods to one that also produced wants. Karl Marx had seen all of this coming, noting that:

> Modern bourgeois society ... a society that has conjured up such gigantic means of production and of exchange, is like the sorcerer who is no longer able to control the powers of the nether world whom he has called up by his spells.

Like the fable of Frankenstein's monster, a creation of man that turns the tables and overpowers its creator, consumption-driven capitalism became the dominant theology of our time, overthrowing the old pieties, and refashioning humans in its own, all-consuming image.

Buyology

As Marx observed, industrial capitalism acts as a sledgehammer on the social order, but it can also be remarkably subtle – influencing our desires and creating a world after its own image. It atomises individuals by corroding social capital, by encouraging specialisation, and by promoting a narrative that we are conscripts in a Hobbesian war of all against all. And, cleverly, capitalism then exploits what classical economic theory largely ignores – that human beings are in fact social beings – to encourage superfluous consumption. In an increasingly fragmented and globalised world, in which we do not necessarily know our neighbours and perform daily on the world stage, it is largely by the accumulation of wealth that we declare our social standing. 'Positional goods' – a holiday house, a ridiculously expensive sports car, designer handbags, and the like – convey information about ourselves, semaphoring where we sit in the social hierarchy. All animals are conscious, but humans are self-conscious also – and Adam Smith's 'impartial spectator', yammering away at the back of our mind and restraining some of our worst impulses, also provokes us towards acts of competitive display. As Smith commented in *The Wealth of Nations*, 'With the greater part of rich people, the chief enjoyment of riches consists in the parade of riches'.

There was no better analyst of 'the parade of riches' than Thorstein Veblen, writing at the turn of the twentieth century in the closing stages of America's Gilded Age. Perhaps the world's first satirical economist, Veblen's imagination was as fertile and as unforgiving as the Midwest plains on which he was raised. He coined the phrase 'conspicuous consumption' and saw the modern world as an arena in which individuals fought for recognition and status, and in which the true value of 'pecuniary success' was not raw purchasing power but rather the social rank it conferred. Veblen observed that ostentatious idleness – the performance of 'a substantial and patent waste of time' – could be a status symbol itself, commenting for example that the expensive and cumbersome skirt of a society matron 'incapacitates her for all useful exertion' and flags her as one insulated from the need to earn a living. As in the natural world, costly signalling is credible signalling – and just as a peacock's unwieldy tail conveys a snapshot of fitness to curious peahens, so too the geysering of champagne in VIP nightclubs and other demonstrations of waste concisely telegraph a story about relative material wealth.

In his *The Theory of the Leisure Class* Veblen noted that 'with the exception of the instinct of self-preservation, the propensity for emulation is probably the strongest and most alert and persistent of the economic motives proper'. Adam Smith made a similar point in *The Theory of Moral Sentiments*, when he observed that: 'When we consider the condition of the great, in those delusive colours in which the imagination is apt to paint it, it seems to be almost the abstract idea of a perfect and happy state'. Keeping up with the Joneses has always been a preoccupation for social creatures like us – and even more so in today's age, when flickering images on our TV sets or an Instagram feed on our phones act like glossy photos from a brochure for a better life. Our desires are inflamed by the lifestyles of others, and capitalism has co-opted advertising to ensure that in the material world our reach always exceeds our grasp.

Capitalism relies on our expectations not being fulfilled – as a General Motors senior executive observed a century ago, 'the key to economic prosperity is the organized creation of dissatisfaction'. Never-ending consumption is only possible if our wants are never satisfied, and the yin-yang of capitalism requires a constant striving for more goods and services in order to devour the things pouring from the globe-girdling productive machine. The writer and historian Lewis Mumford commented in the late 1960s that the capitalist spirit had 'transformed five of the seven deadly sins of Christianity – pride, envy, greed, avarice, and lust – into positive social virtues', apparently believing that sloth and wrath had been spared capitalism's attention. But now even sloth has been commodified, with advertisements assuring consumers that 'you deserve it' – that a luxury holiday or a spa session are essential for those fortunate enough to be able to afford them. Our modern economy has evolved from a system for satisfying needs to one also creating needs, a mass manufacturer of wants as much as goods.

Thorstein Veblen's antipathy to pecuniary pursuits was matched by his incompetence in them – he died in August 1929, at the zenith of the Wall Street bubble, just before the Great Crash that made his stock holdings largely worthless. He was not around to witness another incarnation of constantly evolving capitalism – the shift among the very rich from conspicuous idleness to conspicuous activity. In America, for example, the share of high-income workers who averaged more than 50 hours of work a week almost doubled in the quarter of a century from the 1980s. Rather than Maynard Keynes's predictions of a 15-hour working week by 2030, capitalism had instead pulled off a neat trick. Not only did it successfully inveigle individuals to consume more by offering seductive new products, but it also managed to maintain the Protestant work ethic – this time without the fastidious asceticism of past generations for whom thrift was a virtue and excess consumption the height of vulgarity.

The power of now

Adam Smith was wary of Big Business's instinct 'to widen the market and to narrow the competition', and this monopolising impulse has also been evident in the battle of economic ideas. By the mid-1970s the phenomenon of 'stagflation' – consistently rising prices amid increasing unemployment – was visited on much of the industrialised world. Seemingly unable to adequately explain or resolve stagflation – caused in part by supply shocks such as the 1973 OPEC energy crisis, but also because the economic engine was being run too hot by fair-weather Keynesians – the miracle decades of Keynesianism faded. Replacing managed capitalism as the ruling ideology was 'neoliberalism' – which celebrates individualism, deregulation and small governments – with Britain and the United States leading the charge. Margaret Thatcher, in between breaking the coal mining unions and privatising state-owned industries, maintained that 'there's no such thing as society … and people must look after themselves first', while Ronald Reagan asserted in his inaugural presidential address in 1981 that 'Government is not the solution to our problem, government *is* the problem'.

One-time market infidels also defected to a form of capitalism during the early years of the neoliberal ascent. On the passing of Chairman Mao in the late 1970s, China implemented a range of market-led reforms in an attempt to shake the country out of the economic sluggishness arising from collectivism. China's paramount leader at the time pragmatically declared that 'It doesn't matter whether the cat is black or white, so long as it catches mice', and the country was opened up to foreign investment, special economic zones were created, and agriculture and other enterprises were freed from the heavy hand of state control. The result was the most rapid and comprehensive industrialisation of any nation in history. Observing a type of Moore's Law for economic development, it had taken around 30 years for Britain's economy to double in size from 1830, and just under two decades for American output to double in the late nineteenth century, while the Chinese economy has more than doubled in each full decade since 1980.

As China was becoming the new workshop of the world, however, Adam Smith's Invisible Hand flexed into a fist for many workers in more developed economies. For much of the twentieth century the West's Faustian pact with capitalism had been set against the ostensibly more fraternal ideals of communism, and developed economies were not above implementing socialist solutions from time to time to smooth capitalism's hard edges. But when China embarked on its economic reforms in the late 1970s and the Soviet bloc finally disintegrated in the early 1990s, the need to inoculate against the perceived communist threat fell away. Unmoored from the competitive tension exerted by a true ideological rival, and outcompeted by the flood of low-cost goods from factories in China and other emerging economies, wealth inequalities that had narrowed in the Western world over the post-war period began to blow out. As a result, industrial capitalism increasingly acted as both a mesh and a sieve – uniting economies in a planet-spanning market, while inequality levels in many nations widened the gap between the have and have-nots.

At the same time wealth inequalities were expanding, the accession of China to the world market also contributed to what has been termed 'The Great Moderation' – a roughly 20-year period, beginning in the mid-1990s, characterised by low inflation and unusually stable markets. In a display of mutual but premature back-slapping, many of those in power at the time claimed that this period of steady growth was attributable to the wise stewardship of central bankers and neoliberal policies such as deregulation. The business cycle was declared dead by market triumphalists, and interest rates declined due to a perceived reduction in risk levels and a glut of savings from new recruits to the capitalist club. Spurred on by low interest rates, the avid embrace of the consumerist gospel and stagnating real incomes for many workers in the West, borrowing levels spiralled over the course of the Great Moderation, and global debt now sits at roughly 50 per cent higher in real terms than in the mid-1990s.

A curious hybrid – a corrupted Keynesianism that mutated from a short-term intervention into a doctrine for growth at all costs, combined with a neoliberal mindset that ignored Keynes's counsel that the excesses of the market should be actively countered – ushered in a culture of overconsumption and excess debt across much of the world. A steady decline in interest rates – the reward paid to those delaying immediate consumption – reduced the incentive to save, and brought forward spending over the course of the Great Moderation. Lower interest rates, in turn, reduced debt servicing costs and allowed even more debt to be accrued, leading to dangerously elevated borrowing levels that increased the fragility of the financial system. In 2008 the long term finally arrived in the form of the sub-prime mortgage crisis that was capitalism's most serious financial emergency since the Great Depression. The crash of 2008, and subsequent events such as the European sovereign debt crisis beginning in 2009, all had the same ultimate cause – people, companies or nations borrowing more than they could ultimately pay back.

The English writer Samuel Johnson observed in the mid-eighteenth century that 'the future is purchased by the present ... [and it] is not possible to secure distant ... happiness but by the forbearance of some immediate gratification'. However, when the future purchased by the present is the future itself – when we borrow to consume today rather than invest for tomorrow – then we have a problem. To keep the capitalist machine running the developed world has gone on an almighty borrowing bender and has been living beyond its means, including at a government level where many states have sponsored stimulatory budget measures in an effort to grow economies and pay back debt, which in turn accumulates even greater levels of national debt. As a result, rather than Adam Smith's promise of universal opulence percolating down to the masses, there is a rapidly expanding segment of global society that borrows from the future just to finance immediate consumption. But eclipsing this borrowing binge in the financial markets is humankind's ecological debt – a largely unaccounted drawdown on the natural world that gives the appearance of wealth being created when in fact much of it is being destroyed.

6

THE BUCK STOPS HERE

Capitalism's Ponzi play on the natural world

Lord of the files

The art of government has always relied on effective quantification. The anthropologist James C Scott describes the state as 'a recording, registering, and measuring machine' – rulers use rulers, and the city-states that emerged during the Agricultural Revolution were those that could most ably assess, tax and commandeer a surplus of products. In our far more complex modern society, the task of measuring overall economic activity has largely been delegated to a single indicator, 'Gross Domestic Product', which in broad terms tallies the monetary value of the final goods and services produced in a given country during a given period. The concept of GDP was first developed in the United States in the mid-1930s and was very much a product of its time – when the principal concern of governments was to monitor and fine-tune spending during the doldrums of the Great Depression, and later in the 1940s when it was recruited for large-scale war-planning purposes.

GDP has many recognised flaws – it focuses on average income, not income distribution; it is generally better at quantifying the value of goods rather than services, especially in our increasingly online world; and it solely measures activity mediated by the market. This means that things such as unpaid housework and growing one's own food are not included in

GDP numbers, and it also has the perverse effect of valuing harmful social actions that nevertheless are transacted on-market. Almost a century before GDP was formally introduced as our snapshot of economic progress, Karl Marx noted sardonically that:

> The criminal produces not only crimes but also criminal law, and with this also the professor who gives lectures on criminal law and in addition to this the inevitable compendium in which this same professor throws his lectures onto the general market as 'commodities'.

As foreshadowed by Marx, GDP measures 'bads' as well as goods – illegal activities such as drug trafficking are often included in GDP calculations, while natural disasters and spending on warfare can significantly boost GDP in a particular period.

GDP, then, is just another story, and a one-sided story at that. The giveaway lies in the word 'Gross' in Gross Domestic Product – GDP is not a net measure, subtracting those things detrimental to wellbeing, but rather treats all market transactions equally and assigns the same value to goods and bads. Junk food processed in factories adds to overall GDP, and the resulting increase in obesity and diabetes rates lead to higher healthcare costs – which in turn further increases GDP. And not only does GDP assign a value to socially reckless or questionable behaviour, but it also fails to account for those things that are truly important to most people. In the oft-quoted words of Robert Kennedy, this measure

> does not allow for the health of our children, the quality of their education or the joy of their play. It does not include the beauty of our poetry or the strength of our marriages, the intelligence of our public debate or the integrity of our public officials. It measures neither our wit nor our courage, neither our wisdom nor our learning, neither our compassion nor our devotion to our country, it measures every-thing, in short, except that which makes life worthwhile.

As Simon Kuznets, the father of national accounts, noted back in the 1930s, 'the welfare of a nation can … scarcely be inferred from a measurement of national income' – GDP, he advised, should never be confused for a proxy for societal wellbeing.

But despite these cautionary words from Kuznets, GDP is the mark by which almost all economic progress is now assessed. It has become another form of positional consumption, of competitive display, with countries smugly trumpeting their superior GDP growth rates in the economic arms race. GDP represents the ultimate victory of the market over the non-market domain, fulfilling Charles Dickens's dystopian prediction in *Hard Times* that 'Every inch of the existence of mankind, from birth to death, was to be a bargain across the counter'. This mercantilisation of mankind is perhaps not surprising – economists have long craved the crystalline clarity of physics, seeking to straitjacket the world into a set of numbers, and accordingly made the simplifying assumption that only what can be counted actually counts. Like capitalism, GDP serves a purpose, but continual economic expansion as tracked by national output has become a dogma of its own – and accordingly GDP, like the markets it measures, has switched from servant to master.

The Gospel of Growth is not a wholly false doctrine. GDP is highly correlated to indicators such as the Social Progress Index, which measures the extent to which countries provide for the social and environmental needs of their citizens, but only up to a point – after a certain income threshold is reached then the relationship rapidly falls away. And because GDP is an aggregate figure it measures only 'average opulence' and has nothing to say about income and wealth distribution – in the United States, for example, the average pre-tax income of the top 10 per cent of earners has doubled over the last 40 years, and that of the top 1 per cent has more than tripled, while the average pre-tax income of the bottom half of Americans has largely flatlined. For a while, the promise of perpetual growth sustained the fiction that material wealth would eventually trickle down to those at the bottom of the pyramid – neoliberal economists argued that if we can all benefit from a constantly growing pie then we should not be too concerned if some are given larger servings at the banquet of life. The growth mantra provided a convenient excuse to avoid difficult questions around inequality by offering the illusion that, to paraphrase John Steinbeck, we are all temporarily embarrassed millionaires – merely pre-rich, and that one fine day, if we work hard enough, our ship will come in.

But that future payday of prosperity for those not at the top of the capitalist tree may prove elusive. Capitalism's bounty is unevenly distributed, with the bulk of prosperity channelled to just a small percentage of already affluent citizens while a larger cohort endures stagnant or declining real wealth. It is true that some degree of trade-off between economic growth and wealth equality can be expected in a capitalist system – individuals need to be able to keep a meaningful proportion of what they earn in order to encourage innovation and risk-taking, but if this happens then inequality results. However, over the last half century or so the rising tide of prosperity, rather than lifting all boats, has tended to buoy only the superyachts, while those left behind are often kept afloat only by high debt levels. The Western economic miracle – premised on consumption-driven economic growth and largely funded by the savings of emerging Asian economies – now teeters atop an immense bubble of borrowings, but outstripping by far our debt spree in the world of finance is the enormous overdraft taken out on the natural world.

Handmade tale

Our ecological debt arises partly because GDP is a woefully inadequate metric of overall economic health. After the Second World War, GDP became the indispensable yardstick for Keynesian policies targeting macroeconomic flows of money – aggregate income and expenditure within an economy – and underlying capital balances were largely ignored. This focus on 'flows' of money rather than 'stocks' of assets means that GDP is necessarily backward-looking, giving an aggregate of market-intermediated transactions in a past period, while saying nothing about whether an economy is running down its asset base in order to produce this output. Capital stocks, on the other hand, constitute the true wealth of nations, corporations and individuals – they are a forward-facing indicator of future returns, comprising assets likely to yield goods or services into the future, and it is for this reason that businesses prepare not only income statements but also balance sheets recording the current value of income-generating assets. No responsible business ignores its balance sheet, but this is standard practice at a national level – conventional economists, it turns out, make very poor accountants.

If this selective accounting were to be abandoned for a more comprehensive form of bookkeeping then the global ledger would look very different. For while the world's manufactured capital such as machinery and infrastructure has approximately doubled on a per capita basis over the last few decades, 'natural capital' – that is, the world's nature-based assets, including air, water, soil, plants and animals – is estimated to have declined by around 40 per cent over the same period. In perhaps the ultimate demonstration of our egocentricity, only those things brought into being by human hands are accorded any formal value in the calculation of GDP. Delegating GDP as our catch-all indicator of economic health implies that, for example, the entire Amazon ecosystem has an effective economic value of zero – while Amazon.com is valued by financial markets in the trillions of dollars, and exploitable oil reserves lying beneath the 'overburden' of the Amazonian rainforest are recorded on company balance sheets in the billions.

Natural capital generates what economists clinically call 'ecosystem services' – those dividends from nature that directly contribute to human wellbeing, such as clean air, fresh water, the pollination of crops, and the renewal of soil fertility. Ecosystem services are effectively free labour extracted from the natural world, and although completely unrecorded in the calculation of GDP they are far more than a sideshow in terms of economic value creation. The economist Robert Costanza estimated in 2011 that global annual ecosystem services were valued at a colossal $125 trillion, almost double the prevailing world GDP at the time. As the American ecological economist Herman Daly commented, 'the economy is a wholly owned subsidiary of the environment, not the reverse' – the market economy is only a subset of the wider world of goods and services, and all human prosperity depends on nature and the benefits it provides.

In feeding off nature's bounty the economy is in effect parasitising the natural world, but our modern variant of capitalism – which depletes natural capital far beyond sustainable levels – is now breaking the first rule of successful parasites: do not kill your host.

Although the human-created supply chains girdling the world today are incredibly productive, they are nevertheless still inferior to those in the natural world. But when economists and business leaders talk about economic growth they are almost always referring to industrial and financial growth, and very rarely turn their attention to changes in natural capital stocks. Only those things that can be exploited and transacted on a market are recognised in conventional national accounts, and natural capital, like social capital, has largely been overlooked in our market-centric society. By putting a value only on those commodities that are wrested from nature and fed into the market machine – that is, pricing natural resources at extraction cost rather than replacement value – the modern world is cooking the books on a global scale. We are in effect treating the planet as a business in liquidation rather than as a going concern, and if this fire sale of the natural world is to stop then nature must somehow be put on the global balance sheet.

There are many who are squeamish about placing a monetary value on the natural world by pricing the priceless. They argue that we are meekly waving the white flag for the final victory of neoliberalism, and opening the door to a form of 'totalitarian capitalism' in which everything will be commodified. When everything has a price, they contend, then everything is tradeable, and those at the pinnacle of the economic pyramid will continue their program of appropriation – resulting in a twenty-first century version of the enclosure movement. They rightly note that putting a number on nature is crude and crass, and that many of the benefits provided by the natural world, such as oxygen from plants, have no substitutes at any price. They compare mainstream economists to Oscar Wilde's cynic, one who knows the price of everything and the value of nothing. But the truth is that by not putting a price on something we are in effect putting a zero price on it. The overconsumption of natural capital, unrecorded in conventional economic accounting, provides a temporary boost to income but erodes the underlying asset base needed to generate future returns. Our apparent transformation from scarcity to abundance is therefore deceptive – and 'free' is simply much too expensive in the long run.

Futures trading

Earth's stock of natural capital is analogous to a trust fund in which humans and other living organisms are the beneficiaries. However, by burning through nature's bequest humankind is acting like a trust fund kid carelessly blowing an inheritance – destroying natural capital for a one-off windfall, rather than living off the repeated benefits available when the capital base remains intact. But perhaps a better analogy for our current form of capitalism – which eats into irreplaceable reserves of natural capital, calls the result income, and fails to register the decline in underlying benefit-producing assets – is to picture it as a type of planetary Ponzi scheme. A Ponzi scheme is a form of fraud that lures new investment with the promise of high returns, and then uses these inflows to pay profits to earlier investors. These swindles provide the illusion of high returns due to savvy decision-making or privileged admission into the Next Big Thing, but in fact the returns arise in large part from consuming the asset base itself. The game lasts only as long as there are inflows of capital, and when new capital dries up then the structure collapses.

Due to our failure to assign a value to natural capital, our economic system is a Ponzi play on the natural world – one in which the returns extracted from nature are unsustainable but temporarily masked by new entrants offering up fresh contributions in the form of unexploited resources. These new entrants are often poorer countries drawn by the promise of a First World lifestyle, and they are being doubly gamed because natural resources are significantly undervalued by the market as there is no price placed on primary materials other than the cost of extraction. As the US Securities and Exchange Commission cautions in another context, 'Past performance is no guarantee of future results', and this warning applies equally to our dealings with the natural world. If we continue to consume more than nature's yield – if withdrawals are not supported by underlying capital replenishment – then we will eventually bankrupt the biosphere.

Unlike other pyramid schemes, the Ponzi play on nature is supported, or at least tacitly sanctioned, by those in power. Because GDP measures only activity and not underlying balances, our economic system fails to make a distinction between creative growth – that generated by technological innovation, specialisation and exchange – and mere parasitic growth derived from eating into capital stocks. GDP ignores the steady build-up of liabilities that will be handed down to later generations in the form of a diminished natural asset base, and this depletion of natural capital in turn reduces the amount of ecosystem services that can be provided in the future. Businesses are required to make an accounting entry offsetting asset depreciation expenses against revenue, which has the effect of reducing reported income, but this is not done with GDP calculations. Not only do GDP measures overstate short-term economic performance because there is no corresponding debit for asset depletion, but there is also no strong economic incentive to conserve productive capital – instead, there is a bias to short-term gains rather than long-term maintenance of infrastructure.

Although the words 'economics' and 'ecology' are both derived from the Greek word *oikos* – 'dwelling place' – this common origin is not reflected in conventional economics, with the natural world treated as a mere input into human production processes and a receptacle for the resulting waste. Nature has been treated as a free resource, quite literally a free-for-all – the natural world's life-giving benefits generally only count, and are counted, in economic terms when they are destroyed, whether it be rainforest felled for lumber or fish dredged from the ocean or wilderness groomed into farmland. Rather than national accounts being docked for the costs of growth, these losses are unrecorded, or – worse still – added in as a contribution to GDP growth when markets are obliged to clean up the damage inflicted on the natural world. The modern world is therefore not only blowing its inheritance, but is also leaving a huge bill for younger generations and the yet-to-be-born – and as a result, industrial capitalism has colonised the future as well as the present.

7

COWBOYS & ASTRONAUTS

The cowboys commandeering Spaceship Earth

The Wild West

The astronaut John Glenn was the first American to orbit the Earth and the first to take colour photographs of our home planet from space, using a cheap 35mm camera purchased at a drug store a few days before lift-off. After a hair-raising five-hour flight and re-entry, Glenn emerged from his capsule in early 1962 as a national hero – the latest poster boy in the Space Race against the Soviet Union, lauded and awarded by President Kennedy, and honoured with a ticker-tape parade in New York. Later, when asked what was going through his mind while listening to the countdown, he didn't wax lyrical about the wonder of catapulting a human into space or the feat of moving from the Wright Brothers to spacecraft in under six decades. Instead, he replied, 'I felt exactly how you would feel if you were getting ready to launch and knew you were sitting on top of two million parts – all built by the lowest bidder'. Capitalism – a marvel of complexity and co-ordination, driven by the profit motive, and marshalling the skills of thousands of individuals – had, it seemed, once again proven itself against the competition by constructing the most advanced machine ever known to humankind.

John Glenn's flight occurred at the midpoint of the post-war economic miracle, when Keynesian-managed capitalism reigned in the West.

Less well quoted is Glenn's addendum that *Friendship 7* was built by myriad parties 'under a government contract' – Uncle Sam was the very visible hand behind this project. The state has always had a symbiotic relationship with 'free markets' – as a distributor and enforcer of property rights, for consumer protection, and often to provide essential research and infrastructure. During the Second World War markets were actively managed to serve the needs of the wider community rather than the owners of capital, and governments continued to play a leading economic role for the following few decades. But over the last half century free market fundamentalism has once again infiltrated almost every aspect of modern life. The relentless dynamic of neoliberal capitalism – with the market as preferred middleman in human relations and an unremitting focus on growth – has been abetted by the fixation on GDP, while the money economy diverts the lion's share of material wealth to a fraction of the global population. Governments, previously essential partners in the middle way of managed capitalism during the post-war Golden Years, are now largely derided as bit players by free marketeers, only demanded in times of crisis.

Free markets have undoubtedly delivered substantial benefits. Not only is there a logical link between capitalism and liberty – for if individuals are to fully pursue their own interests then they must be given unfettered freedom to do so – but the discipline exerted by the price mechanism filters out inefficient businesses and drives innovation. Industrial capitalism has generated a cornucopia of material wealth unimaginable to previous generations, and its essentially decentralised character most closely mirrors the vast emergent system that is the globalised world. As observed by Vaclav Havel, the Czech Republic's first president following liberation from Soviet shackles, capitalism is 'the only natural economy, the only kind that makes sense, the only one that can lead to prosperity, because it is the only one that reflects the nature of life itself'. But although the free market system now seems more natural than nature, ironically it fails to value and maintain natural capital – our biggest source of wealth, integral to all human life and flourishing – and in consequence industrial capitalism is eating itself from within.

Capitalism also corrodes social capital, the intangible bonds that tie a community together. It diligently works to shape its subjects into its own image, and if we are not already the atomistic entities that neoliberal economics assumes us to be then the system does its best to mould us into the cold-blooded calculating machines of theory. In testament to the power of stories, research demonstrates that economics students, even after accounting for selection bias, tend to become more self-interested and less altruistic than others over time, while other studies indicate that the majority of citizens in industrialised countries have shown marked increases in individualistic attitudes in recent decades. Additionally, capitalism's storytellers are an unrepresentative lot – economics is the most male-dominated academic discipline, even more so than the STEM quartet of science, technology, engineering and mathematics, and practitioners from the industrialised West enjoy a near monopoly in the discipline. Tending to come from near the peak of the social pyramid where the principal beneficiaries of capitalism also reside, they add weight to the argument that conventional economics is little more than politics in disguise.

The Gospel of Growth, the cult of individualism and the relegation of the natural world as a mere footnote to mainstream theory has resulted in what the economist Kenneth Boulding called a 'Cowboy Economy', in which ever-growing consumption is fuelled by opening up new horizons for resource exploitation. In the Cowboy Economy, Boulding explained,

> consumption is regarded as a good thing and production likewise; and the success of the economy is measured by the amount of the throughput from the 'factors of production,' a part of which, at any rate, is extracted from the reservoirs of raw materials and noneconomic objects, and another part of which is output into the reservoirs of pollution.

Like the romanticised renegades of the past, many capitalist cowboys see themselves as rugged individualists, always on the move, pushing forward the frontiers of conquest, seeking their fortune under the guise of progress. But the cowboys in the Old West often lived outside the bounds of law, whereas our modern cowboys are the ultimate insiders. The capitalist cowboys have co-opted a story that legitimises their actions – a tale, however, that is no longer fit for purpose.

Science fiction

Economics and the hard sciences have, almost since the inception of modern economics, indulged in a great relay race of stories. Thomas Malthus, writing at the beginning of our fossil fuelled age, viewed life as a perpetual fight for scarce resources. In turn, the theory of natural selection was, as Charles Darwin observed in *On the Origin of Species*, 'the doctrine of Malthus applied with manifold force to the whole animal and vegetable kingdoms'. Darwin originally saw evolution, like capitalism, as a form of creative destruction, in which 'from the war of nature, from famine and death, the most exalted object which we are capable of conceiving, namely, the production of the higher animals, directly follows'. In his own rendition of the invisible hand, Darwin argued that natural selection 'works solely by and for the good of each being, [and] all corporeal and mental endowments will tend to progress towards perfection'. Out of this fierce struggle for existence would emerge 'endless forms most beautiful and most wonderful' – culminating, as Victorian Britain no doubt saw it, in the miraculous transformation from ape to Englishman.

Despite his salute to self-interest and competition in the natural world, Darwin was a shy and retiring homebody, happy to focus on his barnacles and finches and earthworms, and to let others fight the good fight on his behalf. Thomas Huxley, known as Darwin's Bulldog, described nature as a 'gladiator's show' and brought that spirit of combat to debates against those still anchored to the biblical conception of creation, with later disciples simplifying the evolutionary story still further. However, in *The Descent of Man* – written in 1871, a dozen years after *On the Origin of Species* – Darwin presented a much more nuanced account of natural selection, one in which 'those communities, which included the greatest number of the most sympathetic members, would flourish best, and rear the greatest number of offspring'. Moving away from a focus on individuals to a focus on the collective, Darwin observed that intergroup competition favours species with a greater proportion of altruists – that is, selfishness might beat selflessness at an individual level, but not at the group level. Evolution, it turned out, was as much, if not more, about co-operation as competition.

Modern science has backed up Darwin's later intuitions. Adam Smith was in fact mistaken when he asserted that the 'propensity to truck, barter, and exchange' is an exclusive trait of humanity – 'nature' is a verb as much as a noun, a vast network of trade, collaboration and, sometimes, competition among living creatures. Only now, as the intricacies of the natural world are truly being fathomed, are we realising that symbiosis and interdependency, rather than domination and hierarchy, are the norm in nature. Perhaps more importantly, nature also offers a very basic lesson in sustainability – other than the occasional meteorite arriving and spacecraft departing, the natural world is a completely contained system, one that not only recycles all outputs, but in fact converts them to higher and ever more complex uses. Our Cowboy Economy does the exact opposite, extracting the Earth's bounty and then discarding the waste in the atmosphere, the oceans, in rivers, and on land, all the time methodically chiselling away at the natural capital that underpins human wealth.

In the Cowboy Economy described by Boulding, consumption is assumed to be a rough indicator of the standard of living, and consumption for consumption's sake is celebrated. Boulding contrasted this global Wild West to an alternative vision – that of the 'Spaceman Economy', in which:

> The essential measure of the success of the economy is not production and consumption at all, but the nature, extent, quality, and complexity of the total capital stock, including in this the state of the human bodies and minds included in the system.

In a Spaceman Economy the aim is to optimise wellbeing within a given level of sustainable consumption – to make the most of the least – with consumption 'regarded as something to be minimized rather than maximized'. Along with other environmental economists, Boulding implied that his mainstream peers had confused the journey for the destination, had prioritised means over ends, by focusing on income at the expense of underlying wealth.

Boulding made the observation – obvious to most, other than market-fixated economists – that the Earth is a closed system, a lonely wandering voyager in space, and that exponentially increasing consumption of natural resources on a finite planet is impossible in the long run. But the frontier logic of Cowboy Capitalism – which favours those who can capture and exploit the greatest bounty, regardless of waste – is destroying the ecosystems and limited reserves of natural capital that support our planetary lifeboat. As recently as 1950, at the beginning of the Great Acceleration, the global economy was living within its means and consuming a sustainable yield from the natural world. However by the early 1980s the demands on natural capital began to surpass Earth's regenerative capacity, and it is estimated that humans are now consuming nature at almost twice the rate that the planet's ecosystems can be renewed. Our unique planet – the only one, as far as we know, in the entire universe with fire, surface water, and living creatures – is being recklessly dismantled in an ever-accelerating race for material wealth.

Anthropoid asteroid

The capitalist locomotive initially driven by coal was later turbocharged with the injection of oil and natural gas into the energy mix, and riding astride this machine the modern world massively increased its program of exploitation and extraction. Now, almost 250 years after the red-letter year of 1776, Man the tool-making animal has co-opted the entire planet as its tool – so much so that many scientists propose that our current epoch be named 'the Anthropocene', the age of humans. Although opinions vary as to the start date of the Anthropocene, the most popular suggestion is the mid-twentieth century, in line with the first stirrings of the Great Acceleration. Since this time we have witnessed not only a huge increase in population and global output, but also the emergence of clear human-caused geological indicators within the Earth's crust – radioactive debris from A-bomb explosions, fly ash from power stations, widespread microplastics pollution, and even vast catacombs of chicken bones. In addition to this sad sedimentary signature, these future fossils, other markers less legibly etched into the planet – such as burgeoning greenhouse gas levels, acidification of the ocean, and extensive habitat and biodiversity loss – serve as eloquent testimony to the world-altering impact of humanity.

Of the past five mass extinctions on this planet, only the most recent, around 66 million years ago, was caused by an intergalactic intruder. All other extinction events were triggered by significant climate change, mostly due to giant volcanoes pouring out carbon dioxide and other heat-trapping gases into the atmosphere. By unleashing the explosive power of hydrocarbons, humanity has itself become a type of supervolcano, and what were once Acts of God have now instead become Acts of Man. So much coal, oil and natural gas has been exhumed from the Earth's crust that we have unbalanced the planet's most vital system of exchange – the carbon cycle, the in-breath and out-breath of the Earth as a whole. Plants, algae and some forms of bacteria take in carbon dioxide and, using the sun's energy, combine with water to produce carbohydrates and oxygen. Closing the circle, other living creatures consume oxygen and carbohydrates, and exhale carbon dioxide. In this way, the Earth's fixed supply of carbon ceaselessly pulses through the atmosphere, the oceans, the soil, and all living things.

Humans are firmly embedded in this eternal dance – we are in effect internal combustion engines fuelled not by the hydrocarbons demanded by our machine creations, but by carbohydrates in the form of food. To sate our machines, billions of tonnes of fossilised carbon are disinterred from the ground each year and then excreted into the atmosphere, resulting in a lopsided carbon cycle that is likely to have already brought the long spring of the Holocene epoch – at 12,000 years, no more than a blink of an eye at a geological scale – to an end. In turn, global heating caused by elevated greenhouse gas levels is driving more extreme weather events, desertifying sprawling tracts of land, and placing acute pressure on freshwater resources. Adding to this are fossil fuelled fishing and farming practices that empty the seas and flay the earth, while the polluting byproducts of carbon-fired capitalism inflict further damage on marine and terrestrial environments.

In consequence, humans today are living through what has been called the 'Holocene extinction', the sixth mass extinction event in Earth's history, with species die-offs occurring at a speed thousands of times higher than the historic background rate. And the pace of annihilation ratchets up further each year as the planet's resources continue to be overconsumed within a system already weakened by climate change and disintegrating webs of life. A paper published in 2022 found an average 69 per cent decline in the abundance of monitored wildlife populations since 1970, while other studies suggest that around one million plant and animal species may vanish within the next few decades. The soil that directly or indirectly supports most of the planet's life is eroding so quickly that the UN's Food and Agriculture Organization predicts that 90 per cent of the world's topsoil is likely to be at risk by 2050 if intensive farming practices are maintained. The oceans that spread across more than two-thirds of the Earth's surface and contain almost a third of its species are facing their own great extinction, with warming waters killing coral reefs, acidifying seawater hampering the ability of creatures to form shells and skeletons, and overfishing rapidly emptying the seas. These are not 'natural disasters' in the true sense of the word, for there is nothing 'natural' about their ultimate origin.

The good news is that this calamity unfolding before us is not attributable to raging volcanoes or a rogue rock bearing down on Earth – it is a human-caused predicament that can be solved by humans. The bad news is that the pressing problems of the world are not as conventionally dramatic as an approaching asteroid or a flaring mountain range – rather, they are more like a stealth predator, whose gradually shifting baselines lull us into kicking the can down the road just a little longer. Compounding this is the narrative confusion generated by what has been labelled 'the environmentalist's paradox' – that is, while often substantial improvements in average human wellbeing are readily apparent, collapsing ecosystems are far less obvious to the average person on the street. But these apparently contradictory trends are in fact two sides of the same coin – humankind's heedless disruption of nature's intricate webs of mutuality, co-evolved over aeons, has delivered material riches, but is also desolating planetary health.

Joan Robinson, something of an agnostic in the Holy War between capitalism and communism during the twentieth century, asserted that 'the purpose of studying economics is not to acquire a set of ready-made answers to economic questions, but to learn how to avoid being deceived by economists'. Knowledge is power, and although Adam Smith's Invisible Hand has delivered staggering material wealth to billions today, it also picks the pocket of our future-selves, later generations and the natural world, while permitting the transfer of wealth from the many to the few and the disposal of waste from the few to the many. Orthodox economics and our present form of capitalism are not aligned with the needs of our living systems, and we must therefore reconsider how we do business with nature. The operating manual for Spaceship Earth is out of date, the cowboys have been at the helm for far too long, and it is time now for a crew change.

AIR

AIR

8

EMISSION POSSIBLE

Fire 2.0 and atmospheric pollution

Pyromania

In late June 1988 the Director of NASA's Institute for Space Studies, Dr James Hansen, was invited by a US Congressional Committee in Washington to provide a summary of his findings on climate change. On the day of the hearing, as if nature had conspired to drive home Hansen's message, the temperature in the nation's capital peaked at just over 100 degrees Fahrenheit. Wiping the sweat from his brow, Hansen departed from his profession's customary restraint and stated baldly that 'the greenhouse effect has been detected, and it is changing our climate *now*'. When quizzed further, he explained that NASA was 99 per cent confident that global heating was due to a build-up of carbon dioxide and other greenhouse gases – this was no random fluctuation, he asserted, and human-induced alteration to the global climate would affect life on Earth 'for centuries to come'. Hansen's testimony that the Earth's atmosphere and climate was changing due to the burning of fossil fuels was decisive in moving the global warming debate from the rarefied realm of science into the public arena.

Humankind has always been a fire species, burning things to suit its ends. While many of what were once considered to be humanity's unique traits – toolmaking, trading, even farming itself – have now been ceded to other species as our knowledge of the natural world deepens, fire-making remains our one distinctive attribute among wider creation. Evidence suggests that our distant ancestor Homo erectus was opportunistically using fire more than a million years ago, and had harnessed flames into campfires around 400,000 years before present. Fire not only provided protection against nocturnal predators and the cold, but may have fast-tracked the development of speech as early hominids clustered around night-time hearths and exchanged tales. Assisting the development of language were the increased calories and cognitive horsepower made possible by fire – the process of cooking not only sterilises food and neutralises toxic compounds, but also makes food easier to chew and digest, boosting the amount of nutrients available. By co-opting fire for cooking, humans in effect outsourced their gut, and energy otherwise taken up by the laborious task of digestion could instead be channelled to the brain. As a result, over time our digestive system shrunk while our brains grew.

Fire formed modern humans, and it also shaped our landscapes. Our big-brained forager ancestors mobilised their advanced language skills and ability to tame fire to implement their own form of creative destruction – burning and clearing land to improve hunting odds, to foster new growth to lure prey, and to encourage the emergence of food-bearing plants. As a result of these 'firestick farming' techniques, much of the inhabited planet was converted into a mosaic of grasslands, and over time an increasing proportion of the world's flora and fauna comprised fire-adapted species. The Agricultural Revolution significantly ramped up land-clearing activities, while later enterprises such as metals smelting consumed enormous quantities of wood and further denuded the terrain. As far back as two-and-a-half thousand years ago, Plato lamented the degradation of the countryside in his native Attica due to deforestation and agriculture:

What now remains, compared with what existed, is like the skeleton of a sick man, all the fat and soft earth wasted away and only the bare framework of the land being left.

Humanity, the pint-sized Prometheus, seized the gift of fire, but like in the ancient Greek myth, a curse lay embedded within this apparent boon.

Fire 2.0 – the exploitation of fossil fuels to power globalised industrial capitalism – marked a new assault on the natural world, but one far more insidious than earlier incursions. By drawing oil, coal and natural gas from the Earth's crust, and then burning it to secure superhuman levels of energy, modern man has knocked the carbon cycle wildly out of balance. Carbon is a shapeshifter, nature's own incarnation in which spirit becomes flesh – atmospheric carbon in the form of carbon dioxide is captured by light-eating plants and some other organisms through the process of photosynthesis, then converted to carbohydrates, which in turn are consumed and become the building blocks of all other creatures. But carbon also has another, equally important function in the creation of life. Not only does it constitute the raw material of every known biological entity – essential scaffolding for the complex adaptive system that is an individual organism – but atmospheric carbon also plays a vital role for the living world by creating the climatic conditions necessary to maintain the Earth at a stable overall temperature.

Although classed as an 'impurity' in the Earth's atmosphere – making up a mere 0.04 per cent, or one part in 2,500, of the total – carbon dioxide exerts a hugely disproportionate effect on the climate. This near-phantom trace compound helps provide an atmospheric blanket for our planet through the operation of 'the greenhouse effect' – the process by which water vapour and some gases in the atmosphere trap solar energy reflected from the Earth's surface, in the same way that the glass walls of a greenhouse retain the heat of the sun. Put simply, if there were no greenhouse effect, there would be no life – the Earth would just be another ball of rock and ice silently spinning in space, rather than a life-thronged planet flourishing at an average temperature of 15 degrees Celsius. Although water vapour and clouds are the largest contributors to the greenhouse effect, they increase in line with temperature and tend to act as climate stabilisers, as clouds reflect sunlight and usually have a net cooling effect. Carbon dioxide and other greenhouse gases are the swing factor – and during the recent geological period have anchored the Earth in a Goldilocks Zone of not too hot, not too cold, but just right. There can, however, be too much of a good thing, and our fossil fuelled growth spurt has upset this finely calibrated dynamic equilibrium established over millennia.

For most of the Holocene epoch carbon dioxide levels in the atmosphere hovered at just under 300 parts per million and this stability also contributed to a steady climate, creating the conditions necessary for the Agricultural Revolution. However, since the Great Acceleration beginning in the 1950s carbon dioxide levels have increased at a compounding rate, in line with other markers of modernity such as population and output growth, and now sit at well over 400 parts per million, around 50 per cent higher than the Holocene average. The Earth has warmed by approximately 1.2 degrees Celsius since accurate thermometer readings began in the mid-nineteenth century, with further heating literally baked-in as the climate system plays catch-up with the huge volume of atmospheric carbon already poured into the sky. Past shifts in atmospheric carbon levels – even those triggered by abrupt geophysical events such as volcanic eruptions – happened relatively slowly, and changes to the climate were correspondingly slow. But now, in the Age of Humans, the Earth is heating many times faster than at any time since the demise of the dinosaurs.

Sources and sinks

The idea that our planet has experienced wild changes in its composition over unimaginably vast spans of time is a relatively recent one – for most of human history the Earth was commonly thought, in the West at least, to be no more than about 6,000 years old. In the mid-seventeenth century, for example, the Irish Archbishop James Ussher claimed to have deduced the exact date of Creation after conducting a detailed study on the chronology of the Bible. By adding up the genealogies of Adam and his brood, and painstakingly cross-referencing these against other classical texts, Ussher declared that the world saw its first sunrise on Sunday 23 October 4004 BC. Working from this absolute base, he could then calculate other key dates from Genesis – Adam and Eve, for example, were ejected from Paradise on 10 November 4004 BC, and Noah's Ark finally bumped into Mount Ararat on 5 May 2348 BC, a Wednesday. Sadly for the Archbishop, his calculations turned out to be a colossal underestimate, and from the late eighteenth century the concept of 'deep time' – the idea that the age of Earth should be measured in millions or even billions of years – gradually usurped the ecclesiastical exactitude of the Old Testament.

One of the first to publicly venture that the Earth was far older than the stories told in the Bible was James Hutton, a contemporary and close friend of Adam Smith. Reading rocks rather than the Good Book, Hutton observed that geological formations around his home town of Edinburgh exhibited what he called 'unconformities', and reasoned that these were due to a long-running cycle of silty deposits, mineralisation and erosion, interspersed with the occasional tectonic upheaval. By asserting that the Earth had been subject to constant change since the depths of remote time, Hutton not only upended the Creationist narrative of Earth as merely 200 or so generations old, but he also challenged the prevailing reductionist mindset by arguing that biological and geological processes are entwined. Natural systems such as the climate, Hutton argued, had shaped and continued to shape the Earth's surface. However, it would take another two centuries for scientists to prove that the process also ran in the opposite direction, and that the Earth's surface can influence the climate.

The Earth's crust plays a key part in the carbon cycle through the process of rock dissolution and creation. When certain rocks erode they combine with carbon dioxide to form new compounds, sucking carbon from the air and locking it into the crust. In periods when temperatures and rainfall are higher, which typically coincides with higher atmospheric carbon levels, the rate of erosion accelerates and carbon take-up is correspondingly higher, eventually countering high temperatures due to lower greenhouse gas levels. Conversely, in low atmospheric carbon periods, when temperatures and rainfall are generally lower, then erosion rates fall and less carbon dioxide is sequestered. The Earth's crust and the atmosphere perpetually exchange carbon – the land capturing carbon from the air through the weathering of rocks, while sometimes the dynamic is switched when volcanic eruptions spew large amounts of carbon into the atmosphere. This see-sawing system of checks and balances has helped keep temperatures relatively constant for extended geological periods, acting as a type of global thermostat until some external event disrupts the equilibrium.

For most of the Earth's history, the planet has recorded much higher carbon dioxide levels, and therefore far warmer temperatures, than today. Immediately after the last great extinction event 66 million years ago it is estimated that – due to the asteroid vaporising carbonate-rich rocks on impact, and then triggering wildfires in up to 70 per cent of the world's forests – atmospheric carbon levels were somewhere in the order of 1,000 to 2,300 parts per million, between roughly twice and five times more carbon in the air than today. The global thermostat, however, works at an indiscernibly slow pace for mortal beings, and it took the planet another 50 million years to reduce carbon dioxide levels to around 400 parts per million. Over vast expanses of geological time jostling continents floating atop molten rock would not only open the volcanic spigots every now and then, but would also stopper fountaining supervolcanoes or buckle into huge mountain ranges such as the Himalayas. These mountain uplift events provided newly exposed mineral surfaces that over time became giant carbon sinks, and by the dawn of the Industrial Revolution the level of carbon in the air had fallen to around 280 parts per million.

The living world has also played a role in shaping the climate. Prior to the appearance of photosynthetic single-celled organisms around 3.5 billion years ago, free oxygen was virtually non-existent in the atmosphere, and instead was locked in a tight bond with other elements such as carbon. Over immeasurable aeons evolving organisms took in water and carbon dioxide and respired it as oxygen, and as a result the element now comprises just over 20 per cent of Earth's atmosphere. The 'Great Oxidation Event' of around 2.5 billion years ago began in the waters of the world, but over time plants, fungi and other organisms crept on to land and began to erode rock formations, in turn drawing down more carbon dioxide from the atmosphere. A biological thermostat – with plants sequestering more carbon dioxide as atmospheric carbon and temperatures increased – complemented the geological thermostat from the weathering of rocks. The air we have today, then, is the product of life itself, and the Earth was transformed into an exquisitely tuned system in which life summons life.

A tough bitch

The individual who more than anyone advanced the idea that Earth was a type of self-regulating superorganism – an evolving complex adaptive system that creates the conditions of its own flourishing – was the English scientist James Lovelock. Forsaking the modern trend towards specialisation, Lovelock ranged widely in his academic and professional pursuits – studying chemistry and later medicine at university, and working stints at organisations as diverse as NASA, the British counterintelligence agency MI5, and the oil company Shell. A free spirit who never accepted a university-tenured position, Lovelock was also a supreme gadfly. But despite often being at odds with the environmental movement – in one interview he lamented that 'it's become a religion, and religions don't worry too much about facts' – this outsider may have had a greater positive impact on the natural world than any other scientist.

In the late 1950s Lovelock jerry-built on his kitchen table a small contraption that could detect minute amounts of pollutants in gases. This device, which he called the Electron Capture Detector, was later modified by the US Food and Drug Administration to test for toxic chemicals in food, providing empirical ammunition in the early 1960s for Rachel Carson's argument in *Silent Spring* that pesticides were seeping into the wider environment. Later that decade, using his Electron Capture Detector on the western Irish coast, Lovelock discovered that what was considered to be clean air was in fact carrying human-created compounds known as chlorofluorocarbons. These contaminants, commonly referred to as CFCs, had been used extensively by industry as a refrigerant and for aerosol sprays, and initially Lovelock believed that there was no cause for alarm. However, subsequent studies showed that airborne CFCs, when broken up by ultraviolet radiation, released chlorine atoms which in turn destroyed ozone molecules. As a result, the Earth's protective ozone layer, which shields the planet from harmful ultraviolet rays, was becoming pockmarked and perforated by giant holes.

Lovelock's invention demonstrated that manmade chemicals were infiltrating and damaging the planet on a global scale – not only in the atmosphere, but also in animal tissue, from penguins in Antarctica to human breast milk – but it was another insight that brought him to widespread public attention. Working for NASA as a foot soldier in the Space Race, he turned his mind to the question of whether there might be life on Mars. The Martian atmosphere is largely static and made up almost entirely of carbon dioxide, and, following the scientific adage that an organism at absolute equilibrium is a dead organism, he concluded that the planet was lifeless. Lovelock then conducted a thought experiment, asking himself how Earth might look to an extra-terrestrial observer. In contrast to Mars, Earth's atmosphere is in a state of constant flux, perpetually exchanging different gases, including far greater concentrations of oxygen and methane than would otherwise be expected. Lovelock realised that Earth's organisms were generating and maintaining this dynamic balance – that Earth is a living planet that, in effect, breathes.

Lovelock argued that, by maintaining atmospheric chemistry at a steady state and regulating temperature, these organisms were instrumental in creating

a complex entity involving the Earth's biosphere, atmosphere, oceans, and soil; the totality constituting a feedback ... system which seeks an optimal physical and chemical environment for life on this planet.

Rather than prosaically labelling his theory 'earth systems science' as originally intended, Lovelock took the advice of a neighbouring novelist and named it after the Greek goddess who shaped the living world from Chaos – Gaia. The Gaia hypothesis became a sort of New Age religion for some in the 1970s, but Lovelock resisted these woo-woo tendencies. The atmosphere, he said, is a biological construction – 'not living, but like a cat's fur, a bird's feathers, or the paper of a wasp's nest, an extension of a living system designed to maintain a chosen environment'. The Earth in totality was not a conscious entity, he emphasised, and his personification of it was just a metaphor – no more serious, he observed, 'than the thoughts of a sailor who refers to his ship as "she"'.

Despite his resolute rejection of the notion that Earth was conscious, there is something almost holy about the Gaia hypothesis. Everything is connected, and just as the Sun and its planets are tied together in a cosmic dance by the invisible strings of gravity, so too on Earth all things are intertwined in an intricate self-supporting web. Lovelock's vision – emphasising the links rather than the separations, the system rather than the components – was an affront to the reductionism of classical science still in thrall to the discovery of that molecular package known as DNA. Lovelock had used a telescope to arrive at his theory of Gaia, and was later aided in his research by a scientist wielding a microscope. The biologist Lynn Margulis contributed her expertise on microbes to explain how they affect the atmosphere and the Earth's crust, and she also demonstrated how life evolved from simple bacteria to Darwin's endless forms through a process known as 'symbiogenesis' – a process in which evolution is driven not just by gradual mutations, but also through symbiosis that merges organisms into new forms. Margulis asserted that, just as life unfolded and became more complex due to co-operation between different organisms, so too planet Earth was 'symbiosis seen from space' – a miraculous self-righting latticework of interactions and feedback effects in which the system as a whole hovers around a set point.

Margulis also made the observation that 'Gaia is a tough bitch'. Like the human body – another emergent system comprising human cells and other forms of life such as bacteria, parasites and viruses, and typically working towards a homeostatic set point – Gaia can lose some cells and still survive. Gaia may be a religion to some, but it differs from most other belief systems in one key respect – it does not elevate Homo sapiens as a favoured species among the other animals, and does not claim that Mother Earth was benignly created for human hegemony. James Lovelock noted that humankind is a relatively recent arrival to the community of the living, little more than 'the froth on top of a glass of beer', and that there should be no expectation that Gaia has a particular favourite among its millions of species. The Gaia hypothesis offered a twist on received Darwinian wisdom – for not only does the environment shape living creatures, but life also shapes the environment. And it also provided a warning – our particular species of bipedal ape, although granted almost godlike powers through the gift of fire, could also be the agent of its own demise.

9

THE EFFLUENT SOCIETY

The playbook of denial, division and delay

Heisszeit

Like James Lovelock before him, James Hansen was a NASA employee who, seduced by the sheer variability and beauty of our home planet, turned his attention away from the original subject of his study. In Hansen's case the celestial body in question was Venus, the hottest planet in our solar system due to an atmosphere filled with carbon dioxide, but his focus later switched to Earth because 'a planet changing before our eyes is more interesting and important'. Earth is a fire planet because it is also an air planet – by producing both oxygen and carbon-based fuel it creates the conditions necessary for combustion, whether that be the flamboyant conflagration of a wildfire or the slow-burn of animal respiration. However, the modern era of fossil fuelled capitalism, a mere one-fiftieth of the 12,000-year-old Holocene epoch, has set aflame the world's delicate carbon cycle.

Hydrocarbons are everywhere in modern society – we burn them to power our machines, we wear them as synthetic fibres such as nylon, and we indirectly eat them via an industrialised farming system that is absolutely reliant on fossil fuel–based fertilisers. They comprise around half the world's commercial tonnage, and have been a key enabler of modern globalisation by powering sea, air and road transportation. Oil, the reigning Carbon King, is the lifeblood of the modern world – each day 100 million barrels of the dark, viscous fluid pump through the economic circulatory system – and to satisfy our ravenous carbon cravings humanity is literally going to the ends of the Earth, to previously pristine areas such as the Arctic, in search of this fossilised sunlight.

Fire feeds off air and returns a new compound into the atmosphere, and modern humankind's reliance on fossil fuels has driven a rapid expansion in atmospheric carbon levels since the start of the Industrial Revolution, with concentrations of carbon dioxide increasing by around 50 per cent and methane by more than 150 per cent since Adam Smith published *The Wealth of Nations*. These accelerating levels of greenhouse gases have already contributed to increased global heating, and are on track to lift global average temperatures by at least 3 degrees Celsius by 2100 if present rates of hydrocarbon exploitation continue. Adding to the carbon that is burned by humans and pumped into the atmosphere are other manmade actions pushing the global carbon cycle further out of balance, such as land clearing and intensive agriculture that release stored carbon. Previously the carbon cycle was moderated by feedback effects such as increased plant growth and carbon dioxide uptake during warmer periods, but now 'positive' feedbacks are overwhelming the climate system. Despite the label, there is nothing positive about these processes – they amplify the effects of the initial change, and can lead to a tipping point in which the Earth's climate moves abruptly to a new set state.

Potential triggers for climate tipping points include the loss of ice which reduces the ability of Earth to reflect sunlight, shifts in ocean circulation due to melting ice sheets, and the detonation of dormant 'methane bombs' as permafrost thaws in the far Northern Hemisphere. These ramifying loops of knock-on effects can not only set off an irreversible step-change in the climate system, but they also make the task of modelling climate change infinitely more complex. Like human society and the markets nested within them, the global climate system is an emergent system in which apparently small changes to constituent elements can exert a disproportionate effect on the whole – where, apocryphally at least, the beat of a butterfly's wings in the Amazon can lead to a tornado in Texas a few weeks later. Although climate change is not a newly recognised phenomenon – back in 1951 the writer and biologist Rachel Carson concluded that 'now in our own lifetime we are witnessing a startling alteration of climate' – only in recent decades have we developed the computational power to attempt to accurately model its likely effects.

In the late nineteenth century, when carbon dioxide levels were still less than 300 parts per million, Swedish chemist Svante Arrhenius calculated that if atmospheric carbon was to double then Earth would warm by around 5 degrees Celsius. For Arrhenius this was purely an academic exercise, as he never expected carbon dioxide levels to increase by that amount – like many others, he suffered from a failure of imagination and grossly underestimated the potential of fossil fuelled industrial capitalism. However, projections by the UN and other bodies predict that carbon dioxide concentrations of 600 parts per million could in fact be breached some time around 2050 if the world continues to consume hydrocarbons on a 'business as usual' basis – levels not seen for 50 million years, a time when the Earth was completely iceless. It is no comfort that, to date, climate scientists have been depressingly correct in their projections, with a study published in 2019 showing that the overwhelming majority of climate models had correctly forecast temperature increases within standard error bars.

Although the raw processing power of supercomputers now permits accurate estimates of likely changes in climate over time, it is incredibly difficult to model the damage that global heating will inflict on both the human-created world and the rest of nature. Increases in average global temperatures in the order of a couple of degrees may not sound significant, but fine differences can make a huge impact – just as the complex emergent system that is the human body becomes feverish at levels of one or two degrees above the equilibrium point of 37 degrees Celsius, so too the Earth is becoming febrile with the virus that is carbon-fired capitalism. Studies predict that additional warming of two degrees will kill almost all coral reefs and reduce global food availability by around 100 calories a day, while just three degrees of warming would see many island nations submerged and spark a tragic new form of globalisation as millions of climate refugees flee to more hospitable zones. The world has entered into what the Germans call *Heisszeit* – 'the Heat Age', rhyming with, and a counterpoint to, *Eiszeit*, 'the Ice Age' – and what are currently the hottest months on record will be among the coolest for the remainder of the twenty-first century, and far beyond, as anomalies increasingly edge into averages.

Combust and boom

James Hansen, the scientist who brought climate change to the front pages of newspapers around the world, proved to be a modern-day Cassandra – gifted with the power of prophecy, but fated to remain unheeded by those in power. Initially, government support was strong – the first President Bush vowed soon after Hansen's congressional testimony to deploy 'the White House effect' to combat the greenhouse effect, and four years later the US became a founding member of the UN Framework Convention on Climate Change (UNFCCC), which aimed to 'to achieve ... stabilization of greenhouse gas concentrations in the atmosphere at a level that would prevent dangerous anthropogenic interference with the climate system'. The UNFCCC had been spawned by another entity in the alphabet soup of climate acronyms, the IPCC – the Intergovernmental Panel on Climate Change, a UN body tasked with providing regular scientific information on human-caused climate change. Since its inception over three decades ago the IPCC has produced compendium reports compiled by hundreds of scientists scouring thousands of peer-reviewed studies, and with each successive report the prognosis becomes more and more dire.

The IPCC has simulated and forecast global warming with remarkable accuracy, but, despite the increasing level of alarm expressed in its reports, greenhouse gas emissions continue to climb inexorably – since the first IPCC paper was released in 1990, annual global emissions have increased by more than 40 per cent. The stunning lack of action in the face of clear scientific accord is partly due to the nature of the IPCC – its summary reports have to be approved not only by the researchers who collaborated on them but also by almost 200 member countries. This creates a dynamic geared towards gridlock, as those nations with a vested interest in downplaying the threat posed by global warming – not only petrostates such as Saudi Arabia and Russia, but also hydrocarbon-exporting Western countries including the United States and Australia – have some influence over the messaging in the IPCC's assessment reports. Many have suggested that the IPCC's clunky consensus structure is not a bug, but rather a feature – a cynical way of allowing politics to work itself into what should be purely a matter of science.

Political interference may have influenced the IPCC, but it is the fastidious protocols of science that perhaps have had the biggest impact on the tenor of its reports. The scientific method enshrines clinical reasoning tested against relevant data, and bets are hedged until conclusions can be unequivocally drawn. IPCC reports have been criticised for being too conservative, with many impacts of climate change underplayed or under-predicted in hindsight. The American historian Naomi Oreskes has characterised science's tendency to caution as 'erring on the side of least drama', in which 'scientists are biased not toward alarmism but rather the reverse: toward cautious estimates, where we define caution as erring on the side of less rather than more alarming predictions'. Scientists operate in an environment of tentative hypotheses, and they use words like 'uncertainty' to denote a spectrum of outcomes, when 'confidence' would be a much better synonym for the lay public. In this world of shades of grey, their findings are often drowned out by the strident black and white convictions of others.

Those rejecting the scientific evidence, and instead adhering to more faith-based belief systems regarding climate change, claim that the IPCC's warnings are yet another example in a long line of Chicken Littles crying out that the sky is falling. They point to works such as *The Limits to Growth*, written by a group of MIT academics, which predicted 'a rather sudden and uncontrollable decline in both population and industrial capacity' due to the overexploitation of planetary resources. Released just before the 1973 oil crisis and resulting global stock market crash, the book captured the zeitgeist and sold over 30 million copies. The 'cornucopians' – those who argued that continual material progress can be secured by advances in technology, and that resource scarcity would never be a constraining factor for growth – were seemingly vindicated when the global economy resumed its heady ascent from the 1980s. These techno-optimists were fond of citing the fable of *The Boy Who Cried Wolf* to support their case – seemingly forgetting that the story ends when, after several false alarms, the wolf does indeed make an appearance and proceeds to consume the village's flock of sheep.

Talking power to truth

NASA's computing and satellite capabilities were co-opted by the likes of James Hansen, but ironically it was the Big Oil companies, the leading enablers of fossil fuelled climate change, that were at the forefront of climate science in the years leading up to Hansen's testimony. Exxon, one of the world's largest publicly traded corporations, marshalled its deep financial and scientific resources in the 1970s and 1980s to conduct research on rising atmospheric carbon levels and its likely effects. In a presentation to the company's management committee in 1977, James Black, a senior scientist at Exxon, stated that:

> There is general scientific agreement that the most likely manner in which mankind is influencing the global climate is through carbon dioxide release from the burning of fossil fuel ... There are some potentially catastrophic events that must be considered.

The following year Black recapped his earlier briefing in an internal memo to Exxon's top executives, and added that 'Man has a time window of five to ten years before the need for hard decisions regarding changes in energy strategies might become critical ... Once the effects are measurable, they might not be reversible'.

Exxon acted on this warning and modified its own strategy, acknowledging that rising sea levels and thawing permafrost could damage the company's offshore and onshore infrastructure, but noting that on the plus side a heating world would lengthen the survey season and lower exploration costs for its Arctic operations. The company stepped up its research on carbon emissions, launching in 1979 the supertanker *Esso Atlantic* on to the open seas, a vessel replete with cutting-edge sensors and a laboratory to monitor carbon dioxide levels in the ocean and the air. However, while Exxon acted internally on the red flags waved by its scientists, to the outside world it presented a very different narrative. In 1996 the Exxon chairman noted in a speech to the American oil and gas trade association that 'so-called global climate change ... perhaps poses the greatest long-term threat to our industry' and declared that 'scientific evidence remains inconclusive as to whether human activities affect global climate'. Despite the fact that as far back as the 1980s Exxon's scientists had plotted a chart accurately predicting atmospheric carbon levels in 2020, members of the Big Carbon club withheld this data and instead embarked on a concerted campaign of misinformation.

To deflect the bad news filtering through to the community many fossil fuel companies employed the classic magician's trick of misdirection. They sponsored editorials in newspapers querying 'Is eating meat worse than burning oil?', they shifted responsibility to individuals by inventing the concept of a 'carbon footprint', and, most egregiously, they diversified into another line of sales and became merchants of doubt. Adopting the tactics used so successfully by the tobacco industry, hydrocarbon companies embraced the mantra that 'Doubt is our product' and employed PR firms and lobbyists to retail the claim that the jury was still out on climate science – despite studies indicating that over 99 per cent of published scientific literature now accepts the reality of human-caused climate change. Science traffics in scepticism, but only as a means to reach the truth. It has, however, been obliged to battle with vested interests who have weaponised scepticism to present an alternative, self-serving story.

In prosecuting its case that climate science is not settled, hydrocarbon producers have also not been above attacking the scientific messengers. This strategy has a long and dishonourable pedigree – over two centuries ago Adam Smith noted that for those who oppose 'the master manufacturers'

> neither the most acknowledged probity, nor the highest rank, nor the greatest public services can protect him from the most infamous abuse and detraction, from personal insults, nor sometimes from real danger, arising from the insolent outrage of furious and disappointed monopolists.

This 'insolent outrage' has been evident in the climate change debate, and fossil fuel corporations have not been averse to playing the man or woman rather than the ball in an effort to resist regulation and protect profits. Charles Darwin noted resignedly that 'Great is the power of steady misrepresentation', although he added the rider that 'the history of science shows how, fortunately, this power does not endure long'. But Big Carbon – armed with enormous financial, organisational and political resources – has, so far, largely succeeded in pushing back against the established science by proffering alternative narratives.

This contemporary corporate gaslighting would have come as no surprise to Adam Smith. In *The Wealth of Nations* Smith observed that, in respect of what today would be called Big Business,

> their thoughts ... are commonly exercised rather about the interest of their own particular branch of business, than about that of the society, their judgment, even when given with the greatest candour (which it has not been upon every occasion) is much more to be depended upon with regard to the former of those two objects than with regard to the latter.

What Smith was saying in his baroque eighteenth-century way was that companies and their minions are often, and perhaps usually, motivated to look after corporate interests rather than the welfare of broader society. This should not be unexpected – historically companies have been legislatively obliged to maximise profit, anything that impedes that trajectory is viewed as an obstacle, and the wealth of their executives and owners is intimately tied to the financial success of the human-created fiction known as 'the corporation'. As single-minded as the system in which they operate, corporations are the ideal capitalist machines – programmed such that they can only behave selfishly, and with the power to make markets appear where they would like them to, and to avoid market creation when it is not in their interest.

10

POLLUTOCRATS

Privatising profits and socialising losses

Growth mindset

Exactly 20 years after testifying to the US Congress that human-made greenhouse gases were responsible for global warming, James Hansen appeared before a US House Committee to provide an update. The intervening period had only sharpened his criticism of hydrocarbon corporations, with Hansen asserting this time that:

> CEOs of fossil energy companies know what they are doing and are aware of long-term consequences of continued business as usual. In my opinion, these CEOs should be tried for high crimes against humanity and nature.

Hansen seemed to share the view of those who liken the corporation to a type of licensed psychopath – free of the moderating influence of the impartial spectator that is human conscience, by definition antisocial and egotistic, and principally focused on money and market power. Corporations are the closest thing we have to orthodox economists' mythical *Homo economicus* – a completely self-seeking entity that is required by law to maximise its economic interests – and, animated by what Karl Marx called capitalism's 'universal energy', they have become the key players in our global economic system.

Capitalism is premised on continuous expansion – any producer with a competitive advantage has the incentive to sell as much as possible, with uncompetitive rivals either failing or taken over, while consumers are incited by advertising and status-seeking to indulge in superfluous consumption. The promise of compound interest implies that capital will find and extract greater returns over time, and a future horizon of projected corporate profits is almost always a prerequisite for attracting capital to finance even more growth. Sales growth can, in turn, snowball further company expansion due to 'increasing returns to scale' arising from spreading fixed costs over a larger revenue pool, which has the effect of lowering unit costs. Similarly, shareholders have become more demanding and fickle in their search for growth and returns – the average holding period for a security on the New York Stock Exchange, for example, has fallen from approximately eight years in the late 1950s to less than a year today – and this drive for higher dividends and appreciating share prices also extends beyond borders.

The threat of 'capital flight' provides an additional lever to economic actors pursuing profits, with nations forced to compete among themselves to furnish the most favourable environment for business. Footloose capital is aided by a global financial architecture that generally encourages neoliberal policies, with multi-government organisations such as the International Monetary Fund and the World Bank typically prescribing pro-market 'shock therapy' policies to any supplicant economy. The IMF and the World Bank are part of what has been dubbed the 'Washington Consensus' – so named not just because these bodies are headquartered in the US Capitol, but also because the United States has an effective veto right in respect of key decisions made by these institutions. Members of the Washington Consensus usually impose free market measures such as trade and investment liberalisation as a condition for providing financial assistance to countries afflicted by financial crises, which has the effect of drawing them deeper into the growth-driven capitalist system, while potentially crowding out alternative economic and social reforms.

Further fuelling the growth dynamic are continuous productivity improvements, one of the triumphs of questing capitalism. Increases in labour productivity require additional economic expansion just to maintain employment levels, while falling costs from more efficient resource use can have the perverse effect of accelerating the consumption of raw inputs. In the mid-nineteenth century the English economist William Stanley Jevons noted that efficiency gains in the use of coal merely encouraged even more extravagant energy use, because demand for coal would rise as energy prices fell. Jevons concluded that:

> It is wholly a confusion of ideas to suppose that the economical use of fuel is equivalent to a diminished consumption. The very contrary is the truth.

As Jevons noted, an increase in resource use efficiency typically generates an overall increase in the consumption of raw materials, and this 'rebound effect' can cancel out the benefits of any productivity improvements. Counterintuitively, 'the Jevons paradox' – subsequently observed across many other inputs – can speed up the extraction and exhaustion of finite resources even while the efficiency in using these inputs improves.

Further, as Maynard Keynes noted almost a century ago, a lack of economic growth – or even misgivings around future growth – can lead to a collapse in confidence that spirals into a self-fulfilling prophecy, sometimes leading to severe social instability. As a result of all these factors, the creed of compound growth has become institutionalised, and capital ranges around the world looking for superior profit opportunities. In service of this growth imperative, neoliberal economists and business leaders act as a modern priesthood – undertaking interpretations and auguries, offering prophecies, and making sacrifices to the Great God Market when required. Unceasing expansion is now the great monotheism of our age, and story-making humans construct a narrative around human-made finance – 'it was flighty yesterday', 'bond tantrums as the Fed increases rates', 'the Dow is losing confidence', and the like – that anthropomorphise the market and often demand acts of propitiation from broader society.

And at the same time that individuals are increasingly regarded as cogs in the capitalist engine – an 'appendage of the machine' in Marx's words – so too have the economic units known as corporations been treated more and more like humans. A corporation is viewed as a legal person separate from its owners – with the ability to enter into contracts, own property, and sue or be sued – and additionally enjoys the protection of limited liability, which allows shareholders to shelter behind a 'corporate veil' and avoid responsibility for company losses and misdeeds. Principally because of this limited liability status, corporations can pool capital and undertake ventures at a scale previously only possible for nations, and just as importantly they can disperse overall risk. As a result, the tendrils of modern corporations now penetrate almost every facet of the economic system – and because of their size and reach they are arguably the most influential persons in the world today, for both good and ill.

Survival of the fattest

Prior to the nineteenth century, only those enterprises considered to be of national interest were granted the privilege of limited liability. The world's first multinational and first listed corporation, the Dutch East India Company, was born at the beginning of the seventeenth century in Europe's most liberal country at the time, but quickly became a vicious mini-empire of its own. The Company gave credence to the adage that war is capitalism with the gloves off, waging constant battle in the Far East, initially securing a monopoly over the spice trade and later diversifying into other commodities including silver, silk and slaves. It cleared rainforests for plantations, instituted forced labour, and committed acts of genocide against those locals who resisted the Company's advance. Other state-sponsored corporations, most notably the British East India Company, took a lead from the Netherlanders and spun the cynical and spurious Roman Law doctrine of *terra nullius* – 'unoccupied land', free for the taking for anyone who could 'improve' it – from fiction into fact, reducing previously diverse ecosystems into simple monocultures while at the same time brutally evicting or destroying native populations.

A later British imitator, the South Sea Company – established in 1711 to secure a trade monopoly over the Spanish Americas, largely comprising an annual quota of 4,800 African slaves – had the dubious distinction of inflating the world's first stock market bubble. The Company's promoters circulated 'the most extravagant rumours' about the potential value of its trading concessions in the New World and, boosted by stimulant-stoked gossip in coffee houses and wildly optimistic reports in the newfangled medium of newspapers, thousands were caught in the riptide of greed. Stock prices rocketed from £128 per share in January 1720 to just over £1,000 less than six months later, but by December 1720 the stock had plummeted back to ground – describing an almost perfect parabola on a share price chart, South Sea paper traded at exactly the same level as at the start of the year. Isaac Newton, the reputed High Priest of Reason, was one of many burned by the South Sea Bubble, losing around £20,000, or more than $7 million in today's money. Chastened by this demonstration of gravity in the world of finance, and bamboozled by the intrusion of systems complexity into his mechanistic universe, he remarked ruefully that 'I can calculate the motions of heavenly bodies, but not the madness of people'.

The earliest corporations diversified into whatever line of business could potentially make a profit – the British East India Company, for example, would outdo its Dutch competitor in confecting new markets by becoming the world's largest ever drug-runner, aggressively pushing Indian opium into China. However, it was not the grim foundations of offshore exploitation, plunder and subjugation that slowed the rise of corporations, but rather the social dislocation visited on home markets due to periodic booms and busts. Partly as a result of the stock market wreckage wrought by the South Sea Company, it was not until the early nineteenth century that the British Government again permitted the formation of 'joint-stock companies', with some other Western countries implementing the law of limited liability at around the same time. To paraphrase Karl Marx, the upper class have the upper hand, and the biggest beneficiaries of this renewed corporate ascendancy were the very same people who acted as midwives to these new legal persons 'born out of statute'. As a result, the corporation – one of capitalism's most paradoxical creations, an invention that affords people the opportunity to work co-operatively within a self-avowedly individualistic environment – quickly became the dominant force in our modern economy.

Adam Smith – who criticised 'the monopolizing spirit of merchants and manufacturers, who neither are, nor ought to be, the rulers of mankind' – would have decried our modern corpocracy. Despite the caricatured portrayal of Smith as the original champion of untrammelled commerce, he was no zealous apostle of laissez faire economics. Smith ended his days as Commissioner of Scottish Customs, diligently enforcing tariffs and thwarting the free trade efforts of those bent on evading government regulations. He was not a supporter of 'the mercantile system', and *The Wealth of Nations* is in part a polemic against the takeover of the state by Big Business. Smith's precondition for 'universal opulence' in a society was the ability for individuals to act freely in their own interests, without the blockers of state-sanctioned cartels and exclusive trade guilds which were 'a conspiracy against the public'. He also lamented the pernicious results when corporations became effective rulers and legislators, noting that the British East India Company had inflicted 'Want, famine, and mortality' on parts of India by imposing a type of De-Industrial Revolution that converted the country from a major textile processor and exporter to a mere supplier of raw material.

Smith realised that, even without the help of state-sanctioned cartels, corporations were driven to 'narrow the competition' which enables them, 'by raising their profits above what they naturally would be, to levy, for their own benefit, an absurd tax upon the rest of their fellow-citizens'. Accordingly, he suggested in *The Wealth of Nations* that:

> The proposal of any new law or regulation of commerce which comes from this order ought always to be listened to with great precaution, and ought never to be adopted till after having been long and carefully examined, not only with the most scrupulous, but with the most suspicious attention.

Although later beatified by free marketeers, Smith's book was not an argument against state intervention, but rather an argument against state capture by powerful corporate interests. However, despite Smith's wariness of Big Business's motives, we now live in an economic system in which many of the most important societal decisions are outsourced to the legal construct known as the corporation.

Over a barrel

Although just another story, albeit one reinforced by the grant of legal rights and shielded by limited liability, corporations have deployed unparalleled financial and political power to execute their profit-maximising ends. By ceaselessly incanting the Gospel of Growth, by purchasing government policies via lobbyists, and by infiltrating the highest echelons of decision-making, corporations and the individuals standing behind them have created markets when there is the possibility of profit, while markets and regulation are vigorously repulsed when there are potential costs involved. These players in the capitalist system – rationally self-interested as theory demands – are motivated to pursue revenue opportunities while offloading costs onto others, and ultimately everyone pays the price while a select few enjoy a free ride.

Economists label those costs or benefits which are not embedded in prices as 'externalities' – either positive externalities such as the ecosystem services provided by nature, or negative externalities such as air pollution. Negative externalities occur when the costs of an economic activity are not borne solely by the relevant producer or consumer, and cause harm to others for which there is no compensation. The price of hydrocarbons generally only reflects the costs of extraction, processing, transport and other overheads, with as much profit as can be extracted from the market on top – while the costs that come later due to pollution and climate change are not recognised at all in the initial transaction. As a result of this negative externality, the market monarchs preaching most fervently against the evils of collectivism are in fact perpetuating a system that is fundamentally socialist in one key respect – for while profits are subject to rules defending private property, environmental costs are typically dispersed among us all.

This sleight-of-hand arises because the atmosphere is what economists call 'a global commons', a shared resource freely available to all, and suffers from a variant of the economic affliction known as 'the Tragedy of the Commons'. The idea of the Tragedy of the Commons was first popularised by the American ecologist Garrett Hardin, who used the example of 'a pasture open to all' to illustrate his argument. Hardin explained that an economically rational herdsman operating in this environment will seek to maximise his gain by adding more and more livestock, as the benefit of adding extra animals accrues to the herdsman alone, while the costs – the depletion over time of the communally held grazing land – will be spread among all users. In Hardin's formulation, this is a tragedy in the classical Greek sense of the word – foreseeable but inevitable. 'Ruin is the destination toward which all men rush', Hardin concluded, 'each pursuing his own best interest in a society that believes in the freedom of the commons'. Hardin asserted that individuals, acting rationally in terms of their own interests, will in fact act irrationally as a group by destroying a communal resource.

Capitalism is premised on ownership, but this is a category error for things that cannot in fact be 'owned', such as the atmosphere. Because clean air is a free resource it is consumed unsustainably, and when the costs of polluting the atmosphere are negligible so too are the incentives to reduce emissions. However, despite occasional episodes of irrationality, the market is generally very effective in allocating resources – or at least those that are counted – and by not valuing the planet's natural assets and ecosystem services in an economic sense we ensure that they will continue to be consumed profligately. The failure to adequately account for the costs of carbon pollution has resulted in what the British Government–backed Stern Review has described as 'the greatest example of market failure we have ever seen' – the biggest, but perhaps the most easily remedied, flaw in our modern economy.

11

COSTING THE EARTH

Making the polluter pay

The price is right

Although James Hansen's explanation of the principal cause of global heating and his predictions of likely temperature hikes turned out to be remarkably accurate, humanity has in fact released more carbon dioxide into the atmosphere since Hansen's first congressional appearance than during the entire span of history beforehand. And Dr Hansen not only correctly diagnosed the disease, but he also prescribed a simple remedy – as he later commented, with the assurance of one who had worked at NASA for over four decades, 'the solution isn't complicated, it's not rocket science'. He explained that:

> Emissions aren't going to go down if the cost of fossil fuels isn't honest. Economists are very clear on this.

Money talks, but it does not always tell the truth – the current pricing of fossil fuels tells, at best, only a partial story. Not all the costs of exploiting fossil fuels – including damage from extreme weather events, illness caused by air pollution, and the desertification of previously arable land – are factored into its final price, and this form of dishonesty has a significant impact on the natural world, on society, and on future generations.

Hansen suggested a simple solution – 'a steadily increasing fee that is then distributed to the public' to reflect future costs not otherwise factored in by the market mechanism. By levying a charge on fossil fuel products, ideally based on an assessment of the present value of the net harm caused by every tonne of carbon dioxide released into the atmosphere, a carbon tax would account for the otherwise hidden costs of carbon pollution. In ensuring that the producers or consumers of carbon-intensive products pay for all the consequences of its use, such a tax should serve to not only decrease demand for goods and services that produce high emissions and provide incentives to make them less carbon intensive, but it would also make renewable energy sources far more competitive. As noted by William Nordhaus, a Nobel Prize winner for his work on integrating climate change into economic analysis, when there is no carbon price 'being extravagant with your carbon footprint costs the same amount as being careful'. Instead, at present the market is dealing in falsehoods by ignoring the ecological and social consequences of excessive greenhouse gas emissions.

Fossil fuel pollution, in theory at least, is particularly well suited to a government-imposed tax to correct for social costs – it is relatively straightforward to quantify, the tax could be easily levied at first point of sale, and taxes could be standardised to include other greenhouse gases based on their carbon dioxide–equivalent global warming potential. True carbon pricing would exert its own selection pressures and allow the market to apply the Darwinian dynamic so beloved by neoliberal economists – price signals would flag which products are carbon-intensive, in turn providing incentives to consumers to use these products more sparingly and for companies to move to lower carbon intensity processes and goods. Rather than being assailed by a deluge of sometimes conflicting data, or hoodwinked by false pricing, an internalised carbon price would in effect constitute a one-stop shop incorporating all important information regarding fossil fuels' relative benefits and costs. Under such a pricing regime the Invisible Hand would revert to some approximation of Adam Smith's ideal of an efficient allocative mechanism, instead of picking the pocket of the majority by not aligning individual interests with group interests.

In practice, however, the situation is far more problematic. A country that imposes a carbon tax will not only increase costs for its domestic industry, but most of the upside from any resulting reduction in emissions will be enjoyed outside its borders. Further, the costs of higher carbon prices are asymmetrically distributed – there is less at stake for the Western world, as richer countries can better absorb higher prices, while developing countries are still playing catch-up with the fossil fuelled wealth explosion enjoyed by their more affluent peers. The average age of coal plants in Asia, for example, is just over a decade while in the West it is closer to half a century, and the higher sunk costs of these less depreciated new assets makes the transition to other forms of energy far more expensive in relative terms for emerging economies. But perhaps most importantly, the benefits of any reduction in emissions will not be apparent immediately, but rather will only be evident at some stage in the future. Nations as much as individuals are driven by short-term self-interest, and the incentive to take a free ride and defer real action is strong.

The phenomenon of climate change is what economists term a 'wicked problem' – not because of its potentially catastrophic consequences, but because its fiendishly complicated and confounding nature tends to induce a state of inertia. A wicked problem is a social challenge that is difficult or impossible to solve for multiple and often interrelated reasons, including incomplete knowledge, the sheer number of parties involved, and the significant costs arising from any possible solution. The relatively new field of 'behavioural economics' provides further insights as to why the problems of climate change can seem so insoluble. The work of psychologists such as Daniel Kahneman and Amos Tversky demonstrates that humans tend to be more sensitive to near-term losses that seem more certain rather than potentially much higher losses at some stage in the future. In the context of carbon pricing, this means that consumers are generally disposed to avoiding immediate falls in living standards even if the more distant costs of inaction are in fact much higher. In addition to short-term loss aversion, humans also labour under other cognitive biases that complicate climate solutions, including 'optimism bias', which leads us to believe that we are less likely to suffer misfortune than others, and 'confirmation bias' in which we seek out information that supports our sometimes erroneous views.

Climate change is the ultimate wicked problem, suffering not just from the Tragedy of the Commons and human cognitive quirks, but also by what has been dubbed 'the Tragedy of the Horizon'. The bulk of the negative impacts from global heating are postponed, imposing costs on future generations which the current generation – if acting rationally in accordance with the dictates of neoliberal theory – has no strong economic incentive to fix. Although the price mechanism in a free market resembles in some ways a giant democracy, with purchasing decisions acting as votes, it is necessarily myopic – crystallising what was agreed and transacted in a given moment of time by a given group of parties, with future generations by definition not participants and having no say in that particular exchange. In the early twentieth century the English writer and arch-conservative GK Chesterton scorned 'that arrogant oligarchy who merely happened to be walking around' and called for a 'democracy of the dead' to honour traditions painstakingly brokered and accumulated over the centuries, many of which had been bulldozed by the capitalist juggernaut. Looking in the other direction, our modern world now urgently requires a 'democracy of descendants' – a forward-looking system that recognises the future social costs of fossil fuel use, and does not barter the wellbeing of later generations in return for present-day advantage.

Land of the free (lunch)

Climate change policy is where economics, the physical sciences and the brute realities of politics collide, a domain of complexity on complexity in which actors relentlessly focused on revenue expansion and cost suppression have the upper hand. Most economists and central bankers agree that the best solution to the problem of greenhouse gas emissions is adding a fee to the price of fossil fuel products that approximates the future social costs of hydrocarbon use, and the idea of a light touch fiscal instrument should in theory be attractive to free market evangelists. A broad-based carbon tax would not only better reflect the true costs of fossil fuels and minimise the amount of government oversight required, but it would also free capitalism to do what it does better than any other system – to innovate and change direction in response to the market's price signals. There is ongoing debate as to the right size of any carbon tax – some academics suggest an initially modest price, rising over time until emissions reductions goals are achieved – but as Maynard Keynes noted, it is better to be vaguely right rather than precisely wrong, and any carbon price is preferable to no carbon price.

A carbon pricing mechanism would need to secure the participation of at least the major emitting countries or blocs to make a real difference, but to date take-up has been patchy. This is partly due to the self-interest of fossil fuel companies that have been largely successful in resisting regulation, but also because of self-interest played out at a national level. Implementing a carbon tax will put home-grown carbon-intensive companies at a competitive disadvantage to offshore rivals not subject to such a regime, while the advantages of any emissions reduction will accrue to all – including 'free-riders' who benefit from the actions of others without sharing in the costs. Further, as Adam Smith noted in *The Wealth of Nations*:

> The proprietor of stock is properly a citizen of the world, and ... would be apt to abandon the country in which he was exposed ... to a burdensome tax, and would remove his stock to some other country where he could either carry on his business, or enjoy his fortune more at his ease.

Like the spectres that they are, corporations are mobile and elusive, and the regulation of emissions in one country may result in the relocation of operations to places where there is a lower regulatory burden.

To prevent 'emissions leakage' to lightly regulated jurisdictions, which has the effect of punishing those countries seeking to rein in hydrocarbon use through a fossil fuel tax, ideally a carbon price should be equalised and levied across as many nations as possible. But the atmosphere is a global commons, and unlike a local or even national commons there is no ready-made regulatory body to deal with shared global resources.

Voluntary multinational pacts such as the Kyoto Protocol have proven ineffective, as signatories have an incentive to free-ride and there are no penalties for failing to honour obligations. However, there is a way to harness self-interest to enforce co-operative policies. Economists have suggested a carrot-and-stick solution – a 'climate club' comprising those countries agreeing to undertake harmonised emissions reductions, and excluding those that will not meet agreed obligations. Club members could impose sanctions on non-participants in the form of tariffs or trade bans, ensuring that the benefits of being inside the club outweigh any perceived disadvantages arising from the imposition of a carbon price. In the absence of a governance architecture that compels shared responsibility for reducing pollution, this coalition of the willing in terms of emissions reductions would provide incentives that bend self-interest towards societal good.

Although a carbon tax is generally accepted as a superior method of implementing climate policy, another market-based approach is also available. Emissions trading schemes, such as the 'cap-and-trade' system used by the EU, invert the carbon tax dynamic by seeking to set the volume of emissions rather than the price. ETS mechanisms utilise another favoured tool of capitalism – the creation of property rights in previously commonly held assets – to impose physical quotas that provide a high level of certainty around future emissions, but in practice agreement is difficult to reach because participants haggle around each country's emission limit rather than focusing on a uniform carbon price. An additional issue for any ETS system – which essentially converts a right to pollute into a marketable commodity – is that they usually assign a portion of emissions permits to carbon-intensive companies at no cost. Any excess allowances can later be on-sold, and this has the perverse effect of rewarding the heaviest polluters for their past sins by granting them a valuable monetary asset.

A broader objection to market-based solutions, whether it be a carbon tax or an emissions trading scheme, is that these mechanisms are potentially regressive – that is, the tax burden will fall heaviest on low-income households which tend to spend a larger proportion of their income on energy. This potential inequality could, however, be addressed by adopting a 'carbon fee-and-dividend' model that returns 100 per cent of carbon tax revenues to citizens on an equal basis. As the richer cohort of society generally use more energy than the rest in absolute terms, a 'climate bonus' in the form of a carbon dividend should result in a net transfer of money to lower-income households, which would also go some way in rebalancing wealth inequalities. The simple reality is that there is already a carbon price – and although it is not captured by the market, it is paid for by fossil fuel users and non-users alike, including future generations. Milton Friedman popularised the adage that in economics there's no such thing as a free lunch – but to date the underpricing of the true costs of hydrocarbon use has allowed the few to dine out at the expense of the many.

Weirded out

By moving on from outright denial of climate change to more subtle wiles such as distraction and division, fossil fuel companies and other vested interests have delayed the implementation of a carbon tax that honestly prices hydrocarbon costs. These entities have assiduously refocused attention towards individual carbon footprints rather than their own gigantic tread, resulting in 'carbon shaming' and debates around individual lifestyle choices that serve to splinter community consensus while diverting attention away from industry's own actions. And they have been assisted in this exercise by free market fundamentalists who discern a suspicious coincidence in timing between the fall of the Soviet Union and the creation of the IPCC – climate change activism is, they argue, a Trojan Horse for another collectivist project, green on the outside but red on the inside. Many of these vested interests, focused on the short term, seem to fear the proposed solutions to climate change far more than climate change itself.

These latter-day Don Quixotes – errant knights tilting not only at windmills, but solar panels and other forms of renewable energy – can perhaps, however, be viewed as acting rationally in a strictly self-interested sense. For although the wealthiest 1 per cent of the global population is estimated to produce more than twice the atmospheric carbon of the poorest 50 per cent, damage from climate change will fall most heavily on lesser developed countries. In broad terms, the regions least exposed to the adverse effects of global warming are those with mild or cold climates, while tropical countries belted either side of the Equator are the most vulnerable. What has been dubbed the 'WEIRD' family of nations – Western, Educated, Industrialised, Rich and Democratic, and located overwhelmingly in the Global North – is in effect robbing the developed world a second time. Not only is the WEIRD club exploiting and consuming the natural capital of resource-rich emerging economies at an unsustainable rate, but there is also a form of carbon colonisation in which apex consumers are staking a claim to the majority of the global atmosphere, while poorer countries bear the brunt of greenhouse gas pollution.

But although the fortunate rich can install more air conditioners, build higher sea walls, and import more food to temporarily delay some of the impacts of climate change, it is a global problem that will ultimately affect all. Like a supertanker, Earth systems tend to move slowly and are hard to turn due to tremendous latent momentum – and to predict the possible consequences of increased carbon dioxide levels we need to indulge in a form of time travel by looking back to previous eras. The last occasion the Earth had this amount of carbon in the atmosphere was around three million years ago, a period when our early ancestor *Australopithecus* had just clambered down from the trees to tentatively forage on the African savanna. At that time the planet was around 3 degrees Celsius warmer than now, sea levels were almost 20 metres higher, and most of the Arctic was covered in thick forests of spruce, pine and fir. An additional 3 degrees of heating above pre-industrial levels is predicted to result in extreme heatwaves, wildfires and flooding, while large tracts of land will powder into desert, freshwater sources trickle dry, and oceans sour as they absorb increasing levels of carbon dioxide.

The Western world will not be immune to the effects of global heating – under a 3-degree warming scenario low-lying cities such as Amsterdam are expected to be overrun by an incremental but relentless tide, climate refugees will seek escape to more temperate climes, and 100 degree Fahrenheit 'heat emergency' days will become the summertime norm in the US Capitol. And although some countries, such as Canada and Russia, are likely to benefit from increased farm output due to climate change, overall global food production is expected to fall – not only due to heat stress, desiccated soil, and lower volumes of water for irrigation, but also because warming and acidifying oceans will decimate vital marine ecosystems. The time is already out of joint for many of the essential ecosystem services provided by nature – some flowers now bloom too soon for the bees to bless them with the rite of pollination, birds arrive weeks after insect pests emerge from their eggs, and the annual volume of glacier melt quenching downstream farms is falling. In addition to decreased agricultural yields, elevated carbon dioxide emissions will reduce the nutrient density of many staple crops, while extreme weather events and social dislocation triggered by climate change will disrupt the global supply chains that currently provide a large proportion of the developed world's calories.

Although all countries will ultimately suffer from the effects of climate change, the dispassionate findings of scientists have been countered by sinister storytellers who, while now largely accepting that global heating is an established fact, assert that it is caused by factors such as increased solar luminosity or minor changes to the Earth's orbit. These arguments, essentially fiction with footnotes, can be summarily dispatched – for example, only the lower atmosphere has warmed, whereas external events like increased solar activity or orbital shifts would heat the entire atmosphere. Humans, when it suits their interests, can be more adept at rationalisation than rationality – as Adam Smith noted in *The Theory of Moral Sentiments*, 'the desire of persuading ... seems to be one of the strongest of all our natural desires' – and there is a theory that we have evolved to win arguments rather than arrive at the truth. Human-caused climate change is a fundamental challenge for those embracing the narrative of unending growth on a finite planet, a very real lesson in limits, and is therefore viewed by some as the new nemesis of industrial capitalism. In the face of this existential threat the capitalist cowboys have circled the wagons and confected new stories – fake news designed to divert and divide, and to delay regulatory action.

By employing lobbyists and others to peddle the fictitious narrative that the science is not settled regarding climate change, corporations and their enablers have in effect purchased the economic policies that are most congenial to their interests. They have been assisted by those at the very top of the political tree – in 2001, for example, the new US administration led by the second President Bush and Vice President Cheney, both oilmen prior to politics, declined to ratify the Kyoto Protocol committing member countries to reduced greenhouse gas emissions. In parallel, fossil fuel corporations and their assorted PR propagandists have also taken a leaf from the neoliberal playbook by seeking to devolve responsibility to individuals, even though studies show that the average Western citizen has little to no influence on policy outcomes – a paper published in 2014, for example, found that 'the preferences of the average American appear to have only a minuscule, near-zero, statistically nonsignificant impact upon public policy'.

In theory, there is a relatively straightforward policy response at hand – an additional levy on fossil fuel prices that would account for the hidden costs of hydrocarbon emissions and 'internalise' the negative externality of carbon pollution – but to date real action has been frustrated by corporate influence. However, a polluted atmosphere is a communal problem that must be addressed communally – and ultimately only governments, acting as agents for the collective, are capable of transcending powerful private interests. But instead, corporations and other vested interests have devised alternative 'carbon markets' that financialise the natural world for profit-making ends, and that give the comforting illusion of progress in fighting climate change without always making real progress.

12

HOT AIR

Burn now, pay later

Homage to catatonia

Like a spinning top kept upright only through constant motion, capitalism 'must nestle everywhere, settle everywhere, establish connections everywhere', as Karl Marx noted, and new specialisations, goods and services constantly evolve to fill niches previously outside the mercantile domain. Healthcare, education and other social welfare programs are ceded to bottom line–focused corporations, while responsibilities such as childcare, once the sole province of households, can now be outsourced to others for a fee. Eyeballs and attention are commandeered by internet and social media companies to generate revenue, and apps for the dating 'market' have commodified the most basic of human needs, the desire to connect. Human affairs are increasingly viewed through the prism of the market, and reflecting this transactional mindset some economists edge into parody by reducing almost all relationships to self-interested business deals – characterising children, for example, as 'consumer durables' and long-term marriages as generating 'marital-specific capital'. Marx's prediction that industrial capitalism would reshape the world after its own image has been largely fulfilled – we have moved from being a market economy to becoming a market society, peopled by consumers rather than citizens, who in turn are encouraged to focus on 'value' rather than values.

The process of commodification reflects and reinforces the atomising ethos of capitalism, and also largely removes from the public conversation troublesome questions around our obligations to others. As Joan Robinson noted, capitalism

> is an ideology to end ideologies, for it has abolished the moral problem. It is only necessary for each individual to act egoistically for the good of all to be attained.

The market provides a convenient cover story, allowing us to dispense with the need to fully take into account the impact of our actions – it is, as the economist EF Schumacher argued, 'the institutionalization of individualism and non-responsibility'. And capitalism's drive for ever-growing material wealth has not only been secured on the back of a largely unrecorded drawdown on the natural world, a form of freeloading on our future selves and our descendants, but it has fostered an unhealthy focus on the short term. Over time the stolid and upright West has been persuaded to trade the promise of Heaven, the ultimate expression of deferred gratification, for a material paradise in this world – so much so that even Christmas, the celebration of the birth of a man who despised worldly wealth, has now been turned into a carnival of consumption.

The Cowboy Economy – cultivated by the credo of individualism and short-termism, enabled by the fiction that the natural world and its resources are limitless, and powered by fossil fuels – has fenced off and exploited the pieces of the world that are profitable, while at the same time desolating natural systems because the cowboys do not pick up the bill. Literally Earth-shattering communal challenges such as climate change and biodiversity loss can only be solved if societies – rather than markets – come together to agree and execute a radical course correction. Instead, as a community we have lapsed into a form of learned helplessness – lulled by material prosperity, unwilling to confront unpleasant truths, and seemingly unable to influence or change outcomes. And capitalism's program of outsourcing has also extended into the realm of public policy, with important societal decisions devolved to the market while individuals have had a bogus sense of responsibility foisted on them.

Rather than top-down regulation that would force fossil fuel companies to be accountable for all the costs of their product, there has instead been another appropriation by the elite – those who have the most to lose from a more honest pricing mechanism, one that would allow the Invisible Hand to nudge things closer towards the collective 'good, are in effect placing themselves in charge of social change. However, the entities most tightly wed to the logic of self-interest and growth cannot be expected to steer the community in a different direction – rational economic actors are guided by price and cost incentives in their pursuit of profit, and a body formed solely for the purpose of maximising earnings cannot readily violate its own precepts. Rather, if corporate behaviour is to change then the overarching rules governing corporations also need to change – otherwise, companies will continue to seek the highest revenue streams and the lowest cost base, wherever that may be on the planet, while doing their best to escape financial penalties for the despoliation of the natural world.

The law insists that corporations are legal persons capable of entering contracts and owning property, but in some ways many act more like infants – demanding, self-centred, flighty, and, one might add, not toilet-trained. But for all of these shortcomings, corporations are also, potentially, immortal – an entity with constantly replenishing cells in the form of shareholders, and with no fixed end date in prospect until the terminal event of insolvency, takeover or company wind-up. The farmer and writer Wendell Berry noted that, unlike humans,

> a corporation does not age. It does not arrive, as most persons finally do, at a realization of the shortness and smallness of human lives; it does not come to see the future as the lifetime of the children and grandchildren of anybody in particular.

A corporation is not sentimental and is not restrained by the 'impartial spectator' that is human conscience. The celebrated *Homo economicus* of neoclassical economics is an outlier, the sociopathic exception rather than the rule – most humans are prosocial creatures who generally value the good opinion of others. But corporations also value their reputation, if only for ultra-rational financial reasons – and at the very least they must be *seen* to be doing something in light of the ongoing plunder of the natural world.

Prose and cons

Corporations, in theory, should be among the best placed to address the problems caused by fossil fuelled industrial capitalism. Their longevity frees them from the tight election cycles of the Western world and they make investments with multi-decade timespans, and therefore they might be expected to keep at least one eye on the longer term. The pragmatic James Lovelock was not above working for large companies, and he disputed the lazy blanket characterisation of all corporations as global criminals – instead, he observed, they are one of the few organisations in our modern economy that thinks 20 years ahead. Other leading voices contend that only corporations have the heft to truly move the dial in terms of positive action – as the environmentalist Paul Hawken argues, 'business is the only mechanism on the planet today powerful enough to produce the changes necessary to reverse global environmental and social degradation'.

Additionally, the monopolising mission of industrial capitalism has resulted in just 15 asset managers – the BlackRocks and Goldman Sachses of the world – directing over half of all global financial wealth, and the case is sometimes made that as these managers become 'universal owners' they will increasingly be obliged to incorporate externalities into their investment calculations. At the very least, it is asserted, self-interest should encourage corporations to be mindful of the welfare of its employees, wider society and the natural world – otherwise, they may suffer from a 'Tragedy of the Corporate Commons', in which each company's pursuit of short-term self-interest endangers the long-term viability of the entire system. Bringing together these arguments, proponents of 'stakeholder capitalism' – an aspirational ideal in which companies focus on long-term value creation by taking into account the needs of all its partners, including broader society – believe that a form of corporate jujitsu can be effected by using the momentum and power of corporations to transport our market society to a win-win world.

Although many companies demonstrate a sincere commitment to long-term sustainability rather than short-term earnings, other corporations have instead opted for what the climate scientist Michael Mann calls a strategy of 'inactivism' – that is, preventing meaningful regulatory action through strategies to divide, deflect and delay. And even those companies that do not actively seek to influence public policy outcomes are still beholden to what has been characterised as the 'global profit enforcement agency' embedded within the financial sector. Not only do fiduciary duties on company directors enshrine the primacy of profit, but other factors also sharpen the focus on earnings – including the threat of competition, minute-by-minute scorekeeping by the stock market, pension holders demanding high returns, and executive share options linked to financial performance. Despite the wishful thinking of stakeholder capitalism advocates, the inconvenient truth is that profits – rather than people and the planet – usually trump other considerations in the never-ending race that is capitalism.

Instead of governments – the people's representatives – determining communal needs and then enacting top-down reforms to countervail market failure due to externalities, corporations have pre-emptively stepped in and proffered an awkward hybrid. 'ESG' investments – originally designed as a screen to assess a company's exposure to potential financial risks arising from a tightening of Environmental, Social or Governance standards – have now become the go-to category for those seeking to catalyse a more socially responsible form of capitalism. Boosters of this form of 'impact investing' have sold the consoling story that consumers can have their cake and eat it too – that investments in companies rating highly in ESG terms should yield a 'triple bottom line' return, providing not only robust financial rewards but also real environmental and social benefits. For a while this seemed to be the case – many past studies, for example, concluded that high-rating ESG companies tend to outperform their lower-rating peers in terms of profit and share price performance. These companies did well by doing good, it was argued, due to more loyal employees and customers, better risk control and governance systems, or sometimes simply because they are disproportionately represented in high growth 'new economy' sectors such as information technology.

Setting aside the fact that such arguments are at odds with the 'efficient markets hypothesis' – a pillar of mainstream finance theory which asserts that stock exchanges already incorporate all public information that could possibly affect the price of a security – these ESG measures tend to be amorphous and aspirational, while related performance data relies overwhelmingly on selective case studies rather than rigorous research. Many recent studies have concluded that there is little to no evidence that funds labelled 'high sustainability' outperform conventional funds, while these green funds also tend to charge significantly higher management fees to their customers. But, perhaps most importantly, there is a substantial disconnect between finance's use of the term 'ESG' and the perceptions of the lay public – in broad terms, the financial sector views ESG as just one factor in determining risk-adjusted returns, while the average person believes that ESG is a vehicle to promote corporate goals that go beyond mere profit maximisation.

Most retail investors, therefore, have things the wrong way around – ESG ratings do not measure how a company might change the world, but rather they measure how a changing world might impact the particular company. The investment industry has been slow to disabuse the public of this misperception, and although little more than two decades old, ESG-badged investments now comprise many tens of trillions of dollars of assets under management. In reality, ESG is designed to measure a company's exposure to risks arising from climate change or stricter environmental and social standards, rather than to actively minimise any damage from unsustainable or unfair business practices. This fact is reflected in empirical studies which conclude that, although firms held by ESG funds tend to issue a greater quantity of ESG-related disclosures, the quantity of disclosure is in general not correlated with the relevant firms' levels of ESG compliance or success in reducing carbon emissions.

Even when ESG audits attempt to put hard numbers around the social and environmental impacts of a company's operations, the exercise often

founders on the sheer complexity of our globalised economic system – it
is estimated, for example, that some major brands have over 100,000
suppliers and sub-contractors. This ever-branching labyrinth leads into
increasingly opaque dead-ends, severely compromising the effectiveness
of ESG monitoring and reporting. Complicating matters further, the
'E', 'S' and 'G' elements of ESG are inseparably intertwined, are often
in conflict, and their relative merits might change in response to broader
societal shifts – for example, a natural gas company that is marked down
on the environmental metric might find itself a comeback candidate on
social measures if it is providing vital energy to households and essential
industries during difficult times.

ESG, then, is ultimately just another form of storytelling, one that
reinforces the notion that only markets and business can solve pressing
long-term communal problems. Used cynically, ESG serves as one more
distraction, a branding and PR exercise, a form of corporate virtue-signalling
in which companies act like a latter-day Saint Augustine, mouthing fine
words and seeking goodness – but not just yet. ESG measures can also
act as a decoy, luring attention away from tricky topics such as inflated
CEO earnings and corporate tax minimisation schemes, while potentially
camouflaging wider business incompetence. Although green may be the
new black in the investment world, for most corporations profit is still
king in the aristocracy of numbers, and ESG metrics the largely powerless
peons. And the dogma of salvation through spending, of change through
purchases rather than politics, also threatens to compromise another
nascent natural capital market – one that, if done right, could actually
materially assist in the transition to a greener world.

Higher purchase

Although fossil fuel companies and their functionaries have sought to
resist government-imposed carbon taxes, they have actively encouraged
another privatised solution that claims to partly address market failure
arising from underpriced hydrocarbon use. 'Carbon offsets' – payments to
third parties for reducing or absorbing greenhouse gas emissions, whether
that be from renewable energy projects, energy efficiency measures, or land

management initiatives – have been heralded as an efficient way for the economy to reach 'carbon neutral' status. The idea is that by establishing a market in which so-called 'negative emissions' can be traded there will be strong financial incentives for economic actors to find the cheapest ways of mitigating overall greenhouse gas levels – the costs of reducing or sequestering emissions will be lower for some, and these economic actors should logically be tasked with the bulk of the emissions reduction job. In theory, this is a neat solution – not only do offsets assign a monetary value to activities that store carbon, providing a market and rewards where none before existed, but they are almost certainly an essential bridge on the road towards decarbonisation. The modern world has been built around the power generated from fossil fuels and any transition away from this system cannot be immediate, and offsets are viewed by many as a necessary form of triage until an alternative energy system can achieve sufficient scale.

However, unlike GDP, carbon neutrality is a net measure – some entities might reduce their carbon footprint while others continue to pour greenhouse gases into the atmosphere – and at present there is usually no accompanying mechanism to compel emissions reduction by polluting companies. Cynics point out that offsets allow hydrocarbon-intensive industries to continue to burn fossil fuels while giving them the luxury of broadcasting their 'carbon net zero' credentials to the wider world. Brandishing the get-out-of-jail card that is a carbon offset, they argue, allows corporate cowboys to touch down in their private jets and solemnly recite the mantra of net zero to customers and investors, without the bother of needing to take meaningful action on actual emissions reduction. Along the same lines, other critics of carbon offsets contend that they are simply another way for the richest cohort of the global community to buy their way out of communal obligations, comparing them to the papal indulgences of another era – 'forged pardons for real sins' as the Renaissance philosopher Erasmus described them at the time – that absolved the guilty while permitting them to continue their wayward behaviour.

There is certainly something to this criticism. Many studies have shown that putting a price on actions that previously attracted social opprobrium has the effect of legitimising that behaviour – if something can be paid for, then, the logic goes, it must be permissible. Perhaps the most famous example of this tendency is what has become known in economic annals as 'the Haifa daycare experiment'. In the late 1990s, economists monitored an Israeli daycare centre that suffered from a worldwide malady – parents arriving late to pick up their children. As economics is the study of incentives, these academics suggested that the imposition of a fine on tardy parents should encourage them to turn up on time. But rather than improving punctuality, the number of late pick-ups more than doubled – lateness simply became another commodity that could be bought, with the moral stigma of inconveniencing the daycare workers apparently set off or extinguished by the payment of money. By turning what had previously been governed by ethical norms into just another market transaction, the exchange tipped into one ruled by a cold calculation based on price signals.

Further, 'net zero' – where human-caused carbon emissions are purportedly offset by human-induced carbon absorption or the avoidance of emissions – can be little more than a spreadsheet entry that permits emissions to be as large as the theoretical and unverified quantum of carbon sequestration. But these projected drawdowns are highly doubtful at present, as offsets do not achieve enduring 'negative emissions' in the form of greenhouse gases permanently removed from the atmosphere. Only 'carbon capture and storage' technology – which, as the name suggests, captures and stores discharged carbon dioxide before it can be released into the atmosphere – can achieve true negative emissions, but to date there has been nothing invented that sequesters and enduringly retains greenhouse emissions at scale and cost effectively. At the moment, 'nature-based solutions' – most notably, land use practices in forestry or agriculture that absorb carbon or avoid further emissions – are the best method of obtaining meaningful negative emissions, but there is no firm guarantee around the durability of those stewardship schemes. 'Nature-positive' land management practices may, for example, be reversed at some future time or forests may succumb to wildfires that release accumulated carbon. Opponents of these nature-based schemes also note that the cheapest offsets tend to be the ones that would have happened anyway, and that there is nothing to stop extractive businesses simply finding new frontiers to exploit.

A broader criticism of carbon offsets is that they encourage a new form of 'carbon colonialism' – not only does the WEIRD club already lay claim to the majority of the global commons that is the atmosphere through its greenhouse gas emissions, but it is argued that it is now seeking to launder this activity by establishing the bulk of offset projects in less developed countries. Land that could be given over for subsistence farming purposes, or protected for biodiversity reasons, may instead be used to burnish the reputation of polluting companies. Additionally, data from some bodies indicates that significantly less than half the money spent on some carbon offset schemes is directed to the actual offset project, with the remainder pocketed by project promoters, brokers and marketers. At present, there are many carbon cowboys generating low-integrity 'junk credits' that often also benefit from an accounting fudge by immediately booking estimated carbon savings even if it will take years before there is any substantial sequestration of greenhouse gases. Pragmatists counter that the perfect should not be the enemy of the good, and that the best way to minimise the incidence of these sub-standard credits is to develop a more rigorously regulated offset market that adheres to common standards.

Endlessly creative capitalism has, then, not only manufactured a lucrative new market, but it has pulled off yet another clever move by fostering the idea that individuals can use their purchasing power to reshape the world. At the same time, under the sway of powerful vested interests it has largely succeeded in delaying necessary systemic reforms while spawning new markets that do not always address the root problem. Fossil fuel profits are inflated as companies do not pay for the damage caused by hydrocarbon pollution, while the emergence of new offset markets gives those same companies a platform to propagate questionable claims about progress on emissions and sustainability. But there is a simple, although not necessarily easy, solution – pricing hydrocarbons so that the full social costs arising from their use are recognised. This one act would reduce the attractiveness of fossil fuels and provide incentives for other forms of energy to compete on a more level playing field, while also rewarding those who provide negative emissions in the form of long-term carbon sequestration. By enforcing honest hydrocarbon prices, capitalism can do what it does best – innovate and adapt, and perhaps help guide us to a more sustainable and equitable future.

13

PANDORA'S BOX

Making fossil fuels fossils once again

The world is not enough

The *World Inequality Report*, compiled periodically by an international team of economists, estimates that the poorest half of the global population owns just 2 per cent of total global wealth while the top 10 per cent now owns 76 per cent. Although the post-war period from 1945 through to 1980 was a time of narrowing inequality in many parts of the world – not just Western nations such as the US and Britain, but also developing countries including China and India – wealth differences widened significantly following the neoliberal revolution of the late 1970s and early 1980s. The report notes that between 1995 and 2021, for example, the global one percenters captured nearly 40 per cent of the world's incremental wealth while the bottom half picked up a miserable 2 per cent, and that the share of wealth held by the global top 0.1 per cent escalated by almost two-thirds over the same period. Under the sway of neoliberalism, the global citizenry has been sifted into an increasingly polarised group of haves and have-nots, and Adam Smith's promise of universal opulence extending to the lowest ranks of people has become increasingly dubious.

The richest global cohort, which includes the majority of people who live in the industrial West, have not only pocketed most of the world's financial wealth, but they also lay claim to the vast bulk of the planet's natural resources. Studies show that we would need approximately three Earths if American and European lifestyles were to be replicated worldwide, and the US alone consumes around a quarter of global resources while comprising less than a twentieth of the global population. We invent stories to justify our privilege – telling ourselves that we live in a meritocracy and that success is deserved, with the implication that lack of success is equally deserved – while studiously ignoring the fact that most Westerners are winners in what the investor Warren Buffett calls 'the ovarian lottery', and that our good fortune is due in large part to where and when we were born. The 10 per cent of households with the heaviest carbon footprints discharge around four times more emissions in aggregate than the bottom 50 per cent, with offsets and ESG investments sometimes acting as little more than a placebo – offering the comforting fiction that extreme polluters can purchase their way out of guilt, or at least salve their conscience by consuming differently rather than simply consuming less.

Given that the permanent sequestration of greenhouse gases cannot be guaranteed at present, some have recommended that humanity should double down on its domination of the natural world. 'Geoengineering' – the large-scale management of the Earth's climate system – has been suggested as a means of moderating human-caused global heating relatively quickly and cheaply. The most discussed form of geoengineering is 'solar radiation management', which seeks to counter the effects of greenhouse gas pollution by putting even more chemicals in the atmosphere – for example, by spraying aerosols into the stratosphere to reflect sunlight back into space. Such an exercise is not only untested, other than by analogy to the 'volcanic winters' that periodically occur when ash and sulphur gases erupt into the atmosphere, but importantly it also fails to address other destructive effects of carbon pollution such as ocean acidification. Like carbon offsets, proposed geoengineering programs are a balancing mechanism that would allow greenhouse gas emissions to evade any hard limits, and would require ever-increasing amounts of chemicals to be dispersed into the atmosphere. Additionally, geoengineering has the potential to radically recast vital weather patterns on which a large portion of the world relies, including the global water cycle which drives annual events such as monsoon activity, while also reducing photosynthetic activity. Ramping up humankind's program of planetary interference would not only foster moral hazard by encouraging existing polluters to continue their polluting ways, but would also result in countless unintended adverse consequences and likely inflict further pain on poorer nations.

Although it sometimes seems easier to alter the Earth rather than our own improvident behaviour, a radical change to our ways is required. The Cowboy Economy has for centuries drafted developing countries into the global Ponzi scheme on the natural world – first in the brutal buccaneering days of colonialism, more recently by holding out the promise of material riches in exchange for natural resources, often the only tradeable asset in poorer nations. The West has colonised not only lands but also the atmosphere, with most of the planet's 'carbon budget' – the maximum limit of human-caused greenhouse gas emissions that would likely keep global heating to a minimum threshold – already spent by the developed world. As Adam Smith commented in his first book,

> we are but one of the multitude, in no respect better than any other
> in it; and … when we prefer ourselves so shamefully and so blindly to
> others, we become the proper objects of resentment, abhorrence, and
> execration.

However, our economic system has removed much of the moral stigma from harmful activity by dismissing social costs as mere 'externalities', by distancing acts of exploitation behind convoluted supply chains, by creating carbon credits that frequently offset responsibility more effectively than carbon dioxide, and by proffering a tale of never-ending growth to postpone awkward conversations around equality and fairness.

In securing abundance for themselves the WEIRD club has exposed developing countries to the worst effects of climate change, with low-income nations most imperilled by the global heating due to the carbon colonisation of the Earth by rich countries. The latest IPCC report estimates that almost half the world's population, somewhere between

3.3 and 3.6 billion people, live in countries that are highly vulnerable to climate change. People in these regions – mainly sub-Saharan Africa, south Asia, Latin America, and small island states – will, the report notes, increasingly experience 'pressure on food production and access … leading to malnutrition and micro-nutrient deficiencies' while some areas will become simply too hot to live in year-round or will sink under rising seas. The West's debt-driven growth model has bled into the natural world, with a huge overdraft made on the world's carbon budget, and the Faustian pact that sacrifices future prosperity for present-day advantage will disproportionately affect those who are least culpable.

Promising the Earth

To address unsustainable drawdowns on the global carbon budget, economics must refocus on its self-professed mission statement of optimising under constraints. The biggest constraint on long-term global growth and prosperity is the health and vitality of the natural world, but in the same way that nature has largely been pushed to the edges by modern civilisation, it is also a fringe-dweller within mainstream economics – subservient to the industrial process, treated as little more than an input into the machine and a repository for the resulting waste. This has, in turn, allowed self-interested economic actors to unsustainably exploit the gifts of nature and transfer the costs of this plunder on to others, while these entities have also delayed urgently needed structural reforms by waging campaigns of diversion and division. At the same time, corporations and their enablers have propagated the idea that those who helped create this problem are also the ones who will solve it – that, with the notable exception of profit-eroding carbon taxes, the solution to market failure is invariably more markets, and that the right type of consumption can in fact solve the problems of excess consumption.

In an unfortunate quirk of timing, James Hansen's congressional appearance in June 1988 also coincided with the growing supremacy of the neoliberal doctrine. Joining fellow communist heavyweight China in a feint away from a command economy, the Soviet Union had officially launched its own program of economic liberalisation at the start of that year, and perhaps just as tellingly the first McDonald's in a communist country was opened a couple of months later. But although government regulation was out of fashion, and collectivist action increasingly anathema, science would still sometimes trump ideology. Margaret Thatcher, the High Priestess of Hustle and an enthusiastic champion of small government, was the first prominent political leader to call out the potential dangers of climate change. In a speech to the Royal Society, just three months after Hansen's public debut, she noted that 'the health of the economy and the health of our environment are totally dependent upon each other' and 'it is possible that … we have unwittingly begun a massive experiment with the system of this planet itself'. Thatcher, a trained scientist, believed that climate change was as much a menace to the free world as communism or the threat of nuclear war.

Despite this early recognition of the dangers of climate change, international action has been woefully limited in the decades since the alarm was first sounded. There had been some past victories in terms of multinational collective action – most notably the 1987 Montreal Protocol securing a global agreement to phase out the use of CFCs, but these chemicals were easily substitutable, and manufacturers did not have the political sway or the immense financial weaponry of fossil fuel companies. Hydrocarbon producers and other heavy industries have a strong incentive to maintain the status quo – and their power is such that they have not only been permitted to dump waste products into the atmosphere at no or little charge, but they are in fact paid for the privilege. The International Energy Agency, an intergovernmental organisation established to act as policy adviser to member states on energy security, estimates that hydrocarbon subsidies amounted to around $1 trillion in 2020, while the true subsidy figure is likely to be more than $6 trillion once externalities are factored in. Not only does it suit these corporations to not measure certain things, but they have also gamed the system to become the biggest welfare recipients on the planet – scooping up public money to exploit the biosphere, rather than protect it.

Supporting those resisting a straightforward polluter-pays system are the cornucopians who oppose the intrusion of the state and reject the 'limits to growth' thesis, arguing instead that human ingenuity will always find a way forward. The business academic Julian Simon, for example, contended in his book *The Ultimate Resource* that there will never be a natural resource crisis because as a particular commodity becomes scarcer its price will rise, obliging rational economic actors to use it more sparingly, to recycle, or to develop substitutes. The 'ultimate resource', in Simon's formulation, is human cleverness – the capacity to invent and adapt. But the price signals for our other ultimate resource – the natural world and the life-giving benefits it provides – are badly awry, as they do not factor in the social costs of hydrocarbon use. Just as in Keynes's day, an entity that can correct the market's failings is needed – the atmosphere is collective good and requires an agent for the collective, and this should be a government project. Instead, like many other tasks in our modern society, the job has increasingly been outsourced to corporations and their functionaries.

Placing the fox in charge of the henhouse means that corporations have usurped or at least run interference on the rightful role of governments in addressing societal problems, instead conjuring the illusion that things are being done when it is in fact business as usual. Initiatives such as the Kyoto Protocol, premised on voluntary national reductions, are essentially toothless treaties without an enforcement mechanism to compel countries to share the responsibility for managing atmospheric pollution. The fact that the UN has convened almost 30 annual conferences to tackle global heating is evidence enough that the current system is not working – due to the absence of honest carbon pricing, we are effectively zero for twenty-something in our efforts to collectively redress human-caused global heating. Instead, climate 'solutions' are privatised, the broader community has been largely disenfranchised, and government's role as an external agent moderating the excesses and irrationalities of the market much diminished. We need to do one big thing and many little things to help address the problems of excess greenhouse gas emissions – but somewhat paradoxically, while governments have an integral role reining in the excesses of globalised markets, in some areas we also need more markets and more globalisation.

The prodigal sun

A carbon price that reflects the social costs of hydrocarbon use – or even a tax that starts from a low base and then increases incrementally towards a full charge or until emissions reductions targets are met – is the simplest first step. If levied at uniform rates across as many countries as possible, and enforced by a 'climate club' that excludes non-participants through tariffs or trade sanctions, such a tax will increase the costs of hydrocarbon use relative to other forms of energy, and the Invisible Hand of the market can then shepherd consumers and producers towards less carbon-intensive alternatives. Already the innovative and adaptive genius of capitalism has resulted in plummeting renewable energy prices and high rates of adoption over recent years – the IPCC notes, for example, that in the decade beginning in 2010 unit costs of solar energy fell by 85 per cent and wind energy by 55 per cent, while over the same period the number of electric vehicles on the road increased more than a hundred-fold.

The market, then, has already delivered to some extent, but hydrocarbons still account for over 80 per cent of all global energy consumption. Even during the Plague Year of 2020, when much of the world's population was cocooned inside their homes and factories shuttered, global carbon dioxide emissions fell by only 5.8 per cent, less than the average annual rate of reduction required for a chance of limiting future temperature increases to 1.5 degrees Celsius above pre-industrial levels. Given that our global economy is geared towards fossil fuel use – with powerful incumbent companies owning trillions of dollars of hydrocarbon reserves, alongside a complementary network of mines, wellheads, pipelines, power plants, gas stations and other infrastructure – the task of decarbonisation will be immense. The job has, however, been made easier by falling renewable energy prices. Electricity generated from both wind and solar power have reached their own tipping point, and are now cheaper than that derived from most fossil fuels, while the problem of 'intermittency' – fluctuations in renewable energy supply due to external conditions such as the weather – is being remedied by battery storage, which itself has fallen in cost by almost 90 per cent over the last decade.

The International Energy Agency has suggested that by 2050 renewable energy technologies could provide just over half of the world's energy needs and two-thirds of all electricity generation if there is a concerted effort to transition away from fossil fuels. Although there are technical issues in integrating renewable energy sources with existing grids, large electricity networks powered mainly by renewables are becoming increasingly viable – in mid-2019, for example, Britain, the birthplace of fossil fuelled capitalism, generated more electricity from renewables than hydrocarbons. The colossal task of transitioning to low emissions energy sources will also require not only a carbon tax, but other government-mandated measures such as the elimination of fossil fuel subsidies, public research and development funding, tax breaks for early stage 'climate tech' companies, and measures that encourage energy efficiency and conservation.

Such an exercise will entail levels of economic mobilisation not seen since the Second World War, when communal interests were similarly put ahead of select business interests. But although the IPCC estimates that green investment requirements for the decade from 2020 to 2030 will be up to six times greater than current levels if warming is to be limited to 2 degrees, it also notes that the global pool of capital is more than sufficient to meet this investment gap. In addition to providing much of this capital, the private sector can assist by promoting common standards and greater regulation in the burgeoning carbon offset market, which should lead not only to higher quality credits but will also allow a clear hierarchy of carbon offsets to be established, with more permanent credits given a higher value through the action of the price mechanism. In the domain of ESG investments, rather than dealing with a grab bag of qualitative and often conflicting goals and metrics, a better approach would be to focus solely on greenhouse gas emissions – the most pressing market failure, and also the most amenable to standardised measures and quantitative rigour.

The accelerated deployment of renewable energy would result in a redistribution of 'power' in both senses. Not only would the energy balance shift increasingly to low or zero emissions sources, but consumers would also be less beholden to often authoritarian and erratic petrostates – for although the impacts of fossil fuel use are widely dispersed, exploitable reserves of hydrocarbons tend to be geographically concentrated. Many countries graced with substantial fossil fuel deposits show low rates of economic development and social progress, and this national Midas curse can be due to a dependency on offshore capital to develop extractive industries, non-mineral sectors becoming less competitive as domestic currencies appreciate due to inbound investment flows, or political meddling from those nations frustrated that 'their' oil inconveniently lies under the sand of another country. Despotism and hydrocarbon riches tend to exist hand-in-hand because it allows a governing clique to appropriate the bulk of the state's hydrocarbon rents, and this windfall is then funnelled to favoured in-groups. In contrast, renewable energy sources are generally locally based, and are not subject to the whims of autocrats, cartels or geopolitical events half a world away.

In the same way that capitalism works because its essentially decentralised character responds best to the emergent system that is messy, multifarious human society, so too should renewable energy – a network of distributed energy nodes that draws on the eternal energies of the wind, sun and water, and a system far less entangled in increasingly fragile global supply chains. Widely scattered renewable energy sources will also moderate the monopolising tendencies of fossil fuel companies and reduce the scope for Big Carbon interests to influence public policy outcomes, perhaps rejuvenating a political system that many now think is rigged. Studies suggest that around 70 per cent of Americans believe that the 'political system seems to only be working for the insiders with money and power', and this dissatisfaction with the democratic process extends beyond US borders, with only 45 per cent of people polled from 27 nations reporting that they are 'satisfied with the way democracy is working in their country'. A flourishing democracy is also a system of exchange – ideally, a constant feedback loop of communication and consultation with the broad population, and not just the elites. By hobbling the pernicious political power of vested interests, we can ensure that the private returns and social returns from any corporate activity begin to converge.

In the Greek myth of Prometheus, the bringer of fire and civilisation was punished by the other gods for stealing the sacred flame and smuggling it to mortals. A woman, Pandora, was created by Zeus and delivered to Earth with a box holding an 'odious treasure', which when opened unleashed evils and disasters on humanity. One version of the myth has Pandora panicking and resealing the box too early, leaving the blessing of hope – with which humankind would have a chance of triumphing over despair and tragedy – trapped inside the vessel. Like this ancient story, fossil fuels have brought both gifts and afflictions, propelling our modern world to unparalleled material wealth but at huge cost to natural systems.

Hope, however, remains. The ultimate carbon capture and storage 'technology' are those fossil fuels that were locked in the Earth's crust millions of years ago – tremendously stable in the absence of human intervention – and by leveraging human ingenuity and the technological legacy granted by our recent hydrocarbon history we can transition to alternative energy sources, with the market co-opted in this process. But like fire itself, markets work effectively only when harnessed and controlled, and are a danger when left untended. Greenhouse gases and their social costs are relatively easy to quantify and compartmentalise, and a true pricing of their costs and benefits will increasingly favour other forms of energy over time. There are, however, some parts of the natural world that are far less amenable to commodification – where the complexity of nature defeats a simple market solution, and for which non-market measures may be needed to ensure a thriving planet.

WATER

14

LIQUID ASSETS

The ocean, our last frontier and largest carbon sink

The manna of the Mediterranean

In a grotto on the Sicilian island of Levanzo a gallery acts as a mute messenger from the depths of prehistory. Cut into the cave walls are the outlines of horses, deer, and the formidably horned and now extinct auroch, dating from the dawn of the Agricultural Revolution when Levanzo was a hilly promontory attached to the mainland. Alongside these are more recent cave paintings – from around 6,000 years ago, by which time sea waters had risen and a small island formed – and swimming among the black stick figures and plump fertility goddesses is the unmistakeable ellipse of a bluefin tuna. In the liquid continent that is the Mediterranean, the annual run of tuna was once a byword for abundance. Entering the sea in late spring, some migrating from as far as the east coast of North America, the immense shoals of fish were a miraculous draught in a season of drought, a river of life that provided the near-tideless sea with its own internal rhythm. Coastal communities gleaned the flood tide of tuna that appeared with metronomic precision every year, leviathans that could reach 4 metres in length and weigh as much as 10 men.

Classical writers marvelled at the sheer heft of bluefin, 'incredible both in size and fatness' according to Aristotle, and the astounding aggregations that each year would grace the shores of the Mediterranean. An awestruck

Oliver Goldsmith, writing 2,000 years after Aristotle in the eighteenth century, described the advance of the 'living mass' of a school of tuna as a

> murmuring noise, which is heard from afar, is echoed from rock to rock, and repeated from shore to shore, resembling that dull but imposing sound, which during a deceitful calm on a burning summer's day announces the approach of a hurricane.

To observers, the schools of tuna were a freakish natural wonder, and it is no surprise that the bluefin was a symbol of the Greek sea god Poseidon, the Earth-Shaker. The imitative Romans would later appropriate the tuna as an emblem of their own water deity Neptune, and the magic trident common to both gods was modelled on the three-pronged spear used by tuna fishers to impale their prey.

In perhaps the most fitting homage to this apparently inexhaustible bounty, Phoenician colonies from Spain to the Levant struck coins featuring the clean, current-forged curves of the bluefin, for even in antiquity tuna was equated with tremendous wealth. Bluefin tuna was one of the ancient world's most important cross-border commodities – salted, brined, air-dried and smoked tuna, even a questionable concoction of fermented tuna innards known to the Romans as garum, were transported around Europe, North Africa and the Near East. A valuable source of protein for the Roman legions, preserved tuna accompanied the Latin language and civil law to the outer bounds of the Empire, with remains of the blood-and-guts brew of garum found as far afield as Hadrian's Wall in northern England. The processing of this yearly bonanza became one of the first enterprises to be conducted on a truly industrial scale, and, prefiguring the canned tuna of our day, ancient mariners and merchants shipped the cured fish around the Mediterranean in large wooden casks and specially made clay pots.

By the early classical age elaborate traps and large-scale processing plants studded the Mediterranean and nearby waters, and like an undersea Ulysses bluefin tuna were obliged to negotiate scores of snares and obstacles on their counter-clockwise odyssey around the huge basin. Following the fall of the Western Roman Empire in the fifth century, Sicily, a political football at the toe of the Italian boot, again became the plaything of distant lords – the Saracens, the Normans, the Aragonese, and, finally, northern Italian mainlanders. But the tuna traps remained a constant, changing remarkably little from the structures first made by the Phoenicians 4,000 years ago. Each year, as if to show nature's indifference to the follies and ambitions of men, a torrent of tuna would unfailingly pour into the island's network of *tonnare*, six-storey high nets fixed to the sea floor with thousands of stone weights and iron anchors, and stretching as much as a mile-and-a-half across.

The hordes of summer tuna that journeyed around the Mediterranean Sea have now, however, been reduced to a relative trickle, while not unrelatedly what the fishermen of Sicily once received for a ton of bluefin can now be garnered for a single fish. Appropriately for a product that was one of our first cross-border industrialised commodities, the bluefin tuna has become both an emblem and a victim of our globalised world – delicacy of choice for the world's elite, but at times threatened with the same fate as the auroch etched on Levanzo's cave wall. The elemental tale of the bluefin is a prism that vividly refracts many of the problems confronting our fossil fuelled society – including the overexploitation of natural resources, the pollution of the biosphere, and markets outrunning governance – but it may, however, also provide a signpost to a more sustainable future.

Vitamin Sea

Just as Earth is a fire planet, it is also a water planet – the only known astronomical body with permanent bodies of liquid water at its surface. Salty seas cover more than two-thirds of the globe, and although cartological classifiers identify five major oceans, the ancient Greeks had it right. Oceanus was the divine personification of one great river girdling the world, and there is in fact just a single interconnected body of water, a complex system of currents and feedback effects generated by temperature differences, winds, the spin of the Earth, salinity changes, and the Moon and Sun acting at a distance through tides. The ancients were also correct in their conception of the world back in deep time – three billion years ago most of our planet was covered in water, as the Book of Genesis claimed, and only later was the face of waters divided by firmaments in the midst. A terrifying void for most of history, marked only with the occasional 'there be monsters' on maps, the ocean today remains largely *aqua incognita* – more than 80 per cent of the ocean has never been explored, and while the deep blue is estimated to contain over two million species, only around one-tenth have so far been described by scientists.

Life almost certainly arose in this vast expanse, and in an echo of our origins seawater still courses through our veins, a brackish stream that carries essential trace elements in almost the same proportion as the ocean itself. Humans are three-quarters water, and like most significant bodies of water we have always been drawn to the sea – initially, for the abundant food resources found in intertidal and near-shore zones, later as a liquid highway opening up new lands for trade and settlement and conquest, and more recently for socially sanctioned slacking by the seaside. The ocean remains an important food source, with more than 3.3 billion people obtaining at least 20 per cent of their protein intake from seafood, while fishing and aquaculture is estimated to support the livelihoods of around 600 million people globally. The ocean has also been a significant enabler of fossil fuelled industrial capitalism – hydrocarbons make up 40 per cent of all shipping cargo, while the Great Acceleration was itself fast-forwarded by the development of standardised shipping containers that cost-effectively transfer goods around the world. And beyond its role as a larder and thoroughfare, the ocean is also the unsung hero in the less obvious domain of climate stabilisation.

The true lungs of the world, the ocean is home to tiny free-floating algae, plants and bacteria that through the process of photosynthesis draw down immense quantities of carbon dioxide that is then released as oxygen. Studies suggest that these organisms – broadly referred to as 'phytoplankton' – supply at least half the Earth's free oxygen, and a portion of the carbon encased in these and other microscopic creatures later drops into deeper water where it can remain in the ocean depths for centuries. In consequence, not only is the ocean the largest carbon sink on the planet – holding over 10 times more carbon than land and nearly 50 times more than the atmosphere – but it sequesters carbon far longer than terrestrial processes. And the ocean is also the most important element in the hydrological cycle that continually moves water around the globe – comprising 97 per cent of the Earth's entire allocation of water, almost all water vapour is drawn from the sea, and this gaseous and purified fresh water in turn congeals as clouds that help regulate the climate, later to fall to the ground as life-giving rain.

The ocean also soaks up over 90 per cent of excess heat caused by fossil fuel use, but its role as a heat sponge means that seas are rapidly warming – the IPCC notes that, should the world continue along a high emissions path, by 2100 it is likely that the ocean will warm by between five and seven times faster than observed changes since 1970. In addition to taking up this heat, the ocean absorbs around a third of all human-caused carbon emissions, but because warm water is far less efficient at dissolving and assimilating carbon dioxide than colder water, the ocean's effectiveness as a carbon sink is diminishing over time. Warming seas also threaten to slow the currents that convey warm water pole-ward and cold water towards the Equator, giant rivers in a watery world that modulate the climate system by partly offsetting the variable radiation of the sun on the Earth's surface. Faltering ocean currents, such as the Gulf Stream which bathes Europe in warm waters transported from the Gulf of Mexico, could eventually trigger an abrupt tipping point that would severely disrupt local weather patterns and significantly lower temperatures in some higher latitude zones.

Despite its vital importance as a climate regulator, the sea remains largely taken for granted by the tribe of landlubbers that is humankind – its inscrutable surface draws a veil over things below, while the ocean's sheer size seems to offer the comforting consolation that it can never be defeated. As Lord Byron exulted two centuries ago:

Ten thousand fleets sweep over thee in vain;
Man marks the earth with ruin; his control
Stops with the shore …

But notwithstanding Byron's confidence, humanity's disfigurement of the world has not in fact halted at the sea's edge. Industrial capitalism has proven more than a match for the oceanic immensity of the world's seas, and human-caused threats – particularly overfishing, pollution, global heating and acidification – are rendering the ocean increasingly vulnerable to the mutilations of modernity.

Battered fish

The romantic image most of us have of fishermen – a twinkly eyed Captain Birdseye in blue sailor's cap and pea jacket, standing proudly between masts on a wooden ship – is far removed from the reality of industrialised fishing. Fishing boats today are steel behemoths – some almost 500 feet in length, armed with sonar and other twenty-first century weaponry, and raking the ocean with nets hundreds of metres wide – floating factories and slaughterhouses capable of processing thousands of tonnes of 'product' every day. Befittingly for such a concentration of killing power, much of the hardware used by these boats, from radars scanning for flocks of feeding birds to an array of satellite uplinks, was first developed for military purposes. Flying flags of convenience rented from smaller countries such as Panama and landlocked Moldova, these vessels are largely shielded from tax and labour oversight, and their hauls only haphazardly documented. And to meet the world's craving for the fruits of the sea these modern-day freebooters range widely on the high seas in a relentless search for treasure.

Fishermen have always punched above their weight when it comes to political power – they bolster food security, in previous ages they constituted a reliable inventory of naval conscripts in times of war, and in our modern era they trade on their role as one of the last hunter-gatherers, seafarers venturing forth on dangerous expeditions far from land. Accordingly, governments have subsidised commercial fishing operations by providing tax breaks or direct payments since time immemorial, encouraging ever-larger ships to compete on the open oceans for the wealth below. Adam Smith remarked in *The Wealth of Nations* that 'it has, I am afraid, been too common for vessels to fit out for the sole purpose of catching, not the fish, but the bounty', and the practice continues today, with global fishing subsidies estimated to total around $35 billion a year. The bulk of these payments, which can only be afforded by richer countries, are directed to capital-intensive fishing fleets – thereby continuing industrial capitalism's campaign of concentration and corporatisation, with the overwhelming majority of the world's wild caught seafood now netted by large companies in developed countries.

Economics is about economising on the limiting factor – and here the scarce resource is the natural capital of fish stocks rather than the manufactured capital of fishing boats, fish rather than fishing capacity. Subsidies to commercial fishing operators are, therefore, a perverse economic policy response to the reality of declining fish stocks. The world's wild fish catch plateaued in the mid-1990s, and the UN Food and Agriculture Organization estimated in a 2020 report that more than a third of global fish stocks are now fished at biologically unsustainable levels, up from only 10 per cent in the mid-1970s. 'Fishing effort' – a measure of fishing intensity that gauges the quantity of fish landed relative to the number of days spent fishing, vessel tonnage, engine power, and other factors – has increased markedly since the early days of the Great Acceleration, as stocks diminish and boats are forced to travel further afield. In the natural world, when a particular food becomes harder to find, predators will 'prey-switch', shifting to alternative food sources that entail a lower expenditure of energy. In the money economy, however, the scarcer a desired product becomes the more it is worth – and this dynamic, combined with the cushioning effects of subsidies, drives ever greater exploitation in certain fisheries.

Fishing in the open seas is a textbook example of the Tragedy of the Commons. Rather than Garrett Hardin's example of a herdsman who adds more and more sheep to a commons, pocketing all profits accruing from his extra animals while dispersing ecological costs among the wider community, with fishing we have the inverse situation – vessels taking as many fish from the ocean as possible in the race for profits. But the outcome in both scenarios is the same – individuals or corporations acting 'rationally' in the pursuit of self-interest act irrationally as a group by potentially exhausting a communally held resource. Economists identify two broad categories of natural resource – 'non-renewable resources' such as hydrocarbons, which cannot be replenished within any human timeframe, and 'renewable resources' which in theory can be tapped repeatedly. Fisheries are considered a renewable resource, but if stocks are exploited faster than they can reproduce then at some point renewable flips into non-renewable.

Catch records from the *tonnara* on the island of Favignana, just south of Levanzo, extend as far back as the late sixteenth century and, almost uniquely among ecosystems, provide a reliable historical chronicle of changes in biomass of a particular species. Within the space of a lifetime, numbers of landed tuna fell from the many thousands each season at an average size equivalent to two or three men, to the grim and ominous year of 2003 when for the first time not a single fish was caught. Because of the unquenchable demand for bluefin, waters that had been sustainably fished for thousands of years, where human history and natural history were so inseparably intertwined, have more recently hovered near the point of collapse. As Kenneth Boulding is reputed to have remarked, 'anyone who believes in indefinite growth in anything physical, on a physically finite planet, is either mad or an economist', and this fish story illustrates his point vividly. It is a cautionary tale against 'uneconomic growth' – the steady depletion of natural capital in return for short-term gains – and a reminder that while some things in nature are well suited to a market solution, many are not.

15

A MOVEABLE FEAST

Kindling desires and demand in a globalised world

Fashion victim

Until recently, the *tonno* harvest at Favignana had been a seemingly timeless ritual in an otherwise rapidly changing world. A large cross stood watch over the tonnara like a seafaring scarecrow, while on shore the village women would direct their prayers to a statue of the Madonna, who cradled not the infant Jesus but a bluefin tuna, and like all other residents of Favignana stared seaward expectantly. When summoned by the *rais*, the head man, the boat-borne *tonnaroti* would crowd around the final compartment in the maze of mesh and floats – the *camera della morte*, the chamber of death. The rais would lift his hand, the *prima voce* begin his song, and the rest of the crew then added their weight to the lilting incantation. The men uttered ancient words and phrases they no longer understood, a barely remembered echo of their Phoenician and Arabic past. As the thrashing tuna were ratcheted upwards in time with the fishermen's hymn the tonnaroti asked forgiveness for what they were about to do. In a fury of blood and motion, the fish would be pickaxed and gaffed and dragged aboard the gathered boats. The slaughter complete, the tonnaroti would then leap into the wine-dark water in ritual absolution.

The Favignana tonnara saw its last *mattanza*, the annual tuna slaughter, in 2007, and while the men of Favignana still occasionally sing their fathers' songs for the summer visitors, they now raise empty nets from the clear blue water. Today the community is geared towards the annual migration of tourists rather than tuna, and the islanders play at being fishermen – what was once a vital tradition, an enterprise involving the entire community, is little more than a theme park performance. The most immediate explanation for the collapse in the Mediterranean bluefin population is that the full arsenal of industrial fishing has been trained onto the fish, and the destructive might of technology has overwhelmed even the prodigious productivity of the bluefin. The vessels scouring the million-square-mile Mediterranean for the last of the tuna are so large and efficient that, in theory, the fleet could exhaust the bluefin quota in just two days.

The sheer magnitude of resources devoted to the capture of bluefin tuna is testament to its unlikely transformation from cheap canned food to a luxury good, and the genesis for this shift can be traced back to another group of islands half a world away. Japan, a mountainous archipelago that has always looked to the sea to provide the bulk of its protein, acquired a taste for the fattier meats favoured by its American occupiers in the immediate post-war years. The dark buttery flesh of the bluefin became prized above all other fish, and *honmaguro* rapidly switched from poor man's food to 'diamond of the sea'. Forced to fall back on its own relatively meagre natural resources during the Occupation, with Japanese boats tethered to their home coast under the terms of surrender, this passion was initially a purely domestic affair. However these vessels soon overfished local waters polluted with the byproducts of the country's economic miracle, and when the ban on offshore fishing was finally lifted in the early 1950s the Japanese looked beyond their borders and led the modern age's belated thrust into the Mediterranean. The array of tonnare around the Mediterranean gave way to a flotilla of factory ships from distant shores, and, submitting to the more efficient predator, the remaining tuna traps closed down one by one.

The Favignana tonnara, once the largest in the Mediterranean, was also one of the last to close. In times gone by, Favignana's first tuna of the season was reserved for the Madonna, but all others were unsentimentally dedicated to Mammon. Slain fish would be hauled by the barrowload to the island's cathedral-like cannery, a curious combination of Gothic arches and towering smokestacks, where bluefin would be once again transformed into cheap and portable protein. But the Favignana cannery succumbed to the ways of the modern world in the late 1970s, to be replaced by Japanese buyers who carefully scrutinised the landed bounty, shrouding the best fish in rice paper and cradling them in ice. These flying fish would be dispatched to Narita airport, which became Japan's largest fishing port in terms of seafood landed, and then on to Tokyo's Tsukiji fish market where the frozen bluefin were solemnly dissected into logs of glossy crimson, to be wholesaled not only in Japan but increasingly worldwide.

Although Japan remains the beating heart of the global bluefin trade, absorbing over three-quarters of all bluefin landed worldwide and 90 per cent of those caught in the Mediterranean, the 1990s saw new markets for sushi and sashimi open up in other countries. One man's fish is another man's *poison*, and the anthropologist Claude Levi-Strauss's facile distinction between the raw and the cooked – 'barbarity' versus 'civilisation' – has been inverted in the case of sushi. The consumption of raw fish – especially bluefin, which is highly perishable due to its fattiness – requires advanced infrastructure, including cold chains and efficient distribution networks. Sushi became a proxy for economic development and sophistication, a cultural phenomenon, and a signature food of the aspirational global middle class. Bluefin tuna, the premier ingredient in sushi and sashimi, was in turn elevated from humble sandwich filler to one of the world's most expensive delicacies, so much so that the creature that accelerates faster than a Porsche can now cost more than one. In today's globalised world, the ocean-crossing animal that began its pilgrimage off the east coast of America might complete its post-mortem journey there, this time as a few fleshy fingers of *toro* in an upmarket New York restaurant.

The Middle Kingdom

The bluefin's transition from commodity to connoisseur's choice, and the resulting impact on prices and fish stocks, is a prime example of the intertwined phenomenon of cultural and economic globalisation. In his

History of the Decline and Fall of the Roman Empire, the first volume of which was published in the same year as *The Wealth of Nations*, Edward Gibbon wryly observed how the decree of a medieval Mongolian monarch impacted the price of fish in England:

> In the year 1238, the inhabitants of Gothia (Sweden) and Frise were prevented, by their fear of the Tartars, from sending, as usual, their ships to the herring-fishery on the coast of England; and as there was no exportation, forty or fifty of these fish were sold for a shilling. It is whimsical enough, that the orders of a Mogul khan, who reigned on the borders of China, should have lowered the price of herrings in the English market.

Globalisation is by no means a new phenomenon, but the entanglements of our times are now immeasurably deeper and more diffuse. Charles Darwin noted that all living things are interdependent and 'bound together by a web of complex relations', and although the focus of Darwin's attention was firmly on the natural world, the same observation holds true in the manmade construct of commerce and trade.

The rise of what has been termed the 'global middle class' exemplifies not only the links within the human-constructed world but also the knock-on effects to natural systems. The middle class are largely middlemen – functionaries required to attend to the paperwork of modern capitalism, such as contracts, invoices, lawsuits and government services – and this pen-pushing caste use education as one of the main escape routes to a better life. This, in turn, has resulted in lower family sizes over time due to the expense of schooling, greater female participation in the workforce, and the reduced need for children to provide labour in non-farming areas. In consequence, the global fertility rate has more than halved over the course of the Great Acceleration, from an average of 5 children per woman in 1950 to 2.4 children today. But although family sizes have rapidly decreased due to the world's burgeoning middle class, the resource footprint of these smaller households has increased exponentially. This is because the middle class is also a consuming class – using its discretionary income to acquire energy-intensive manufactured goods, to travel to far-away places, and, not least, to eat more animal protein.

The American think tank the Brookings Institution estimates that the global middle class – broadly defined as those earning somewhere between around $10 and $100 per day – grew from 1 billion in 1985 to 3.8 billion by 2017. Asia has been the biggest beneficiary of this increase in living standards – as recently as 1997, for example, just over 40 per cent of the people in China and India were living in conditions of extreme poverty, whereas only 20 years later that share was reduced to less than 1 per cent in China and 12 per cent in India. In many ways, this is a reversion to the historical norm – for much of the last two millennia, China and India together accounted for more than half of global GDP, and it is expected that by 2030 the middle class in China and India will once again spend more than the middle class in the US and Europe. The additional billions moving towards developed world lifestyles are, however, placing further pressure on the Earth's natural systems, including the ocean and its inhabitants. Seafood has recorded the highest growth in consumption of any animal protein since the start of the Great Acceleration, with the average global citizen now eating almost twice as much seafood as half a century ago, while in China annual consumption has increased 10-fold over the same period.

Thomas Malthus's grim global reckoning had been premised on a mismatch between the Earth's finite resources and compounding population growth, but he was only half-right – growth in consumption, far more than population, is placing increasing pressure on the world's natural resources. Emerging economies unsurprisingly seek to emulate First World levels of development and consumption, and China is the best case study in this regard – to cite just one indicator of the pace of materials use, it is thought that in 2017 and 2018 alone China manufactured more cement than the US made in the entire twentieth century. China's growth imperative is unlikely to dwindle any time soon, as improvements in material standards are the principal source of legitimacy in autocratic regimes. The Chinese leadership has the tiger economy by the tail – the Middle Kingdom has become middle class, and like much of the emerging world, it expects a First World lifestyle.

China now accounts for around 30 per cent of global manufacturing output – the same share as the next three largest manufacturers, the US, Japan and Germany, combined – and emits a commensurate amount of carbon dioxide each year. However, China's growing impact on the natural world is not limited to the atmosphere – to service the appetite of its protein-hungry middle class, it is thought that around 17,000 Chinese fishing boats comb the open seas, humankind's final frontier of Earthly exploitation, compared to less than 300 vessels for each of the US and the European Union. China is far more than just the new workshop of the world – its huge distant-water fleet captures almost half of all wild fish landed globally, and more broadly it is also the world's fastest growing consumer market and second-largest importer. And China has been transformed by its new-found wealth – eating more seafood in aggregate than any other country, with its tastes increasingly leaning towards expensive imported food and foreign cuisines.

Raw deal

The sushi trains of Japan – conveyor belts bearing bounty to seated customers at carefully calibrated speeds, and expressly modelled on the production line – are the perfect symbol of our globalised and ostensibly ultra-efficient world. As Marx and Engels noted in *The Communist Manifesto*, industrial capitalism and its close confederate globalisation have 'given a cosmopolitan character to production and consumption in every country'. Seafood is the world's most traded animal protein, and the bluefin's circumnavigation of the world – from icy New England waters, to the warm Mediterranean, to Tokyo's sprawling fish market, and then on to its final incarnation as a sliver of protein sitting atop vinegared and sugared rice in a restaurant in Mumbai or Moscow or Miami – is testament to both the organisational feats of our modern economic system and its ability to kindle new desires. However, wild fish stocks, like all forms of natural capital, are different to most other goods, as total supply cannot be easily boosted to meet increased demand. Instead, there is a vicious circle in which higher demand leads to higher landing prices, putting more pressure on supply and further increasing the price, in turn leading to even greater exploitation. This 'perverse incentive' in the human world of the markets is the exact opposite of the dynamic in the natural world – as a hunted species becomes scarce predators will prey-switch, allowing the pursued to return to some state of population equilibrium. For a long time, most 'experts' complacently asserted that fish stocks were as vast and limitless as the sea itself, and that a form of prey-switching would also operate in the commercial world. In 1863 Thomas Huxley, Darwin's faithful Bulldog, was appointed as a Royal Commissioner to investigate claims by artisanal fishermen that trawlers were not only taking too many fish but also destroying the sea floor by carrying out the marine equivalent of clear-felling. Huxley was unmoved by the protests of those clinging to the old ways. 'Any tendency to overfishing', he declared, 'will meet with its natural check in the diminution of the supply [and] this check will always come into operation long before anything like permanent exhaustion has occurred'.

Although an accomplished biologist, Huxley was a woefully inept student of commerce. He took insights gleaned from his studies of the natural world – that an increase in hunting effort for a particular prey species will result in reduced predation, allowing depleted stocks to recover until the 'great powers of multiplication have made good their losses' – and applied them wholesale to the world of markets. Huxley reasoned that:

> If any trawling ground be overfished, the trawlers themselves will be the first persons to feel the evil effect of their own acts. Fish will become scarcer, and the produce of a day's work will diminish until it is no longer remunerative.

Huxley and his fellow Commissioners proffered a classic neoliberal prescription, advising 'that all Acts of Parliament which profess to regulate, or restrict, the modes of fishing in the open sea be repealed; and that unrestricted freedom of fishing be permitted hereafter'. However, the elegant stabilising dynamic seen in nature does not always apply in the human construct of the market. Apex consumers – that relatively small proportion of the global community that can pay for luxury goods, and indeed may welcome a reassuringly expensive item as a marker of status – can incite a race to the bottom to capture an ever-dwindling stock of a natural resource.

Until recently, large aquatic animals had avoided the fate of terrestrial megafauna because they were less accessible, and the seemingly imperishable abundance of the sea was thought to be enough to protect fish stocks from humanity's greed and mismanagement. But technology has now outrun nature and the ocean has been largely sifted clean of large predatory fish – some tuna and shark stocks, for example, are estimated to have fallen by approximately 90 per cent since 1950 – and the plunder of the world's seas has not been limited to its most economically prized inhabitants. Globally, almost 10 per cent of creatures caught by humans are thrown back into the ocean because they do not yield a profit. These 'discards' – including non-targeted fish species, dolphins, turtles, and sea birds – are collateral damage from ostensibly 'efficient', but recklessly indiscriminate, fishing methods such as longlining and driftnetting. The overwhelming majority of discards, more than 90 per cent, come from industrial fishing, with destructive bottom trawling that reduces three-dimensional habitats into two-dimensional wastelands having the highest wastage rate – more than half the catch from shrimp trawls, for example, is dismissively labelled as 'bycatch' and cast back in the water.

Adding to the fishing pressure of the factory fleets are multinationals of a different hue, 'pirate fishers' who evade quotas and government oversight by trans-shipping illegally caught fish and then landing them in inspection-light countries. Illegal and unreported fishing tends to be prevalent in lesser developed countries where fishing pressure is most intense – especially fisheries in Africa, Asia and Latin America – but even in areas such as the Mediterranean the practice is widespread. In past years, for example, Japan's inbound Atlantic bluefin tuna supply has exceeded legal quotas by up to 50 per cent, with these additional thousands of tonnes of bootleg bluefin trafficked by organised crime networks that are as voracious and nimble as the fish itself. Pirate fishers are economically rational agents, and higher prices encourage heavier resource exploitation, which can lead to reinforcing feedback loops of higher prices and ever-diminishing fish stocks. This perverse market incentive reaches its absurd endpoint with what has been called 'extinction speculation'. In the case of bluefin tuna, for example, it has been noted that a small number of multinational conglomerates have effectively cornered the market by building 'strategic reserves' of deep-frozen fish, and are therefore positioned to benefit financially from any collapse in bluefin stocks or the commercial extinction of the species.

Driven by a growing global appetite for animal protein, enabled by the overwhelming power of modern technologies, aggravated by illegal and unreported fishing, and spurred on by government subsidies and other perverse economic incentives, many aquatic lifeforms have been herded towards their own fatal final chamber, the mesh steadily tightening as humans overexploit the world's marine resources. Longer-term sustainability has been sacrificed for short-term volume, the overfishing of some target species has led to a tipping point in which stock size falls below critical replenishment thresholds, and this overexploitation can have damaging knock-on effects for other species within the particular ecosystem. As the web of human relationships becomes more complex, the web of nature is losing its diversity and complexity – and as a result, the super-predator Homo sapiens may be inadvertently engineering a descent back towards the primordial soup of plankton and other simple organisms from which all life originally emerged.

16

NEXT LEVEL

Wearing thin the fabric of life

Red alert
Like many humans, bluefin tuna are drawn to the Mediterranean each summer by warm waters and, if lucky, the opportunity to mate – they spawn in great schools, the females laying around 40 million eggs each year, and ironically it is this very act of generation that exposes the bluefin to mortal danger. Riding the Gulf Stream from the other side of the Atlantic, they join company in a dance around the Mediterranean – a chevron of fish, like birds in flight, bulleting around the inner sea. Visible to overhead spotter planes, the aggregations of tuna are easy meat for the armada of boats in eager pursuit. This bluefin blitzkrieg not only brought the species close to commercial extinction, but it has also impacted broader ecosystems, including the human world. To cite just one relatively trivial example, tuna feed on smaller animals, including jellyfish, and reductions in bluefin numbers – combined with the overfishing of forage fish that compete with jellyfish for plankton – has resulted in increasingly frequent invasions of stinging jellyfish on the Mediterranean coast. Now, around the Mediterranean seaboard, the water periodically turns red not from the *mattanza* of the tuna harvest but from the crimson tide of jellyfish blooms.

Charles Darwin understood earlier than most that in the natural world everything is inseparably connected, and that pulling one thread in the warp and weft of life could rent the entire ecological fabric. Although Darwin made his name circumnavigating the world on the HMS *Beagle*, he was at heart a terrestrial and non-migratory creature, and after his youthful escapade stuck closely to his own patch of ground on the periphery of London. In the meadows on his small country estate he observed that bumble bees were necessary for the pollination of certain types of clover, and that the number of bees in a given district tended to be inversely related to the number of field mice, as mice destroy bees' nests. The number of mice, in turn, is inversely correlated to the number of cats, and Darwin therefore concluded that 'it is quite credible that the presence of a feline animal in large numbers in a district might determine, through the intervention first of mice and then of bees, the frequency of certain flowers in that district'.

The phenomenon that Darwin observed was later given the name 'trophic cascade', derived from the Greek word *trophe*, meaning 'nourishment'. A trophic or feeding cascade describes the trickle-down dynamic in which predators influence the density and behaviour of prey, which ultimately determines the abundance and diversity of the prey's prey. Carnivores that keep herbivores in check, thereby limiting the unbridled consumption of plant and algal matter, are considered a 'keystone species' – that is, an organism that maintains the entire ecosystem in a state of balance. All animals are in effect plant parasites, living off the energy initially provided by the miracle of photosynthesis which conjures life from thin air – they are either vegetarians or, in one sense, vegetarians at a remove. But plants also need meat-eaters to prosper – the world is green because marauding carnivores restrain runaway consumption by the plant predators better known as herbivores. In nature's version of a negotiated peace reinforced through constant skirmishes, perpetual competition and predation at an interspecies level leads to stability at a systems level.

Thomas Huxley fancifully added another layer to Darwin's bucolic food chain when he observed that

> old maids keep cats, and ... the economy of the British Empire was
> based on roast beef eaten by its soldiers, and cattle rely on clover, so

[we must] conclude that the prosperity of the British Empire was thus dependent on its population of old maids.

Although this extension of Darwin's logic was made in jest by Huxley, he edged towards a real truth about human impact, both inadvertent and intentional, on ecosystems. Humans, the ultimate predators, have long shown a preference towards hunting other apex predators – whether that be to protect life or property from perceived dangers, to provide a community-sized protein windfall, or simply for the prestige of slaying a beast bigger than themselves. But by selectively killing off large animals humans have triggered a trophic cascade that has degraded some of the most productive ecosystems on the planet.

The collapse of the Canadian Atlantic cod industry, once one of the world's largest fisheries, is a bleak case in point. Powered by ships that could trawl further, deeper and for longer, and using new filleting and freezing machinery to manufacture uniform fish sticks for the mass market, landings of Canadian cod grew exponentially in the first two decades of the Great Acceleration, climaxing at just over 800,000 tons in 1968. The reduction in the number of cod, the prime predator in the North Atlantic, resulted in an increase in smaller fish which in turn fed on cod eggs and larvae. This shift in the balance of power, combined with rampant overfishing of mature stocks, created a runaway feedback effect. Within a decade of the late 1960s peak the cod catch had fallen by 80 per cent, and in 1992 the fishery was closed when it was determined that cod biomass had fallen to just 1 per cent of historical levels. A 500-year-old fishery, the riches of which had drawn the first Europeans west to North America, had been declared commercially extinct, and many human communities that had co-evolved with this ecosystem quickly went the same way as the cod.

While stocks last

The once fecund Black Sea provides a similar cautionary tale in this regard. In much the same way that enormous shoals of cod would lure Basques and northern Europeans to the New World many centuries later, mercantile-minded Phoenicians and Greeks pursued sea-roaming tuna to previously unexplored reaches of the Mediterranean and the Black Sea during the classical age. Many of the city-states of this era – strewn around the seaboard, as Plato noted, 'like frogs on a pond'– relied heavily on local tuna fisheries in their early days, including the great city of Byzantium, later rebadged as Constantinople and later again as Istanbul. Strabo, the Greek historian and geographer writing 2,000 years ago, contended that Byzantium's Golden Horn, a chokepoint between the Mediterranean and the Black Sea, was so named because of the profusion of tuna that would crowd the bottlenecked inlet – so many that, 'due to the narrowness of the area, they are even caught by hand'.

Today, however, the river of summer tuna that would unfailingly stream into the Black Sea to spawn is no more. The narrow strait separating the Mediterranean Sea from its northern offshoot is one of the world's busiest shipping lanes, with an estimated 1,000 tankers transporting oil and grain and other products each week, and these vessels dump not only waste and fuel, but other stowaways from their ballast. In the early 1980s the Black Sea, weakened by both overfishing and pollution, was overrun by the introduced North American comb jellyfish. Within the last four decades the comb jelly has multiplied from a handful of individuals to an aggregate weight that can on occasion reach an estimated 1 billion tons, at times comprising around 90 per cent of the total biomass of the Black Sea. Combined with 'marine mucilage' – microorganisms more descriptively known as sea snot, which thrive in conditions of nutritional overload – this alien invasion has rendered much of the rich fauna of the Black Sea functionally extinct, and no bluefin have emerged from this once thriving fishery for over 30 years.

Jellyfish are the great survivors of the natural world. They have been around in their present form for at least around half a billion years, far earlier than the first dinosaurs appeared on Earth, and have outlasted every one of the last five mass extinction events. Jellyfish are found all over the planet – in the open ocean, in coastal zones, and some in fresh water – and they feed opportunistically on a wide range of animals, including plankton, fish eggs, small fish, and even other jellies. They are also what is known as an 'indicator species' – an organism whose population changes can act as a flashing red warning that an ecosystem is approaching a tipping point. Blooms of jellyfish have increased in size and frequency in recent decades, not only due to the overfishing of their predators and competitors for food, but also because they are well adapted to other human-caused disturbances to the marine environment – they thrive in turbid conditions because they hunt by touch rather than sight; they are generally more tolerant of warmer and more acidic waters than other aquatic lifeforms; and they also have relatively modest oxygen requirements. This last attribute, in particular, has allowed jellies to thrive in our Anthropocene age – even in the vast 'dead zones' that most spectacularly illustrate the impacts of extreme aquatic pollution.

These dead zones are seeded by excess nutrients flowing into the world's seas – mainly nitrogen from fossil fuel–derived fertilisers leaching from farms, and phosphorus from human sewage and concentrated animal waste – that stimulate the eruption of algae. Like plants, algae are photosynthetic organisms that play a vital role as both an oxygen producer and as the foundation for many food chains, but there can be too much of a good thing – and when algae grows unchecked it foments its own Malthusian catastrophe, not only choking off sunlight to other organisms, but once dead it is decomposed by bacteria that in turn create de-oxygenated expanses. More complex lifeforms cannot survive because of low oxygen levels, and those unable to migrate can suffer mass mortality events. Compounded by a feeding cascade in which overfishing of predators leads to more forage fish that eat zooplankton, resulting in less algae predation, this can lead to a proliferation of toxic tides. A vicious cycle is activated, in which creeping dead zones exacerbate an already unbalanced ecosystem, keystone species are weakened as food webs shrink, and large patches of the world's seas and rivers become deserts of water – ecologically impoverished and increasingly inhabited by simple organisms.

This process of winding back the evolutionary clock through overfishing and pollution may not only result in some fish species becoming the latest of the megafauna extinctions, but it has also forced humans to fish further down the food web – to eat, in the words of one marine biologist, what our grandparents used as bait. Everything is connected, and the targeting of large predatory fish has resulted in knock-on effects that reduce biodiversity and increase fragility across marine biological communities. Studies have concluded that declining species diversity is strongly correlated to increasing rates of fisheries collapse, while also reducing water quality, ecological stability and the recovery potential of fish stocks. Just as in the world of markets, richly diverse environments – with their intricate network of interrelationships and stabilising feedback effects – tend to be far more robust than simplified systems dominated by just a few players.

Circular argument

These collapses in ecosystems are becoming increasingly common, both in the seas and on land. With all the generative power of an algal bloom supercharged by excess nutrients, humankind has gorged on fossil fuels and spread across the Earth's surface. At the time of Adam Smith's birth in the early eighteenth century, around 10 per cent of the world's inhabitable land was used by humans, increasing to 15 per cent by the end of the nineteenth century, and jumping to approximately half today. Humanity's campaign to rid the planet of other large living beings has gone on even longer – hundreds of the world's biggest animals were driven to extinction between 50,000 and 10,000 years ago, with humankind's onward march swiftly followed by megafauna die-offs. Modern humans were therefore not the first of their species to employ frontier-busting, unsustainable practices, but after this initial assault pre-agrarian societies tended to reach some sort of post-battle stalemate with the natural world. However, the explosive power granted by fossil fuels – which is destabilising the amiable Holocene spring by enabling the mechanised plunder of the world's natural resources – has exponentially escalated the war on nature, and extended the field of combat to places such as the deep ocean, where fish are slow-growing and slow to replenish.

The ecologist Aldo Leopold noted that 'to keep every cog and wheel is the first precaution of intelligent tinkering', but humankind's clumsy disruption of the living world's intricate webs of mutuality is fracturing ecosystems and compromising planetary health. In *The Wealth of Nations*, Adam Smith argued that 'The division of labour ... occasions, in every art, a proportionable increase of the productive powers of labour', and this observation also holds true in the non-human world. As organisms become more specialised and diverse then ecosystems become more productive, capturing more of the Sun's immediate energy supply and accessing greater quantities of nutrients. Compared to a biologically impoverished ecosystem, a richly diverse system is far more efficient at absorbing atmospheric carbon, and a proportion of the embodied carbon will be locked away and taken out of the carbon cycle. In aquatic environments the 'biological pump' drives some of this sequestered carbon to the ocean depths to become sea floor sediments, thereby increasing the planet's overall carbon storage potential, while in healthy terrestrial systems a similar mechanism sequesters carbon into the soil.

Diverse ecosystems are not only more productive and more efficient at storing carbon, but they are also more resilient. The tighter the weave, the sturdier the ecological fabric – and like almost all highly diversified systems in which no one actor is dominant, self-correcting feedback loops within a biodiverse community tend to be more stable. In nature, as with all complex adaptive systems, the whole is greater than the sum of parts, and self-correcting feedback loops drive sturdier and steadier systems. Symbiosis and exchange, more so than domination and hierarchy, are the norm in the natural world, and typically only the introduction of an external factor disrupts a biosphere in equilibrium. Industrial capitalism's crusade of concentration and homogenisation is, however, overwhelming nature's drive towards diversification and complexity, while the tendency towards runaway destabilising feedback effects in the world of markets is bleeding into the natural world.

The American economist Hyman Minsky achieved immortality of sorts when he gave his name to what became known as a 'Minsky moment', the tipping point when reckless speculative activity in financial markets reaches an unsustainable extreme and rapidly unravels into a collapse. Like his intellectual hero Keynes, Minsky did not just view markets from the elevated heights of academia – in addition to his day job as a Professor of Economics, Minsky sat on the board of an American bank and saw up close and personal how financial markets worked and sometimes did not work. Rejecting the complacent assumption that markets tend towards equilibrium, he discerned that they were not always rational and efficient, and that factors such as easy credit and intoxicating new narratives could greatly amplify business cycles. Echoing the views of Marx, Minsky thought that 'instability is an inherent and inescapable flaw of capitalism', and that upheavals in the human world of money can have damaging impacts in the real world. Minsky, like Keynes before him, therefore advocated counter-cyclical measures to dampen runaway feedback loops that cause modern economies to lurch from crisis to crisis.

The countervailing force of regulation is required in the financial sphere to moderate positive feedback effects, and as human-created markets increasingly annex the natural world so too some sand needs to be thrown in the wheels of the capitalist locomotive to head off ecological Minsky moments. Industrial capitalism is premised on productive power, but there are parts of the economy where the pursuit of short-term 'efficiency' is absurd – not only in areas such as child and elder care, but also in other endeavours such as fishing. An oversized and hyper-efficient fishing fleet, often subsidised by governments, represents a gross misallocation of resources, mortgaging the future by exhausting the natural capital of some fish stocks well beyond sustainable levels. In an ideal world, capital would instead flow to solutions that restore rather than deplete natural capital. Instead, the decimation of fish stocks is leading to giant blooms of single-celled and other simple organisms as aquatic ecosystems break down, all with the tacit support of equally spineless creatures who should – in theory at least – be acting to arrest this decline.

17

NET LOSS

Oceanic waste and warming

The Plasticene Age

The bluefin tuna is a poster child of cultural and economic globalisation, but although humankind performs remarkable deeds of collaboration and exchange to convey the ocean-voyaging bluefin to dining plates around the world, the web of co-operation has proven much flimsier at the state level. The Mediterranean is crowded around by more than 20 countries on three continents, and, as with international efforts to rein in greenhouse gas emissions, national self-interest provides incentives to free ride and defer meaningful action. The UN Food and Agriculture Organization notes that, of all the areas it monitors, the Mediterranean has one of the highest proportions of fish stocks – almost two-thirds – that are exploited at unsustainable levels. The body charged with protecting Mediterranean bluefin stocks, the International Commission for the Conservation of Atlantic Tunas – better known by its acronym ICCAT – has in the past been widely derided as the 'International Conspiracy to Catch All Tunas' due to its sometimes lax enforcement of quotas and disregard for scientists' recommendations. Like with many other collective action problems, national and multinational agencies have been derelict or actively stymied in carrying out their obligation to ensure that bluefin are sustainably fished, and quotas have frequently overshot most independent recommendations.

On the 'high seas' – that part of the ocean that sits outside a particular country's jurisdiction and control – there is an even more extreme manifestation of the Tragedy of the Commons. Like the atmosphere, it is a global public good, and any instance of governance has generally dawdled a long way behind the goldrush. Although there have been some rare victories for the marine environment, it is usually because of market-driven factors rather than any concerted regulatory effort. One of the most unsustainably extractive industries in the nineteenth century, whaling, was only reined in when whale blubber used for lamp oil was superseded by hydrocarbons. In the more confined domain of the Black Sea, which is encircled by seven countries, its waters were temporarily restored to some semblance of their previous vitality in the early 1990s, but this was mainly because the collapse of the Soviet bloc in 1991 resulted in many farmers being unable to afford polluting synthetic fertilisers. More often than not, the imperatives of profit trump those of the planet, and unfortunately in the world of fisheries management it often seems as though red herrings are the only species that is thriving.

Humankind's unwillingness or inability to collaborate in tackling global problems similarly manifests in the 'trash vortexes' spreading across the world's oceans. These slicks of waste – another expanse of microscopic flotsam, like algal blooms but much larger – eddy into huge aggregations such as 'the Great Pacific Garbage Patch', estimated to be three times the size of France and expanding at a steady rate. Pushed by the same currents that concentrate plankton and drive the weather-moderating oceanic circulatory system, 'microplastics' – tiny plastic fragments from sources such as food packaging, fibres from synthetic textiles, and microbeads in cosmetics – swell into a gigantic slurry. Plastic – a product of our fossil fuel age, derived from petroleum or natural gas – is everywhere, whether that be polystyrene for containers, nylon for stockings, polyester for clothing, PET for plastic bags, or PVC for that passport to consumerism, the credit card. It is inexpensive, lightweight and flexible, and these attributes can deliver significant environmental benefits – for example, plastic packaging extends shelf life and therefore decreases food waste, while vehicles made with plastic parts are lighter and reduce fuel consumption. But another great advantage of plastic, its durability, is also its biggest flaw – plastics decompose exceedingly slowly, or not at all.

The UN estimates that less than 10 per cent of all plastic is recycled while around 14 per cent is incinerated – which in turn can lead to atmospheric pollution in the form of carbon dioxide and chemical additives. The remaining mass of plastics, around 5 billion tonnes in total, still exists in some form, either as landfill or litter. Although many governments have adopted measures such as banning single-use plastic packaging and utensils, implementing deposit refund schemes for plastic containers, and encouraging recycling by consumers, the volume of plastic pouring into the oceans from rivers and cities is increasing at a compounding rate. Annual global production of plastics has soared from around 2 million tonnes at the start of the Great Acceleration to almost 500 million tonnes today, and it is projected that without a meaningful course correction the rate of plastics pollution into the ocean will double by 2030. Plastic waste is scattered from the Antarctic Ocean to the Mariana Trench and, in one of the most graphic markers of the Anthropocene age, the World Economic Forum predicts that if trends in plastic consumption continue then by 2050 there will be a greater mass of plastic than fish in the planet's oceans.

Microplastics are believed to interfere with animals' metabolic and reproductive systems, and zooplankton – tiny aquatic creatures such as crustaceans, molluscs, worms and single-celled animals – are the first link in a chain that allows plastics to infiltrate and accumulate in the bodies of predators at the top of the food web, including humans. This process of 'biomagnification' – the steady accretion of toxins in the tissues of organisms at higher levels in the food ladder – smuggles not only land-based but also airborne pollutants into the food chain. For example, a proportion of the mercury emitted as a byproduct from coal-burning power stations eventually falls into the ocean, is converted to methyl mercury by phytoplankton, which in turn is consumed by grazing zooplankton, and the residual mercury concentrates as it funnels up the food chain. In consequence, some apex marine predators can record mercury levels up to a million times higher than the waters around them, and are so contaminated with heavy metals that when washed ashore they are treated as toxic waste.

Large predatory fish such as bluefin tuna are a living barometer of the airborne pollution generated by humankind's fossil fuel binge – the canary in the coal mine carrying a warning about coal mines – and perhaps the best illustration that in this world everything is connected.

Polyp friction

Just as the bluefin is a victim of many of the byproducts of industrial capitalism, so too is another marine creature. Corals are a strange beast – an invertebrate with an outer skeleton, and an animal that is also usually part algae. It is what is known as a 'colonial organism' – comprising a tentacle-mouthed polyp, typically around 2 centimetres high, that absorbs microalgae into its tissues in order to cadge part of its energy requirement from photosynthesis. The algae residing within the animal feeds on the polyp's waste products, and in turn the carbohydrates produced by the photosynthesising algae nourishes the polyp and allows it to build a carbon-based exoskeleton. These 'compound animals', as Darwin called them, are a microcosm of the wider world, a network of individual organisms absolutely dependent on each other, which together make up a larger symbiotic whole. And in the same way that jellyfish and apex predators are indicator species, a living gauge of human-inflicted pollution, coral reefs are 'sentinel habitats' – sensitive not just to the impacts of excess greenhouse gas emissions, including heating waters, rising sea levels and ocean acidification, but also to the effects of pollution and overfishing.

Coral reefs – the cumulative product of patient stonework by countless polyps over thousands of years – are often called the 'rainforests of the sea'. This is not only due to the incredible biodiversity and biological productivity of these ecosystems, but also because of their technicolor brilliance. It is the algae embedded within the coral organism that gives coral forests their primary colours and softer pastel hues – but when coral is stressed due to the surrounding water becoming hotter or more acidic, or when water made turbid by pollution obscures the sunlight needed for photosynthesis, or when marine herbivores are overfished and harmful algae settles on the coral, then the palette of natural pigments can turn a sepulchral white. This coral bleaching is a result of polyps expelling algae from their safe harbour, and although bleached coral can later re-absorb the algae on which it depends, if this 'dysbiosis' goes on for too long then the polyps will weaken and eventually die.

The principal cause of coral bleaching is marine heatwaves. The IPCC estimates that, due to the Earth's oceans absorbing more than 90 per cent of the excess heat in the climate system, it is likely that the rate of ocean warming has more than doubled over the last 30 years. Marine heatwaves – officially defined as a period when the local sea surface temperature exceeds the 99th percentile over a past benchmark – have become more frequent, more intense and more pervasive. The IPCC concluded that it was very likely that up to 90 per cent of marine heatwaves in the period from 2006 to 2015 were attributable to human-caused global warming, and the incidence of these heatwaves is climbing. The world's largest structure made by living organisms, the Great Barrier Reef off the north-east coast of Australia, was subject to just one mass coral bleaching during the 10-year period surveyed in the IPCC study, but since the publication of the report it has recorded four bleaching events in seven years. In this ever-hotter world, it is expected that coral bleaching on the somewhat less-Great Barrier Reef – which has already lost more than half its corals since 1995 – will soon become an annual occurrence.

Ecosystems such as coral reefs – once thought of as near deathless, with timescales beyond mortal man – may now have the same terminal horizon. Some studies predict that the Great Barrier Reef will be largely dead by as soon as 2050, with coral cover declining to less than 5 per cent by that time. Unlike more mobile organisms such as fish and crustaceans, which can move poleward as the oceans warm, corals are anchored to their limestone dwellings and may be outrun by rapidly warming waters. Another consequence of heating oceans is sea level rise due to the phenomenon of 'thermal expansion' – in addition to ice loss on land, the oceans are rising because the volume of a given quantity of water increases at higher temperatures. Seas rose rapidly after the last 'glacial maximum' 20,000 years ago – the most recent time that ice sheets were at their greatest extent – increasing by over 100 metres in response to a warming world, and due to lag effects only stabilised approximately 10,000 years ago. For most of the subsequent period, sea levels have been almost constant, the rising trend only kicking in again around the turn of the twentieth century. Since this time, the rate of annual global average sea-level rise is estimated to have almost tripled, with further rises built in due to the delayed action of global heating on the ocean.

The rising seas that created the islands of Favignana and Levanzo also birthed the Great Barrier Reef we know today, as corals colonised slowly submerging hills. For almost all of the last 8,000 years the Reef benefitted from largely unchanged sea levels, but over the last century or so the sea level has started rising at an accelerating rate. An island in the Great Barrier Reef has already recorded the first known mammal extinction as a result of sea level rise, and corals – which tend to be very slow-growing, reaching up towards the water's surface at an average pace of only a centimetre a year – are similarly threatened. The IPCC notes that 'the rate of sea level rise is very likely to exceed that of reef growth by 2050', and this projection is based on relatively conservative warming scenarios. The IPCC's models do not take into account runaway feedback loops – including ice loss reducing the ability of Earth to reflect sunlight and related ice sheet instability – that would lead to even faster sea level rise. Some studies predict that a combination of these feedback loops could lead to the sea level increasing by more than two metres by 2100, not only wiping out most coral reefs but also threatening coastal areas that much of humanity presently inhabits.

Shell shock

These impacts in the marine world will also, over time, increasingly affect land-based humans. It is estimated that around two-thirds of the world's cities with five million or more people are located in low-lying coastal areas. A remorselessly rising tide and more extreme weather events due to global heating will increase the incidence of flooding in these places, with one review of recent scientific papers concluding that lifting sea levels will result in 'tens or hundreds of millions of people exposed to coastal inundation and coastal flooding for different timeframes and scenarios'. Rising seas will not only intensify the prevalence and severity of flooding, but will have other adverse impacts, including coastal erosion, 'saltwater intrusion' into groundwater supplies, and the contamination of arable land. River deltas that support huge human communities will be among the worst affected, and small island states are in danger of being swallowed by the sea. Natural systems, too, are vulnerable to the steady creep of salt water – and although some ecosystems can move inland in parallel with the high-water mark, many will be subject to what has been called 'coastal squeeze' arising from human-made and natural barriers.

This coastal squeeze will affect habitats sitting at the margins of the ocean – mudflats, marshes and, most importantly, mangroves. Mangroves grow in the intertidal zones of tropical and subtropical coasts, and are of high ecological value – they serve as a home and nursery to many aquatic species; their branching network of stilt-like roots trap sediment and help prevent erosion; they provide a buffer against storms and floods; and they store up to four times more carbon than a comparable terrestrial area. As coral reefs sink under rising seas the role of mangroves in shoreline protection becomes even more important, because, if unhindered by coastal squeeze, they can grow with the rising waters. Evolved to tolerate wide swings in salinity, temperature and moisture levels, mangroves are incredibly tough plants, but their ability to adapt to the modern world is being severely tested. Manmade structures limit the scope of mangroves to migrate inland, while every year substantial swathes of mangrove forest are cleared for aquaculture and other developments.

Coastal systems are also under attack from industrial pollution. Sediment runoff from nearby farms reduces the amount of light available to marine organisms, decreasing the energy that can be extracted from their environment, while fertilisers leaching into the ocean can seed blooms of phytoplankton that overwhelm the ecological equilibrium. Almost all the pollution and decline in water quality seen on the Great Barrier Reef, for example, is attributable to farming practices, with hard coral numbers almost double on those reefs that are far from agricultural areas. But the ocean's greatest pollution threat is also its least visible – the acidification of the seas due to the increasing absorption of carbon dioxide. A third of all atmospheric carbon is soaked up by the ocean, with this dissolved carbon dioxide then reacting with ions in seawater, and as a result the chemical balance of the water becomes more acidic. Due to excess greenhouse gas emissions, ocean acidification has already increased by 30 per cent compared to levels at the start of the Industrial Revolution, and some studies suggest that by 2100 the oceans of the world could be approximately 1.5 times more acidic than pre-industrial levels.

A more acidic marine environment interferes with the ability of certain animals – including corals, molluscs and crustaceans, but perhaps more importantly some types of zooplankton that constitute the foundation of marine food webs – to form skeletons and shells. Due to steadily increasing acidification, these 'calcifying organisms' can exhibit slower growth rates, their exoskeletons may become more brittle, and in conditions of extreme acidity their shells might in fact dissolve faster than they can grow. And at the same time the seas are souring due to higher carbon dioxide levels, the amount of dissolved oxygen in the Earth's oceans is decreasing. Warmer water holds less oxygen than cold water, and because it is lighter it also tends to rest above cooler layers, slowing the transfer of atmospheric oxygen to lower depths. Faltering oxygen circulation can produce its own dead zones in deeper waters, and the warm-blooded bluefin tuna, which swims open-mouthed to obtain enough oxygen to power its free-roaming ways, will be particularly affected. Not only does their high metabolism render them especially sensitive to a decline in oxygen, but tuna and other pelagic fish species are now staying closer to the ocean surface, and therefore are more exposed to the predations of vigilant fishing fleets.

The IPCC notes in its latest Assessment Report that at warming levels beyond 2 degrees Celsius by 2100, the 'risks of extirpation, extinction and ecosystem collapse' escalate rapidly in marine environments. The oceans of the world – which support more animal biomass than on land – have slowed the rate of global heating by absorbing huge amounts of carbon dioxide and excess heat, but they also bank future global heating. Warmer oceans lag a warmer atmosphere, and climate change effects in this domain are only now becoming truly apparent. Used heedlessly as a receptacle for waste and ravaged for its protein – and suffering also from noise pollution and 'biological pollution' in the form of invasive species carried by globe-ranging ships – the ocean is beginning to buckle under the impacts of industrialisation. The profusion of plastics, the most visible but not the most pressing problem arising from our industrialised system, is perhaps the ultimate expression of the short-termism of modern society – often used for just one fleeting moment, these hydrocarbon derivatives can remain in the environment for many human lifespans. But coral – a symbiotic superorganism in which individual lifeforms come together for mutual benefit – also provides a metaphor for a new way of looking at things, and perhaps an outline towards more effective forms of collective action.

18

PLEASANT ISLAND

Non-market solutions for shared resources

Excremental growth

The story of modern Nauru – a small island sitting just south of the Equator, north-east of New Guinea and more than 300 kilometres from its nearest neighbour – is in many ways a bleak parable for our globalised world. Settled by seafaring Micronesians over 3,000 years ago, the island remained largely untouched by the outside world until the late eighteenth century, when a British whaling ship sailed past after dispatching cargo to the fledgling penal colony of Sydney. In the businesslike ship's log, clinically recording latitudes and longitudes and affixing English names to each new territory, Captain John Fearn lapsed into a rare rapture, describing the island as 'finely ornamented' with trees 'of a beautiful deep green foliage' and having 'houses in great numbers, the capacious size and regularity of which bespeaks the possessors not meanly lodged'. The ship was greeted by outrigger canoes, in which the captain observed no weapons, and the behaviour of the natives 'was very courteous, and they strongly invited us to anchor on the island', waving coconuts and breadfruit as a sign of goodwill. Captain Fearn named this Pacific paradise 'Pleasant Island'. The locals called it *Anáoero*, which means 'I go to the beach'.

The Nauruans lived off fruit from trees, seafood from the surrounding ocean, and milkfish captured as juveniles and then carefully nurtured in the island's brackish lagoon. In the nineteenth century Nauru became a stopping-off point for traders and a refuge for European runaways, the islanders receiving palm wine and firearms in exchange for food and water. In the late 1880s, after negotiating respective 'spheres of interest' in European meeting rooms, Germany claimed Nauru as a possession of its Pacific empire. Later, at the turn of the twentieth century, enormous reserves of 'guano' were discovered on Nauru, the cumulative result of thousands of years of droppings from migrating seabirds that also valued the island's food and water resources. Guano comprises concentrated quantities of phosphorus, nitrogen and potassium – essential elements for plant nutrition and a valuable fertiliser for depleted soils – and a monopoly was incorporated to mine these rich deposits, with phosphate rock sent from this isolated speck of land in the middle of the Pacific to farms around the globe.

Following the First World War, Nauru was wrested from Kaiser Wilhelm and delivered into the hands of his cousin, His Britannic Majesty George V, and in a game of imperial pass-the-parcel was later gifted to Australia. The Second World War saw Nauru subject to another invasion, this time by the Japanese, who deported 1,200 residents to work as labourers in the Chuuk Islands to the west, almost half of whom died while slaving for the Nippon Empire. By the mid-1960s, mining had reduced the interior of Nauru to a barren moonscape of craggy limestone pinnacles, some almost 20 metres high, while a large proportion of marine life in the nearshore sea had been destroyed by silt and phosphate runoff. The Australian Government, believing that the island would be uninhabitable by the 1990s, offered to relocate the locals to a similarly sized Australian island. The Nauruans, however, rejected this proposal and were finally freed from the colonial yoke in 1968, purchasing the assets of the phosphate company and intensifying the extraction of the island's principal tradeable commodity.

For a brief period it seemed as though the island that had been pooped on twice – first by countless generations of seabirds, later by extractive colonialism – would at least prosper from the first dump. As a result of the flow of royalties to the state-owned Nauru Phosphate Corporation, Nauru was one of the richest countries in the world on a per capita basis by the mid-1970s, second only to a Saudi Arabia riding the tailwinds of the OPEC oil price spike. Recognising that the economic life of its phosphate reserves was limited, the Nauruan government established a national trust fund to invest the mining proceeds. The fund was spectacularly mismanaged – investments included the epic West End theatrical flop *Leonardo the Musical* – and was also subject to fraud and embezzlement, and as mining royalties declined and fund money was squandered on bad investments the country became increasingly indebted. By the 1990s the national fund was effectively bankrupt and creditors seized all of its assets, including Air Nauru's sole passenger plane.

To earn much-needed income, Nauru became something of an outlaw nation – a money laundering and tax evasion hotspot, while at the same time hawking citizenship to foreigners and votes to the highest bidder on the international diplomacy market. The most recent insult to be visited on Nauru happened in the early 2000s, when the country became the Alcatraz of the South Seas – agreeing to host an offshore immigration detention facility for Australia, a country that itself had started its European history as a far-flung prison. Mirroring its economic decline, the people of Nauru have also become some of the world's poorest and unhealthiest – dependent on foreign aid, and with almost 90 per cent of all adults classed as overweight or obese and more than 40 per cent of the population suffering from type 2 diabetes. Compounding these social problems are the mounting impacts of climate change – not just rising sea levels that threaten to submerge the island over time, but also more local effects due to a column of hot air that rises above the barren interior and has the effect of pushing away rain clouds. But although the tale of Nauru is one of extraction and exploitation – peopled by rogues, vandals and victims – nested within this doleful account is a guide for an alternative way to manage natural capital.

Commons sense

Nauru is the third-smallest country in the world in terms of area, just behind the Vatican City and Monaco, and with slightly over 10,000 residents is the second-smallest by population after the headquarters of the world's first multinational, the Roman Catholic Church. Over the last two centuries the nation's natural resources have been pillaged and pilfered, with the needs and preferences of the local community largely disregarded. With its phosphate reserves now almost exhausted, the island that had been self-sufficient for thousands of years has flirted with other extractive ventures, such as seabed mining, that would further hollow out its natural capital base. The country that exported fertility around the world itself became largely infertile, and almost all that was left was the abundant tuna in its waters. Until relatively recently foreign fishing boats carried out the aquatic equivalent of the strip-mining seen on the island, with huge quantities of tuna dredged from Nauru's waters, trans-shipped to larger refrigerated vessels, and then ferried to foreign ports for processing and sale. Nauru, without the capital resources to fish the waters of its exclusive economic zone, was instead forced to compete with nearby island states to sell catch rights to offshore corporations.

This race to the bottom led not only to unsustainable and largely unregulated fishing of regional tuna stocks, but also resulted in just a small sliver of income flowing to the Western Pacific nations whose waters provide somewhere between a quarter and a third of the world's annual tuna supply. But in the early 1980s these countries – which together administer 14.3 million square kilometres of ocean, an area 50 per cent larger than the United States – began to work as a collective to sustainably manage the riches of their seas. 'The Nauru Agreement Concerning Cooperation in the Management of Fisheries of Common Interest' saw a move away from nations undercutting each other in attempts to secure short-term revenue, and towards a more collaborative approach focused on the long-term management of tuna stocks. The Nauru Agreement stipulated a minimum mesh size for nets and an independent observer on every fishing boat, implemented a no-discard policy, and the amount of total fishing effort was limited so as to ensure a sustainable fishery across the entire region. Forty years later, and as a result of these protocols, the Nauru Agreement was declared by the UN Development Programme to be 'one of the most effectively managed large-scale fisheries in the world'.

The achievement of Nauru and its neighbours is a rebuttal, at least in part, to Garrett Hardin's Tragedy of the Commons. Hardin's argument that multiple actors motivated by self-interest will ultimately deplete a shared resource has become entrenched in mainstream economics – his article is one of the most-cited academic papers ever – and provided intellectual cover for those agitating for the further enclosure and privatisation of communally held property. As John Kenneth Galbraith drily noted, 'Economists are economical, among other things, of ideas; most make those of their graduate days last a lifetime' – and it was decades before the Tragedy of the Commons was challenged as the only paradigm of human behaviour in respect of communal resources. It would take an outsider, in every sense of the word, to propose another economic story – one founded on co-operation rather than competition, a system that was kept in check by social norms rather than price signals.

Elinor Ostrom operated on the margins of mainstream economics – she was a woman, at the time a relatively rare occurrence in what was largely a fraternity; she had studied political science rather than economics at university because maths was not her strong suit; she worked collaboratively with other social science disciplines such as anthropology and ecology, instead of remaining siloed within the economics faculty; and her theories were informed by observing actual human behaviour, rather than making deductions from the ivory towers of academia. But these attributes were her superpower, and in 2009 Ostrom was finally embraced by the Establishment – becoming the first female to receive the Nobel Prize in Economics, with the Royal Swedish Academy of Sciences observing at the time that her work 'teaches us novel lessons about the deep mechanisms that sustain co-operation in human societies'. Countering Hardin's deterministic, Malthusian view, Ostrom argued that the tragedy of resource depletion was not inevitable in respect of commonly held assets – if resource users decided to co-operate, and could effectively monitor and enforce rules for the sustainable management of that resource, then Hardin's tragedy could be averted. There were, Ostrom argued, alternative ways of self-organisation that did not necessarily require the parcelling up of shared resources into individual property rights and the operation of the Invisible Hand.

Conventional economics, as evidenced by the fixation on GDP and the relegation of social capital and natural capital to the margins, focuses overwhelmingly on activity that is channelled through markets. In contrast, and perhaps because of her background, Ostrom was far more interested in collectives where the market mechanism was not dominant – within households, among associations, and in long established traditional cultures. Ostrom's extensive fieldwork led her to the conclusion that the Tragedy of the Commons typically occurs when those outside the community impose new paradigms or change the rules to suit their own interests. Rather than a remote top-down approach, Ostrom argued that sometimes a decentralised model – in which management decisions are made by those closest to the communal resource, and solutions co-evolve with a particular ecosystem – can best guard against the overexploitation of common resources and ensure fairness for all users. Good fences, it turns out, do not always make good neighbours – Hardin's account was just another story, albeit one eminently well aligned to the interests of the powerful.

Too big to bail

Ostrom received her Nobel Prize a year after the collapse of Lehman Brothers, the nadir of the sub-prime mortgage crisis that starkly illustrated the shortcomings of capitalism's perpetual pursuit of growth. Fuelled by a combination of factors – including a lack of regulation, predatory lending practices, and excessive risk-taking by company executives focused on near-term profits and stratospheric compensation packages – markets experienced a classic Minsky moment when overleveraged bets rapidly unwound. Maynard Keynes noted back in the mid-1930s that 'when the capital development of a country becomes a by-product of the activities of a casino, the job is likely to be ill-done', and 70 years later the cycle was repeated. Having largely exhausted middle-class demand for borrowings, Western financial institutions had proffered debt products to the 'NINJA' consumer category – No Income, No Jobs or Assets – the last possible frontier in their quest to expand their universe of potential customers.

For a while, amid recriminations and outrage, it had seemed that this evident failure of the market would perhaps reverse the neoliberal hegemony, and Ostrom's award by the Nobel committee was viewed by some as a very public rebuke to free market fundamentalists. But Western governments, previously disdained as impediments to the efficient working of markets, stepped in to once again save their detractors. Banks and other financial institutions were deemed 'too big to fail' – so large and so entwined with the wider economy that their demise could potentially bring down much of the economic ecosystem around them. Accordingly, governments and central banks extended bailouts to faltering financial corporations in a globally co-ordinated response, deploying many hundreds of billions of dollars of public money in an exercise that was unprecedented in scale, only to be exceeded by the state spending and money-printing provoked by the global pandemic just over a decade later. The crash of 2008 emphasised, once again, that the world of commerce, like the natural world, is an emergent entity – everything is connected, and changes to one element can in fact have large impacts on the system as a whole.

In casino capitalism the house usually wins, and in the aftermath of the 2008 Crash banks were able to externalise their losses. The privatisation of profits and socialisation of costs seen in the hydrocarbon sector was replicated in the financial domain, and banks outsourced to the wider community the consequences of bad decisions made in high-risk plays using borrowed money. In addition to the risk of financial contagion, banks were rescued because although they can be considered parasites in one sense – living off the largesse of their host, the real economy – they are often useful parasites, and at their best can act more like the symbionts in a coral colony. Finance allows the pooling and channelling of capital to productive uses; it facilitates the transfer of money, a medium of exchange that permits specialisation and trade; and by offering a repository for savings in return for interest it provides a reward for deferring immediate consumption in anticipation of future benefits. However, the 'financialisation' of the economy over the course of the Great Acceleration has seen the banking and finance sector swell massively – in the United States, for example, the sector's share of GDP has tripled since 1950 – and too often the financial tail now wags the real economy dog.

As a result of this financialisation, our modern economic system has in many ways become more adept at confecting claims on future wealth than producing actual wealth. Debt is, in effect, a claim on an economy's future product, but much of the debt today finances current consumption rather than investments generating future returns. Emerging economies, most particularly China, have in recent decades underwritten Western lifestyles through what is effectively the world's largest vendor finance program, while other developing nations are not only subsidising the consumption of developed world importers – because natural resources are significantly undervalued by the market – but they may also be the last round of investors in a planetary pyramid scheme. Low-income countries, which on average depend on natural capital for almost half their total wealth, have been inveigled into a grand deception that promises endless growth – because financial capital, a human fiction, is expected to grow ceaselessly at compound interest. But humans have confused the symbol for the reality, as we cannot just mint more nature. Rather, it is a slow process of rebuilding natural capital stocks and then living off nature's interest. Despite the hubris of humanity, Mother Nature does not do bailouts, and as a species we are not too big to fail.

Hyman Minsky – the economist who observed that periods of apparent stability often seeded abrupt instability in heavily financialised economies – noted that 'there is no simple answer to the problems of our capitalism ... no solution that can be transformed into a catchy phrase and carried on banners'. Similarly, Elinor Ostrom's signature slogan was 'No panaceas!' and her findings affirm that market creation is but one instrument in the economic toolkit. The default policy prescription of commodification and marketisation may not always be the optimal course of action – although some commons, such as the atmosphere, are best suited to a market solution, many others are not. Some ecosystems are so intricate, interrelated and particular to their place that they resist a one-size-fits-all solution. Ostrom's vision – a decentralised, community-driven mechanism that sustainably manages shared resources through the exercise of strong local bonds – presents an alternative to the ideology of market supremacism, and a rebuttal of neoliberalism's 'blackboard economics' in which theory often trumps reality.

19

SEA CHANGE

The perils of thinking economically

Rivercide

It has been observed that our planet Earth should in fact be called 'Ocean', as around 70 per cent of its surface is covered by this one giant body of water. The seas of the world play a key role in moderating the worst effects of climate change by absorbing most of the heat generated from excess greenhouse gases, by drawing down immense quantities of carbon dioxide and returning oxygen to the atmosphere, by locking up some of this carbon in the abyssal depths, by contributing to cloud formation, and by smoothing out regional temperature differences through the action of ocean currents. But while the ocean is pivotal in maintaining the climatic conditions to which modern humanity has adapted, and provides a significant portion of our protein, it is the planet's reserves of fresh water that are more immediately critical to humankind.

The overwhelming majority of land-based plants and animals need fresh water to survive, and for humans it is vital not only for everyday hydration but also for food and fibre production – almost three-quarters of global freshwater withdrawals flow to the agriculture sector, and irrigated land now provides 40 per cent of the global grain harvest. But this resource, although continually replenished through the action of the hydrological cycle, is also finite – only 2.5 per cent of all water in the world is fresh. Notwithstanding this scarcity freshwater withdrawals have more than tripled since the beginning of the Great Acceleration. It is estimated that over two billion people live in countries now suffering from 'water stress' – a situation in which demand for usable water exceeds the available amount during a given period – with the problem most acute in the Middle East, North Africa and South Asia.

Most early urban cultures were founded near rivers and lakes that reliably supplied water for crops. The Egyptian Empire, for example, was built on large-scale farming along the Nile River, which towards the end of each summer baptised this low rainfall region with the annual miracle of inundation. Silt-rich water flowing from the east African highlands created a corridor of green between the desert sands on either side, and the ancient Egyptians channelled and stored this resource via a network of raised earthen banks and sluices. The Nile, however, could be both benefactor and destroyer – in high-flow years floodwaters would demolish crops and infrastructure, while low-flow years could result in drought and famine. One of the world's first recorded economic forecasts was Joseph's prediction of seven years of plenty followed by seven years of famine in Pharaonic Egypt, and the Egyptian state, like most other civilisations, has throughout history attempted to regulate these swings by exerting ever-increasing levels of control over life-giving fresh water.

In Egypt, humanity's millennia-old attempts to manage water culminated in the construction of one of the world's largest dams in the late 1960s. The Aswan Dam was designed to not only moderate outlier river flows, but to also provide hydroelectric power for the country's industrialisation drive and irrigated water to Egypt's economically important but thirsty cotton crop. The Aswan Dam brought many benefits to Egypt – including greater certainty around water flows, additional arable land, and improved navigation along the Nile – but it also decreased the natural fertility of the floodplains. The Nile's annual cycle has now been largely stilled, and instead of nutrient-rich floodwaters feeding the river plains, farmers today rely on fossil fuel–derived fertilisers – many of which, ironically, are manufactured using power generated by the Aswan Dam. The expense of acquiring these synthetic fertilisers, combined with a focus on large-scale cash crops such as cotton, has forced most subsistence farmers from the land, and in consequence Egypt – once the breadbasket of the Roman Empire – is now in most years the world's largest grain importer.

Across the Red Sea, another country is even more dependent on offshore carbohydrates. Saudi Arabia, a country with no lakes or rivers, is abundant in oil but not the more precious liquid that is fresh water. In the 1970s, responding to threats of a counter-embargo on grain following the OPEC oil export strike, the Saudi Kingdom embarked on an ill-considered foray into wheat farming by tapping into 'fossil water' reserves deep under the desert sand. For a brief period in the early 1990s Saudi Arabia was the world's sixth-largest wheat exporting nation, but within a decade its ancient aquifers were largely exhausted. The Saudi experience serves as a cautionary tale for the rest of the world – groundwater now supports around two-fifths of global irrigated crop production and supplies drinking water for more than a quarter of the world's population, but many aquifers are rapidly depleting. It is thought that a quarter of all irrigated crop production relies on unsustainable groundwater extraction, with countries comprising half the world's population – including three of the four biggest grain producers, China, India and the US – emptying their aquifers faster than they can be replenished.

Although it is the most plentiful source of fresh water available to humans, comprising more than 30 times the volume of all the Earth's surface fresh water, groundwater is consumed unsustainably in many parts of the world. In India, the world's most populous country and largest user of agricultural water, the consumption of water for farming purposes has approximately doubled since 1975 and, in a stark illustration of the Tragedy of Commons at work, it is estimated that over 20 million unregulated irrigation wells pump water from depleted groundwater sources. Compounding this situation is declining summer snowmelt from Himalayan glaciers – for a period, global warming accelerated the thawing of glaciers and therefore the flow of water to downstream farms, but these glaciers have wilted so much that water flows are now much reduced from historical norms. In a microcosm of the unsustainable pyramid scheme afflicting the wider world, higher liquid water yields temporarily masked the declining physical stock of solid water, but annual freshwater 'dividends' are now declining rapidly as the underlying natural capital base erodes.

Economies of scales

Rivers and other freshwater systems were the first aquatic environments to be severely impacted by human activity, with agriculture and deforestation eroding the soil and clouding nearby streams, while dams that drove watermills blocked the path of migratory species. In Europe, historically a heavy consumer of fish due to Christianity's various proscriptions on eating red meat, the decline of freshwater ecosystems was evident as early as the eleventh century. Freshwater fish as a proportion of the total piscatorial diet fell from 80 per cent to 20 per cent over the course of that century, and in addition to being forced to new saltwater frontiers, there was an increase in freshwater aquaculture, with carp and other species raised in small ponds. Despite this pedigree, aquaculture has, however, only taken off over the course of the Great Acceleration, and mostly in marine environments – global aquaculture production comprised less than 10 per cent of the total seafood catch until the early 1980s, but now the quantity of farmed seafood exceeds that caught in the wild.

The 'Blue Revolution' of the last four decades is in many ways a welcome development – because most fish are cold-blooded and less belaboured by gravity they tend to more efficiently convert feed to biomass; fish farms usually do not crowd out land-based areas; and the cultivation of some species, such as oysters and other bivalves, requires no external feed inputs, and these filter feeders improve surrounding water quality as well as facilitating carbon sequestration through shell building. But there are also downsides to aquaculture – some forms inflict significant unrecorded externalities on the wider world, not just through excessive antibiotic use and the destruction of ecosystems such as the clearing of mangrove forests, but also because huge quantities of smaller fish are required to raise the carnivorous species favoured by humans. In the Mediterranean for example, bluefin 'ranching' has become a major industry, but unlike most farmers these ranchers only reap, and do not sow – juvenile pre-spawning tuna are netted into cartable *camera della mortes* where they are fattened on a diet of wild-caught sardines. These 'baitfish' are perfectly palatable and more wholesome than the bluefin itself, while high-metabolism tuna are extravagantly wasteful converters of feed to flesh, with around 20 kilograms of feedstock required to add a single kilogram to the farmed fish.

Given some of the problems arising from aquaculture production and the declining stock of wild fish, market-based solutions for wild-caught fish have been employed in an effort to combat the Tragedy of the Commons. The most common market regulation has been 'Individual Transferable Quotas', which is essentially a form of enclosure imposed on part of the marine commons. Species-specific ITQs utilise the fishing equivalent of a cap-and-trade mechanism to regulate fishing effort – quotas can be bought, sold or leased, and are designed to promote the conservation of the stock of a particular species by providing a long-term right to fish certain stocks. Rather than property rights accruing only at the point of capture, which leads to industry overcapitalisation and overexploitation, quota-holders in theory have an economic incentive to take the long view and conserve stocks. However, although ITQs in theory discourage the zero-sum imperative of catching as many fish as quickly as possible, they often result in quota consolidation into just a few corporate hands, and studies indicate that in practice this form of privatisation yields only mixed results in terms of rebuilding fish biomass.

Other management regimes have gone in the opposite direction, reversing the trend towards commodifying natural capital and often securing superior outcomes. 'Marine Protected Areas' – zones closed to commercial and recreational fishing, although often accessible to local communities for subsistence purposes – are in many ways a return to a form of pre-enclosure resource management in which common rights prevail over individual rights. Regulators have taken a lead from many small island nations – which in the past relied on local nearshore waters for the bulk of their protein requirements, and very distinctly comprehended the finiteness of their natural resource endowment – to ensure that resources are managed for the long-term benefit of the community. Closed seasons during spawning periods, allowing a portion of the catch to escape, and declaring some fishing areas and species taboo all assist in rebuilding species diversity and abundance, and the presence of marine reserves often has positive knock-on effects for commercial fisheries outside protected zones. A biodiverse local system with more mature fish tends to produce more offspring, and the eggs from these larger fish fan out on ocean currents, in turn seeding adjacent fisheries.

Illustrating the advantages of taking a longer-term view, a report produced by the World Bank in 2012 and updated in 2017 estimated that if global fishing efforts were to be approximately halved then this would eventually double the fishable biomass and increase the sustainable wild catch harvest. The benefits of recalibrating to a longer time horizon, and avoiding a mutually destructive race to the bottom, has been demonstrated to some extent in the Mediterranean bluefin fishery. Due to overfishing, Mediterranean tuna stocks were pushed to the verge of collapse, recording an estimated fall in aggregate biomass of 80 per cent between 1970 and 2010. This precipitous decline prompted ICCAT to set fishing quotas and a minimum landing size, and, after some false starts, efforts to protect the species appear to be working. In a rare victory amid the backdrop of the global extinction crisis, in 2021 the International Union for the Conservation of Nature, citing an increase of stock of more than 20 per cent from levels in the early 1980s, moved Mediterranean bluefin from 'Endangered' to 'Least Concern' on its Red List of Threatened Species.

The fear of all sums

Orthodox economic theory encourages 'economical thinking' – not just through its focus on market-mediated activity, but also by taking a very blinkered view of the world. It favours selective attention rather than a systems-wide perspective – zeroing in on certain easily quantifiable component pieces, largely ignoring key connections and feedback effects, and typically proposing market-based solutions that disregard the intricacies and entanglements of the real world. The key simplifying assumption in classical economic theory, *ceteris paribus* – 'all other things held constant' – although sometimes helpful in discerning broad causal trends, does not apply in practice to emergent entities. Everything is connected in complex adaptive systems, and the nature of the whole is different to, and much greater than, the sum of parts. These sprawling webs of interdependencies do not resemble the mechanistic models seen in the world of Newtonian physics, but rather are organic networks subject to myriad feedback effects – either negative feedbacks that serve to stabilise, or positive feedbacks that can rapidly destabilise, the larger entity.

Mainstream economic theory has become ensnared in what has been called 'the quantitative trap' – attempting to distil all interrelationships and all activities into mathematical models and formulas, while dismissing qualitative elements as unworthy of analysis. But any sum-of-parts valuation that seeks to dissect emergent networks into their constituent pieces will undervalue the whole. A highly diverse ecosystem such as a thriving coral reef, for example, provides benefits far beyond the quantity of protein caught and sold or tourist dollars spent – it also supplies less easily measurable ecosystem services such as coastal protection and, perhaps more importantly, it is an efficient mechanism for carbon sequestration. All carbon is only borrowed – cycling through the Earth's crust, atmosphere, waters and lifeforms – and a healthy ecosystem acts as a carbon pump that absorbs carbon dioxide and converts it to organisms. The robustness and productivity of any complex system is dependent on the healthy functioning of all its components – resiliency is strongly correlated to diversity, and simplified networks dominated by just a few players are not only more susceptible to sudden collapses, but are far less efficient in drawing down atmospheric carbon into living entities that sequester this element.

Elinor Ostrom's findings provide an alternative to the relentless focus on short-term profit maximisation based on market prices. Some things – such as biodiversity, and the associated health and productivity of an ecosystem – may be impossible to properly measure and regulate through external market mechanisms, and their effective management can be much better secured through a decentralised approach that respects the uniquely evolved characteristics of a particular environment. Ostrom's advocacy, in certain circumstances, of a 'moral economy' for commonly held resources – one based on reciprocity, customary rights, and community decision-making – often better reflects the complex webs of mutuality that enfold the natural world and dependent human societies. In uniting the two forms of capital largely overlooked by conventional economics, social capital and natural capital, Ostrom reminds us that markets are just another tool available to humans – useful in some cases, less so in others – and, rather than reflexively becoming the tool of this one tool, other solutions may be preferable.

But just as the dynamics of finance have edged into the natural world – destabilising ecosystems through a ceaseless growth imperative – increasingly the dynamics of the natural world have been imported into the field of financial regulation. Until recently, for example, regulatory agencies focused on individual banks and their stand-alone risk profile rather than considering broader systemic connections, but the nascent field of 'financial ecology' takes lessons from successful fisheries management and encourages regulators to cast their nets much wider. As Alan Greenspan, the former chair of the US Federal Reserve, observed of the bloated banks that were the main vector for financial contagion in the sub-prime crash, 'if they're too big to fail, they're too big' – the real problem was not that some of these large firms were suddenly on the precipice of failure, but rather that they had been allowed to succeed and swell so much in size in the first place. By examining the interconnections between financial firms and the potential for damaging cascade effects, regulators are belatedly mimicking the natural world.

With complex networks, what may be viewed as 'efficient' in the near term can turn out to be tremendously inefficient when timespans are lengthened – natural and human systems can collapse if one particular component is overexploited or pushed beyond its limits, and short-term efficiency gains may prove to be a false economy when long-term resiliency is compromised. The value of taking a systems-wide perspective was similarly seen during the global pandemic, when 'just-in-time' supply chains – which seek to lower inventory costs and waste by reducing excess stock, excess workers, and excess manufacturing time – in effect became daisy chains. These 'lean manufacturing' systems – running on too-fine margins, reliant on inputs from distant contractors, and vulnerable to severe disruption if just one domino in the row topples – are ostensibly efficient, but can also be tremendously brittle. Taking a lead from the natural world, the argument has been increasingly made that 'just-in-case' supply webs – which reduce reliance on a single upstream supplier and mimic the redundant capacity seen in nature – should instead be employed to lessen systemic fragility.

Elinor Ostrom cautioned that there is no single unifying theory around the management of shared resources, and the lessons from successful fisheries management show that a mix of market and non-market solutions may be needed for the effective conservation of natural capital. Ostrom's alternative governance model for certain common property regimes – one that respects tradition and culture, that empowers communities to set their own values and priorities, and that enfranchises those communities as custodians of ecosystem health over the long term – is a reminder that in some circumstances less markets rather than more markets may in fact be the optimal policy response. And for the Mediterranean – both history and harbinger, the cradle of Western culture and a herald of things to come – it can, depending on our choices, either epitomise our overfished, overpolluted and overheated world, or instead be a proving ground for alternative solutions. Continuing recent progress, perhaps one day a multinational effort will establish a tuna reserve in the Mediterranean – sustainably tapped by small-scale, artisanal fishermen – and the islanders of Favignana will once again lift full nets from the surrounding seas.

EARTH

EARTH

20

THE WAR ON TERRA

The fossil fuelled Green Revolution

Paradise lost

In 1880 Charles Darwin embarked on his last book, ponderously titled *The Formation of Vegetable Mould, Through the Action of Worms, with Observations on their Habits*. Revisiting a topic he had broached in one of his first public talks over 40 years before, Darwin wished to bring attention to this 'unsung creature which, in its untold millions, transformed the land as the coral polyps did the tropical sea'. As steady and industrious as the animals he studied, Darwin performed many painstaking experiments on the worms on his property, shining lights on them, offering them different foods, and posing challenges to ascertain how they drag objects into their burrows. Darwin had played the evolutionary game himself by having 10 children, and the bearded patriarch recruited his children to help as lab assistants, one playing a low-toned bassoon and another a piano at high pitch to ascertain whether worms had a sense of hearing. Although he determined that earthworms are deaf as well as blind, by no means were they automatons – Darwin noted that worms 'enjoy the pleasure of eating' and that they 'perhaps have a trace of social feeling, for they are not disturbed by crawling over each other's bodies, and they sometimes lie in contact'. But perhaps most surprisingly, Darwin concluded that the worms 'exhibit some degree of intelligence instead of a mere blind instinctive impulse'.

Darwin published his book in October 1881, just six months before he died and joined the subjects of his final study. Some mocked the great man for spending his last months preoccupied by the humble earthworm, but in many ways Darwin's final book was a fitting coda to his overarching scientific theme – that small, sometimes imperceptible, changes can produce large effects over time. In the last paragraph of his book, Darwin concluded that 'It may be doubted whether there are many other animals which have played so important a part in the history of the world, as have these lowly organised creatures'. Darwin demonstrated not only that 'worms have much bigger souls than anyone would suppose', as he confided to one of his sons shortly before publication, but he also provided an early indication that lying beneath humankind's heavy and oblivious tread there were unheralded marvels and wonders. But despite Darwin's enthusiasm, soil – the foundation for so much life on Earth, and responsible for almost all the calories consumed by humans – has been treated like dirt over the course of human history.

The biblical Garden of Eden has traditionally been identified as somewhere in Mesopotamia, on the eastern leg of the Fertile Crescent, the same area that birthed the Agricultural Revolution 12,000 years ago. Mesopotamia – 'the place between the rivers', the once mighty Tigris and Euphrates – was watered by annual floods and the rich alluvial soil bore not only the first crops and livestock, but other accoutrements of civilisation including the wheel, mathematics and writing. However, within a few millennia of the Agricultural Revolution, much of this terrestrial paradise, the site of the mythical garden surrounding the Tree of Life, was little more than a desert. Overgrazing destroyed once abundant grasslands, the plough tore open the soil and exposed it to the sun, irrigation turned the ground salty, and deforestation stripped the land bare and drove even greater erosion.

Today much of the former Fertile Crescent is a wasteland, fertile only in oil and gas. Many countries in the region now survive through their own particular version of the carbon cycle, trading hydrocarbons for carbohydrates – modern-day Iraq, the successor state to ancient Mesopotamia, is one of the world's largest oil exporters while at the same time relying on imports for the bulk of its total food intake. Middle Eastern and North African countries in the formerly Fertile Crescent have become, simultaneously, beneficiaries and victims of our fossil fuelled age – owing to a geological fluke they have been gifted with hidden carbon treasures, but this has drawn in opportunistic offshore corporations, fostered crony capitalism, and also inflicted some of the worst ravages of global heating on this part of the world. A scientific paper published in 2016 predicted that, unless humanity steers a course away from its current emissions trajectory, large parts of the Middle East will likely 'experience temperature levels that are intolerable to humans' by the end of this century, while already weakened local agriculture will be further compromised by rising temperatures, prolonged droughts and emptying aquifers.

Ironically, much of the food that is imported into the Middle East and North Africa originates, at least in part, from these now arid and desertified lands. The Old Testament declared that all flesh is grass, but today most internationally traded meat, and grain too, is ultimately derived from fossil fuels. Hydrocarbons are the essential feedstock for synthetic farm inputs such as nitrogen-based fertiliser and many pesticides and herbicides, while tremendous quantities of fossil fuels are required to power agricultural machinery and irrigation systems, and to process, pack, store and transport food around the world. The supply chain for industrialised agriculture, starting at the world's oil and gas fields, is driven forward by energy-intensive practices, and it is estimated that food production accounts for approximately 30 per cent of global energy consumption and almost the same proportion of greenhouse gas emissions. As the political philosopher John Gray has noted, 'intensive agriculture is the extraction of food from petroleum' – the outputs of industrialised agriculture are in effect just another fossil fuel derivative, much the same as polyester and plastic bags.

Cereal monogamy

Although the Middle East is a cautionary tale of sorts – sowing the wind in terms of hydrocarbon use, and now reaping the whirlwind – fossil fuels have, over the course of the Great Acceleration, spurred a remarkable transformation in agricultural productivity in other parts of the world.

In the years after the Second World War, the developed world turned swords into ploughshares, training its underemployed arsenal onto the natural world – assembly lines switched from tanks to tractors, sonar scanned for fugitive fish rather than submarines, and demobbed fighter pilots buzzed fields in cropdusters – with energy consumed per unit of agricultural area estimated to have increased 90-fold over the course of the twentieth century. Food production increasingly overrode the rhythms of nature in the quest to prise the fruits of the Earth from the soil, and the industrialisation of agriculture has allowed the world to outpace, so far at least, the dire predictions of Thomas Malthus.

While the global population has broadly doubled since 1970, global food supply has almost tripled over the same period, and the United Nations estimates that the proportion of people in the world with not enough to eat has fallen from more than a third to just over a tenth in the last half century or so. And as a result of improvements in farm productivity, the number of people working in the agricultural sector has plummeted since the beginning of the Great Acceleration, especially in Western nations. In 1950, for example, a quarter of West Germans were employed in farming-related occupations compared to around 1 per cent today, and a low agriculture participation rate is today one of the best proxies for a country's economic development. The twinned phenomena of increased farm productivity and agriculture's decline as a means of livelihood has, in turn, sparked a worldwide population surge from rural areas to cities. The flip side of our intensive industrial food production system is intensive, high-density city living – the number of global citizens living in built-up urban areas has increased from 750 million in 1950 to around 4 billion today, further accentuating the divorce between the human-constructed world and the natural world.

Farms by their very nature are local, but food supply chains are now international. Swelling in lockstep with urbanisation has been a huge escalation in the global food trade – food exports have grown six-fold over the last three decades, and four-fifths of the planet's population now eat calories produced in another country. Volume and efficiency and profits, rather than the health and needs of the local population, tend to be the drivers of what Wendell Berry calls 'the industrial food economy' – a globe-spanning supply chain in which each link is becoming ever more concentrated, from intensive feedlots to supermarket chains to fast food franchises promising 'one taste worldwide' – and a handful of internationally traded commodities have crowded out diverse subsistence farming enterprises that once sustained the immediate community.

Like GDP, industrialised agriculture favours quantity over quality, and on a simple volume basis it can be considered a success. Utilising high-yielding genetics developed during 'the Green Revolution' in the 1960s and 1970s – and supported by fossil fuel–based agrochemicals, irrigation systems and heavy machinery – farms increasingly became factories over the course of the Great Acceleration, and agricultural productivity leapt in Asia, Latin America and, to a lesser extent, Africa. In Asia, the biggest beneficiary of this revolution, cereal production more than doubled between 1970 and 1995, increasing average food calories per person by 30 per cent and cutting the poverty rate by half. And the benefits of the Green Revolution have not been limited to the developing world – households in the US and Britain, for example, now spend only around a tenth of their disposable income on food, compared to a third in 1950. For those in the advanced economies, food has never been cheaper than today, freeing up consumers to spend more on other products and keeping the wheels of the capitalist machine turning.

Partly as a result of the Green Revolution, just three types of grain – wheat, rice and corn – now provide over 40 per cent of the world's calories. And in addition to the 'Big Three' crops, animal production has also become industrialised. Rates of meat consumption are tied closely to wealth, and as the global middle class has expanded so too has its taste for animal protein. Global meat production has more than quadrupled since the early 1960s, with the increase most marked in Asia – escalating 15-fold over the last 60 years, and more than 30-fold in China. Each year 80 billion terrestrial animals are killed and consumed by humans, and to service this appetite what are euphemistically called 'concentrated animal feeding operations' have become the dominant mode of livestock and poultry production. Like all industrial enterprises, these operations are focused on productivity and profit, and animals are treated as little more than factory inputs.

These intensive animal production systems then dispatch their fattened and finished 'outputs' into giant slaughterhouses – disassembly lines that inspired the assembly lines of modern industry. Henry Ford, the father of the modern production line, lifted his revolutionary idea from the overhead trolleys ferrying carcasses to waiting Chicago meatworkers, each of whom had a specialised task on the onward journey towards a cut of protein. Writing at the start of the twentieth century, just a few years before Ford established his first factory in 1913, Upton Sinclair described one meat processing plant as 'porkmaking by machinery, porkmaking by applied mathematics … like some horrible crime committed in a dungeon, all unseen and unheeded, buried out of sight and out of memory'. Over a century later, these facilities have become far larger and more concentrated – it is estimated, for example, that just over 50 plants are responsible for around 98 per cent of all slaughtering and meat processing in the US – and, although protected by fences and cloaked in nondescript windowless walls, the bloody reality of industrial mass carnage has not changed.

Dirt poor

This Food Fordism of gigantic feedlots, mechanised killing and ever-larger processing plants is complemented by increasing monopolisation at both ends of the agriculture supply chain. At the pre-farmgate stage, 40 per cent of the world's commercial seed market is controlled by two firms, four companies account for more than 60 per cent of global pesticide sales, and just four corporations comprise a third of global nitrogen fertiliser production. At the other end of the supply chain, the purchase of international bulk commodities is dominated by just four privately owned firms who together control around 90 per cent of the global grain trade. Big Agriculture has defeated the competitive dynamic that Adam Smith venerated, and the outcome has been much as Smith predicted – a 'contrivance to raise prices', whether that be inputs to farmers or processed products to retailers, while at the same time leveraging overwhelming bargaining power to drive down payments to the far more fragmented primary production sector squeezed in between.

Big Agriculture's instinct to limit competition has also extended to farmland itself. By producing synthetic herbicides and pesticides that kill everything but the crop, and then engineering specialist plant varieties that can repel these chemical assaults, multinational agrochemical corporations have hatched a profitable and mutually reinforcing protection racket. These plant strains – some of which are laboratory-fabricated genetically modified organisms spawned by what has been nicknamed 'the Gene Revolution' – are capable of withstanding the likes of glyphosate, a widely used herbicide that cripples most plants and has been declared as 'probably carcinogenic to humans' by the World Health Organization. The dominance of these herbicides and their co-dependent plants disadvantages farmers who cannot afford expensive agrochemicals, as proprietary crops unsupported by their chemical enablers often produce lower yields than older varieties adapted to local conditions. As a result, industrial agriculture's high-input, high-output business model not only requires more fossil fuel–based fertilisers, pesticides and pumped water, but it has also led to the consolidation of landholdings as farms become more mechanised and capital-intensive.

Industrialised farming has secured impressive improvements in productivity over the course of the Great Acceleration, but at the same time the global food production network itself is becoming increasingly fragile. A handful of large corporations dominate the production of farm inputs, the processing of agricultural commodities, and the on-sale of products to wholesalers, retailers and consumers, while millions of farmers with little bargaining power are sandwiched in the middle. Not only are countries increasingly reliant on food products from other shores, but industrialised agriculture is Adam Smith's specialisation run amok – factory farms tend to be a monoculture within a monoculture, with genetically homogenous crops or animals massed in one small area. This overcrowding and lack of genetic diversity makes modern farming more vulnerable to pathogens, triggering an endless arms race between the natural world and human ingenuity as pesticides, herbicides and antibiotics attempt to outgun constantly mutating Mother Nature.

However, perhaps the greatest threat to our food supply is the very thing that birthed its existence. Agriculture arose because of climate stability and will be one of the main casualties of climate change. Global food production is caught in a pincer movement – productivity improvements have slowed and in some cases gone backward, soil fertility is declining, two-fifths of farmland is classed as 'degraded' or 'seriously degraded' by the UN Food and Agriculture Organization, and freshwater supplies are falling, while the global population is expected to increase by a further two billion by 2050. Half of these additional two billion people will be born in sub-Saharan Africa and another 30 per cent in South Asia – the very regions where the negative impacts of climate change are expected to be most pronounced. Developing countries are expected to experience the sharpest decline in grain yields due to global heating and an increased incidence of droughts, heatwaves and extreme weather events, and while some of the world's northern breadbaskets should benefit from increased wheat production this is highly unlikely to offset declining yields in the Global South.

But at the same time that food production will become one of the biggest losers from global heating and other climate change effects, it is also one of its main agents. Agriculture is second only to the energy sector in terms of greenhouse gas emissions, accounting for around a quarter of annual human-caused carbon dioxide emissions, 70 per cent of human-created nitrous oxide emissions and approximately a quarter of anthropogenic methane emissions. Additionally, agriculture is the principal cause of habitat and biodiversity loss, is draining groundwater and destroying soil fertility, and inflicts 'dead zones' on downstream aquatic systems due to chemical runoff. Industrialised agriculture is locked into a destructive, ever-spiralling cycle – more and more fossil fuels are required to increase or just maintain yields, while at the same time those fossil fuels contribute to global heating and further degrade farmland.

Norman Borlaug, the chief architect of the Green Revolution and a Nobel Peace Prize winner for his work, sounded a cautionary note in 1970 when he observed that:

The green revolution has won a temporary success in man's war against hunger and deprivation; it has given man a breathing space. If fully implemented, the revolution can provide sufficient food for sustenance during the next three decades.

Borlaug's window for action has well and truly passed, and while agricultural output rocketed as a result of the Green Revolution, these gains have been extracted at enormous ecological expense. A 2020 paper in the journal *Science* determined that, even if fossil fuel emissions were to be stopped today, food production on a 'business as usual' basis would alone exceed the remaining global carbon budget by the middle of this century. Like mainstream economics, industrial farming has largely sidelined the natural world, and the industrialisation of eating has distanced consumers from the negative effects of modern food production systems – whether that be in terms of animal welfare, the state of wider ecosystems, or the collateral damage to human health.

21

THE WORLD'S FARE

Monocultures in our fields and on our plates

The way of all flesh

If history is geography set in motion, then geography is agriculture solidified. National frontiers have often been laid down on agricultural faultlines – the Great Wall of China, for example, marked the border between the agrarian civilisation of Imperial China and the nomads to the north, while the bounds of the Roman Empire tended to stick closely to the fertile farmed areas around the Mediterranean. Borders acted as both a moat and a bridge, shielding settled communities from what Max Weber called the 'booty capitalism' of opportunistic plunderers, while also allowing states to control and tax the exchange of goods. Grain – easy to standardise, quantify and store – was well suited to early forms of taxation, and the apparatus of the state developed around those grain-growing communities that generated surpluses of staple crops such as wheat, rice and corn. Today, these three crops continue to provide the bulk of the human world's calories, and what agriculture divided it has also helped stitch together – food trade between states is now an intercontinental phenomenon, embracing the entire planet.

Innovations in the early years of the Industrial Revolution – such as railways, steamships and refrigeration – allowed products from the plains of North America, the pampas of Argentina and the paddocks of Australia to be exported to the Old World. Barbed wire, an invention of the late nineteenth century, permitted further exploitation of rangelands by fencing in not only livestock but people – indigenous populations were extirpated from country that had been theirs for hundreds, sometimes thousands, of generations and garrisoned into reservations by the usurping unsettlers, freeing up the land for European crops and livestock. Other countries were later enlisted into the world market through a more subtle form of colonialism, as multinationals pushed into emerging economies and encouraged a transition away from subsistence farming and towards the production of cash crops such as sugar, soy and corn. Continuing capitalism's program of specialisation, marketisation and globalisation, a large proportion of these undifferentiated bulk commodities are exported to more developed countries where they serve as animal fodder or become the building blocks for processed food products.

The innovations of the Green Revolution were not entirely motivated by philanthropic reasons – the US Secretary of Agriculture frankly admitted in the 1970s that 'food is a weapon', a new front in the Cold War that could avert the threat of a 'Red Revolution' in poorer countries by winning hearts and stomachs – but the industrialisation of food production has undoubtedly succeeded in dragging millions from poverty and hunger. Increased yields from the intensification of agriculture have also reduced the acreage of arable land required to produce a given amount of food calories – for although around half of the world's habitable land is farmed, without the productivity boost provided by the Green Revolution this proportion would be materially higher. Additional agricultural expansion would have resulted in even greater deforestation and land-clearing, and it has been estimated that without the Green Revolution our planet would have lost four times more fertile forest land than has actually occurred.

However, as a large portion of the developing world slipstreams to material prosperity on the tailwinds of the Great Acceleration, its citizens increasingly prefer Western diets high in animal protein. This swing towards a meat-rich diet has undone much of the Green Revolution's good work by encouraging additional land-clearing for grazing pastures and by diverting cereals, soy and other crops from human consumption to animal feed. When cropland used for fodder is taken into account, livestock production accounts for over three-quarters of the world's agricultural land, yet contributes less than 20 per cent of global calories and just under 40 per cent of protein. The average American eats well over 100 kilograms of meat each year compared to less than 5 kilograms per person in India, and if the entire global population were to adopt a meat-rich American diet then the world would need approximately three times the amount of farmland currently used – an impossible ask on this finite planet.

Animals have been integral to most human diets since time immemorial. They convert grass and other plants not digestible by humans into high quality, nutrient-rich protein – meat, dairy products and eggs contain essential vitamins and minerals that complement carbohydrate-heavy staple crops. They can also transform high-energy, low-protein cereals into high-protein sources, although there is significant wastage of energy and total protein in this process. But while it is true that livestock can produce calories on land that is unsuitable for crops, much of the fodder in today's industrialised livestock production system comes from cereals that could otherwise feed humans. Over three-quarters of the world's production of soy, a legume that when consumed with cereals provides a complete protein profile for humans, is used as fodder, and more than 40 per cent of global grain production is fed to animals. Additionally, some species of livestock – such as cattle and sheep – co-opt microbes in their stomach to ferment, break down and absorb plant carbohydrates. Largely due to the methane produced as a byproduct of this process, animal production – when combined with land-clearing for grazing pastures and the shadow carbon footprint from the production of fodder crops – generates up to 60 times more greenhouse gases, on a calorie-for-calorie basis, than an equivalent amount of plant-based food.

Stuffed

As Wendell Berry observed, 'how we eat determines, to a considerable extent, how the world is used'. The Green Revolution's operating manual of fossil fuelled monocultures is degrading farmland, reducing freshwater supplies, and contributing to extreme weather events that chip away at yield improvements, while much of the world's forested land initially spared due to productivity improvements is now being cleared for animal feed crops. Specialisation of food production and specialisation in food consumption are inextricably related, and affluent consumers tend to prefer a large slab of flesh around which a few desultory greens sometimes orbit, rather than Thomas Jefferson's recommendation that meat be used merely as a 'condiment for vegetables'. The suffocating sameness of cash crops and intensive animal rearing operations has replaced diverse farming systems adapted to local conditions, and much of the world's food production has become as mechanised as Adam Smith's pin factory. Landscapes have been radically simplified, most of the world relies on a handful of crops and animals for its sustenance, and these monocultures are often genetically homogenous and ill-equipped to meet the challenges of a heating planet.

The sheer abundance provided by modern agriculture has also led to food providers being taken for granted – another appendage to the machine, as Karl Marx described an earlier cohort of industrial workers. Since the Great Acceleration the average growth in productivity in the agricultural sector has in many nations outstripped even that of the manufacturing sector, but this copiousness has instilled complacency. The perceived 'liquidity' of global food markets promotes a short-term mindset that further distances humanity from its food sources and encourages wasteful behaviour, with the UN estimating that a third of all food produced globally is thrown away. Intricate global supply chains have also obscured the connection between the food we consume and how it is produced, providing an element of deniability to consumers. This is a failure of imagination, or perhaps more correctly a refusal of the imagination – as Ralph Waldo Emerson sermonised, 'You have just dined, and however scrupulously the slaughterhouse is concealed in the graceful distance of miles, there is complicity'. Most consumers seem to accept, tacitly at least, the assumption popularised by the seventeenth century philosopher René Descartes that animals are nothing more than soulless machines feeling neither joy nor pain, and entirely subservient to our appetites.

Such wilful blindness severs the link between a bland fillet of 'white meat' and its origin – an unnaturally oversized chick that never saw daylight, was shuttled from a hatchery to a 'grow-out shed' alongside thousands of other birds on its first day of existence, and 40 days later was transported to a giant processing facility for live-shackle slaughter. There are over 20 billion chickens in the world at any one time – almost three chickens for every human on this planet – but 60 billion are killed each year, testament to both the ruthless mechanical efficiency of intensive agriculture and the truncated lives of these captive animals. This resolute looking away results, in the words of Wendell Berry, in an 'industrial eater' who 'no longer knows or imagines the connections between eating and the land, and who is therefore necessarily passive and uncritical – in short, a victim'.

Industrial agriculture also extracts a price from humans, who – conditioned for thousands of generations to extract the most calories from a sometimes capricious and unforgiving environment – have been hardwired to gorge. In past ages, the diet of omnivorous humans was adapted to local conditions, with those in the tropics relying heavily on plants and those at higher latitudes having a more meat-rich menu. But industrial capitalism's trend towards uniformity, concentration and scale has also resulted in a lack of dietary diversity. Western lifestyles are increasingly embraced by the global middle class, and not only is more animal protein consumed, but highly processed foods have become a significant component in most modern diets. These convenience foods – originally tailored to the tidal flow of commuters and time-harried workers of the industrialised world, and usually packaged in plastics or paper that eventually finds its way to landfill or the ocean – are high in the fats, sugar and salt that were relatively scarce in our hunter-gatherer days, but are now cheap and abundant.

Although ultra-processed foods satisfy basic human cravings, overconsumption of these products has contributed to health problems worldwide. The World Health Organization estimates that globally around 40 per cent of adults are overweight or obese, and that the share of children and adolescents – a particularly attractive market for fast food companies – at an unhealthy weight has more than quadrupled in the four decades since 1975. The proportion of the population that is overweight tends to be higher in more affluent countries – for example, approximately 70 per cent of Americans are deemed overweight or obese – but less developed countries are following a similar trajectory. The simple math of more calories in than calories out – increased consumption of energy-dense processed food, combined with less physical activity due to generally more sedentary lives – has resulted in a rising incidence of 'non-communicable' diseases such as diabetes, cardiovascular disorders and certain types of cancer. Although classed as non-communicable, in reality these lifestyle diseases are highly transmissible – arising from a lack of real food choice, and propelled along the vectors of low prices, slick marketing and increasing ubiquity.

While it is true that the number of undernourished people has generally fallen since the beginning of the Green Revolution, it is thought that around three billion people still cannot afford a healthy diet. Instead, they are limited to cereals and other high-starch food, which can result in deficiencies in protein, essential fats and vital micronutrients. More than two billion people suffer from 'hidden hunger' due to insufficient consumption of micronutrients such as zinc, calcium, iodine and certain vitamins, which in turn can slow physical and mental development. Many countries are also witnessing a strange phenomenon – some of their citizens are overweight but at the same time undernourished, for although they may have access to macronutrients in the form of protein, starch and processed food, they are lacking in essential micronutrients. And just as human health has been compromised by the modern industrialised food system, so too has the health and viability of many of our fellow creatures.

Buzz kill

In the Anthropocene age we have witnessed a new iteration of the Darwinian imperative. Those organisms that adapt best to humankind's schemes and structures – livestock, pets, rats, and certain domesticated grasses such as wheat – multiply, while other species, including the world's pollinators, disappear. Insects are the most abundant family of organisms on this planet, comprising perhaps 90 per cent or more of all animal species, and in the ant kingdom alone some scientists believe that at any given time there may be approximately 20 quintillion members – 20 billion billion creatures, or around 3 billion ants for each human alive. Insects can fly, walk, swim, and a few species walk on water; they are usually solitary, but some have colonies with populations running to the hundreds of millions, practising highly refined specialisations that would dazzle Adam Smith; and they can communicate by flashing light, broadcasting pheromones, rubbing their wings together, or performing elaborate dances. They are often regarded as pests – damaging crops, carrying disease, or parasitically dining on human hosts – but insects are also crucial to the functioning of ecosystems. They turn and aerate soil, decompose organic matter, help control pests, provide nutrition to other organisms, and are essential to the life cycle of almost all flowering plants.

In a classic example of symbiosis, a number of insect groups – including bees, wasps, butterflies and ants – evolved in union with flowering plants, with these insects reaping the benefit of energy-rich nectar in return for porting pollen from one plant to another. This act enhances the ability of flowering plants to cross-pollinate, driving greater genetic diversity and improving the evolutionary fitness of the particular plant species. It is estimated that three-quarters of farmed crops depend on pollinators to some extent, although in terms of total global tonnage only around a third of harvested crops are typically reliant on pollinating insects, mainly because cereals such as wheat do not require this service. Just a handful of cultivated plants – usually cash crops that are particularly important to developing countries, such as soybeans, palm oil, coffee and cocoa – are entirely dependent on pollinators, but if pollinators disappeared there would be a significant decline in overall crop yields. In the human realm, the value of ecosystem services provided by pollinating insects – although not recorded in national accounts – is substantial, with some studies estimating that the pollination of fruits, vegetables and oil crops globally is worth somewhere between $235 billion and $577 billion each year.

Although claims of an imminent 'insect apocalypse' may be somewhat overdone, recent studies have found that the population of the world's terrestrial insects is decreasing by almost 10 per cent a decade. This decadal decimation is due to habitat loss from urbanisation, the increasing use of pesticides and herbicides, and also the effects of climate change. Rachel

Carson called out the knock-on effects from the indiscriminate use of fossil fuel–derived DDT – utilised during the Second World War by soldiers for lice control, and later rolled out to new markets as a farm and household pesticide – in the early 1960s, and the 'toxic load' on many ecosystems has only multiplied since then. Global pesticide use in the three decades from 1990, for example, increased by approximately 80 per cent to just over 4 million tonnes each year, and these pesticides not only eradicate those animals considered counter to human endeavours, but also the pests' predators and other beneficial insects.

The increased toxic load on the environment from pesticides and herbicides has also been accompanied by a reduction in the nutritional quality of human food due to global heating. In what one scientist has called 'possibly the most significant threat that has been documented for climate change', research has demonstrated that although rising levels of carbon dioxide can increase crop tonnage in some circumstances – because atmospheric carbon is the principal feedstock for plants – it can also lead to a reduction in protein and key micronutrients in many staple crops. Higher levels of carbon dioxide may plump plants, but it chiefly increases the synthesis of sugars and starches while decreasing in relative terms the concentrations of zinc, iron, magnesium, calcium and protein. This decline in essential nutrients, in turn, also has knock-on effects for flesh-eaters – as the writer Michael Pollan notes, 'You are what what you eat eats, too', and animals feeding on these less nourishing grains and plants produce less nourishing meat and milk.

The fossil fuelled Green Revolution has driven astounding improvements in the yields of key staple crops, producing more grain from a given area of land and sparing the Earth from even greater human incursions. Likewise, intensive animal production – although bought at a tremendously high cost in terms of animal welfare, the additional acres required to feed our subject animals, and lower micronutrient levels – has vastly increased the amount of animal protein available to the global community. But the increasing uniformity seen on our plates is a mirror-image of the industrial monocultures seen in our fields, and it is estimated that three-quarters of the food eaten by humans today comprise just 12 crops and five animal species. Our simplified diets have resulted in simplified landscapes and decreasing biodiversity, and have weakened ecosystems through the application of pesticides and herbicides. Crops, livestock and humans have been fattened, but nutrient levels are falling at the same time, with even ostensibly healthy food recording falls in key vitamins and minerals. Short-term agricultural productivity has been secured at the expense of long-term planetary and human health – and accordingly, food and fibre production needs, quite literally, a return to its roots.

22

LOSING THE PLOT

Mining the soil for short-term returns

Notes from the underground

After his five-year escapade on the HMS *Beagle*, for the rest of his life Charles Darwin was as barnacled onto his 20 acres of land as the crustaceans-masquerading-as-molluscs he spent almost a decade studying. A dropout from medical school and shying away from an expected vocation as a country priest, he instead joined the ranks of 'parson-naturalists' of the early Victorian era who worshipped the world and its creations in their own particular way. Darwin was a dilettante in the original sense of the word – one who took delight in all things, who comprehended the connections between creatures and their environment, who grasped the 'dependence of one being on another' in the 'recurring struggle for existence'. Allowing his mind to wander and wonder as he ambled laps around the 'thinking path' on his property, his circuitous cogitations eventually alighted on something far closer to home – the green and pleasant fields on his country plot.

Darwin had noted in a book on the fertilisation of orchids that 'the economy shown by nature in her resources is striking'. To frame things in the language of economics, there are no externalities in the natural world, and in the soil lying beneath Darwin's feet there existed a supremely parsimonious underground circulatory system that continually scavenged and re-assembled valuable nutrients. In nature there is no waste – one organism's dregs becomes another organism's sustenance. Performing feats of resurrection every moment, soil that thrums with life converts matter into ever more complex forms, conjuring living beings from thin air through the founding miracle of photosynthesis. And because of all this generative activity, soils are the world's second-biggest carbon sink after the ocean – topsoil contains more carbon than exists in terrestrial vegetation, and almost double the amount that is present in the atmosphere.

However, in our industrialised food production system soil is viewed as little more than a conduit for conveying synthesised chemicals to a particular monocultured crop. Only now, with the advent of new technology, are the complexities and the interdependencies of the subterranean world being fully comprehended. Recent scientific discoveries reveal not only self-interested competition but also strong bonds of collaboration between plants, invertebrates, soil microbes and fungi. A handful of healthy soil – simultaneously solid, liquid and gas, a mix of organic matter, minerals, water and air, the halfway house between geology and biology – comprises an elaborate trophic cascade containing many billions of organisms and thousands of species. Bacteria and fungi feed on plant litter and other dead matter, these organisms are consumed by single-celled animals, which in turn are eaten by tiny worms and arthropods such as centipedes, and the cycle begins again when these animals die and settle into the soil. At the same time, many of the fungi and microbes at the base of the soil food web also trade foraged minerals for plant sugars – on average, around 30 per cent of the carbohydrates produced by living plants are exuded from their root systems for the benefit of these other organisms, currency for one of the oldest exchanges on Earth.

The application of synthetic fertilisers has, however, upset this below-ground bazaar. In the mid-1800s the German scientist Justus von Liebig identified three chemical elements – nitrogen, phosphorus and potassium – that, working in combination with water and carbon dioxide, are essential to plant growth. In a quest to combat the problem of 'soil exhaustion' arising from increasingly intensive agricultural practices, industrialised countries then embarked on a worldwide search for these three indispensable ingredients, which happened to be most richly concentrated in natural form in bones and bird droppings. Napoleonic battlefields and catacombs were raided for skeletons, guano-topped islands were seized by European powers, and in the mid-nineteenth century the United States embarked on one of its first exercises in overt imperialism by instituting legislation empowering the 'annexation of any islands thought to be rich' in this petrified poop. Guano was a concentrated source of not only phosphates and potassium, but also nitrates – useful for green organisms and also gunpowder, with the latter occasionally deployed to support the muscular pro-development policies of voracious Western nations.

Metabolic riff

In Liebig's reductionist paradigm, organic material was seen as playing a negligible role in generating fertility and plant growth, and soil was treated as little more than a substrate for plant roots. Previously farmers had rotated crops across the seasons to restore nutrients removed with each harvest, to moderate the build-up of pests and pathogens that preyed on a particular plant, and to improve soil structure by alternating deep and shallow-rooted crops. In addition to crop rotation, land would also be left fallow for a period to permit the natural regeneration of soil fertility, and livestock often introduced to graze and manure the fields to provide further nourishment. With the identification of Liebig's new wonder trio of macronutrients, however, it was assumed that land no longer needed to be rested and that yields could be maximised merely by applying deficient elements. A new agricultural age was ushered in – a simplified paint-by-numbers approach imposed on previously diverse ecosystems, which seemingly only required the application of chemicals in carefully calculated proportions to produce high-yielding monocrops.

Liebig's discovery sparked not only a landgrab for remote Pacific islands rich in guano, but it also prompted some deep thinking in the Reading Room of the British Museum. Karl Marx, who drew on Liebig's findings, observed that capitalism's impulse towards concentration 'causes the urban population to achieve an ever-growing preponderance', and that this urbanisation prevents the return to the soil of its constituent elements consumed by man in the form of food and clothing; hence it hinders the operation of the eternal natural condition for the lasting fertility of the soil.

In earlier days villages and towns would recycle what was delicately called 'nightsoil' – now more descriptively, but less poetically, known as 'human faecal sludge' – onto nearby fields, while mixed farming systems returned nutrients to the land through the scattering of livestock manure and the planting of nitrogen-fixing legumes. Industrialised agriculture, however, ruptured this natural cycle by embracing a one-way linear system – in which external inputs were ladled onto land, nutrients embodied in food and fibre were stripped away at harvest, and then conveyed to distant urban agglomerations.

With Liebig's breakthrough, industrial capitalism's impulse to create a world after its own image spilled into the ancient culture of agriculture – driving a high-input, high-output factory model focused on maximising near-term volume and profits. Marx asserted that, as a result, industrial capitalism alienated not only workers but also nature, declaring that

all progress in capitalistic agriculture is a progress in the art ... of robbing the soil; all progress in increasing the fertility of the soil for a given time is a progress toward ruining the lasting sources of that fertility.

Dialling up the short-term productive capacity of the agricultural machine not only impoverished the soil and necessitated ever greater lashings of external chemicals, Marx noted, but at the other end of the supply chain it also resulted in expended outputs accumulating as polluting waste. This 'metabolic rift' identified by Marx – the sundering of the previously closed nutrient loop, with nutrient depletion in farming areas indivisibly twinned with waste pollution in the cities – was perhaps the first acknowledged ecological crisis of capitalism.

Cities are like any other living system – drawing in resources and excreting waste – but unlike complex ecosystems such as the soil, which evolved over millions of years to salvage and re-use every available resource, they are recklessly extravagant. Cities are, in effect, just another concentrated animal-feeding operation, taking in energy and materials, and depositing huge quantities of waste. The amount of annual global 'throughput' – raw materials such as fossil fuels, metals and biomass consumed by humans – has more than tripled since 1970, now approaching 100 billion tonnes each year, but less than 10 per cent of this throughput is recycled. Discards only become pollution if they are not metabolised in a meaningful way – it is only waste, after all, if it is wasted – but by opening up separate sources and sinks for raw materials industrial capitalism split one solution into two problems: profligate natural resource depletion, unaccompanied by any meaningful recycling, has resulted in ever-growing reservoirs of pollution.

Marx discerned a direct connection between the level of industrialisation and soil health, commenting that 'The more a country starts its development on the foundation of modern industry ... the more rapid is this process of [soil] destruction'. Marx was not around to witness the advent of intensive livestock operations that now provide a large proportion of global meat production, but these systems replicate and magnify the metabolic rift he diagnosed between town and country. Industrialised animal production takes in soil-depleting fodder from around the world and pumps out staggering quantities of localised animal waste, which can pollute waterways with excess nutrients, antibiotics and pathogens, while also hazing the air with harmful gases and airborne particulates. Like overfishing, modern agriculture was sacrificing long-term sustainability for near-term productivity, destroying fertility in the service of volume, but a fix was seemingly found just in time – the invention of an artificial fertiliser which, for a period at least, seemed to avert the crisis of soil exhaustion.

Dust to dust

Justus von Liebig popularised what is known as 'the law of the minimum', which asserts that plant growth is determined not by total nutrient endowment but rather by the scarcest available single macronutrient. Nitrogen – usually the limiting crop element, the weakest link in the nutrient triumvirate – is needed to make chlorophyll, the molecule that gives plants their green colour and is essential for photosynthesis. But although nitrogen is incredibly plentiful, comprising almost 80 per cent of air, it is not available to plants when in its inert atmospheric form. Instead, bacteria, legumes and rainfall – supported by externally applied substances such as manure, compost and guano – were required to provide 'reactive' plant-accessible nitrogen to the soil. In the early twentieth century, however, Fritz Haber, a German chemist, discovered how to synthetically produce reactive nitrogen by combining atmospheric nitrogen with hydrogen at high pressure. Haber's innovation allowed usually tightly locked nitrogen to be fed to crops at an industrial scale, and provided a final kick to the agricultural innovations that began 200 years earlier with enclosure, land reclamation and improved infrastructure.

Nitrates in the form of ammonia were first commercially manufactured under the 'Haber process' in 1913. In the initial years of production most of this ammonia was channelled to the German Army which, cut off from its offshore guano supplies, desperately needed this feedstock for explosives. But after the Great War ammonia was turned towards peaceful purposes, and the influx of synthetic nitrogen fertilisers resulted in surging farm yields. This green revolution before the Green Revolution, in turn, ignited another explosion, with the global population roughly quadrupling since the mid-1920s. Today, food produced from synthetic nitrogen fertilisers is thought to sustain approximately half the world's people, and the Canadian scientist Vaclav Smil estimates that if average crop yields had remained at levels prior to the invention of the Haber process then around four times more farmland would be needed to sustain Earth's eight billion human residents. In recognition of his feat of conjuring 'bread from air' Fritz Haber received the Nobel Prize for Chemistry in 1918 – an award subject to much controversy, for although his discovery was lauded as 'of the greatest benefit to mankind' by the Nobel committee, the German scientist left a decidedly mixed legacy to humanity.

The synthesis of ammonia not only permitted the production of enormous quantities of explosives, but during the war Haber was also heavily involved in the weaponisation of chlorine and other poisonous gases.

Demonised as 'the father of chemical warfare' – even present at the Ypres battlefield in 1915, the first time chlorine gas was unleashed in combat, to survey his handiwork – Haber's work also wreaked horrific personal consequences. His first wife, a peace activist, killed herself with Haber's own military pistol a few weeks after the Ypres demonstration; his son, who had cradled his mother in her last moments, committed suicide just after the Second World War; and his granddaughter, a chemist who developed antidotes for chlorine gas, took her life in 1949 when she was informed that future research funding would be diverted to the atomic program. In the early 1920s Haber was also involved in the development of pesticide gases, including what would later become Zyklon B – and Haber, who converted from Judaism to Christianity in his early adulthood, would lose members of his extended family when this chemical was later appropriated and perverted by the Nazis to murder millions in the concentration camps.

Fritz Haber's tragic story is in many ways the tale of technology – a double-edged sword that can be both creator and destroyer, helpful and harmful, giver and taker. In agriculture, the application of additional nitrogen, phosphorus and potassium to soils has supercharged productivity and allowed millions to escape the clutches of hunger, but it has also wildly unbalanced global ecosystems. More than half the nitrates and phosphates sprayed onto cropland eventually runs off these farms to pollute aquatic environments, and human-created nitrogen compounds enter the atmosphere as nitrous oxide, a potent greenhouse gas that also contributes to acid rain. On top of the heat-trapping potential of nitrous oxide, the manufacture of nitrogen-based fertilisers requires significant quantities of hydrocarbons in the form of natural gas, and huge amounts of carbon dioxide and methane are belched into the atmosphere in order to synthesise ammonia.

In addition to atmospheric and aquatic pollution, the fossil fuelled depredations of industrial modernity have affected the soil in particular. Industrial farming has inflicted erosion and other forms of land degradation across much of the world, with soil on cropping and intensively grazed lands estimated to be wearing away 100 to 1,000 times faster than natural rates. If the long view is taken, soil is a renewable resource – topped up gradually by rock weathering, the action of soil microbes, and humus formation – but it regenerates even more slowly than fish stocks, and like overexploited fisheries it can become a rapidly depleting non-renewable resource. The degeneration of the Great Plains of North America from breadbasket to basket case in the 1930s demonstrated the consequences of clumsily disrupting co-evolved natural systems. Ornate networks of deep-rooted perennial native grasses were ripped up and replaced with fertiliser-fed cultivars that live fast and die young – focusing their energy on seed production rather than root networks – and the soil was untethered from its sturdy subterranean netting. As a result, up to three-quarters of the topsoil in some areas was blown away, soon followed by blizzards of dust that accompanied the harvest into great urban metropolises such as Chicago and New York.

Crops withered and failed in the 'Dirty Thirties', and farmers became as poor as the soil itself. The banks foreclosing farm mortgages were viewed, as John Steinbeck wrote in *The Grapes of Wrath*, as

> something else than men. It happens that every man in a bank hates what the bank does, and yet the bank does it … It's the monster. Men made it, but they can't control it.

The Dust Bowl coincided with the Great Depression, and both phenomena were due to similar underlying factors – unsustainable consumption within an economy firmly focused on the short term – and like the remorseless banks, the wider capitalist system seemed to many to have switched from servant to master. In his Inaugural Address in 1933, President Roosevelt asserted that 'the money changers have fled from their high seats in the temple of our civilization [and the] measure of the restoration lies in the extent to which we apply social values more noble than mere monetary profit'. But despite FDR's fighting words 90 years ago, the money economy still reigns and profits remain the north star. Just as with fossil fuels, the ecological price of industrialised food is not factored into the final cost, and our form of capitalism is producing meals that, in the most literal sense, are costing the Earth.

23

ROOT PROBLEM

The bridge between planetary health and human health

Ground breaking

Charles Darwin's beloved earthworms are what are known today as 'ecosystem engineers' – they break down organic matter for smaller creatures, create porous structures in the ground for air and water, and improve soil fertility by making minerals and nutrients more accessible to other organisms. Like worms, which undertake 'niche construction' to access food and to keep themselves damp, humans are also ecosystem engineers – we modify the world around us to accommodate our lifestyle. And again like earthworms, we are in a sense 'detritivores' – an organism that feeds on dead organic matter, in our case in the form of fossil fuels. As a result of this predilection, the Earth's terrestrial areas have been decarbonised – not just through the obvious means, by excavating billions of tonnes of coal, billions of barrels of oil, and trillions of cubic metres of natural gas from the ground each year – but also by farming and forestry practices that rob the soil of its carbon reserves. Agriculture not only accounts for nearly a third of global oil use, but it is estimated that between half and two-thirds of the original carbon stored in cultivated soils has been released since the start of the Industrial Revolution, and that up to a third of excess historic carbon dioxide emissions are attributable to the degradation of soil organic matter.

Although this increase in carbon emissions has resulted in parts of the blue marble becoming greener due to 'carbon fertilisation' from higher rates of photosynthesis, other impacts from excess greenhouse gases significantly outweigh the mitigation benefits from a more verdant planet. The global 'leaf area index' – the ratio of plant foliage to surface area – has increased significantly in recent decades, and the good news is that in broad terms more vegetation absorbs more carbon dioxide. Plants also release water vapour into the atmosphere through a process known as 'evapotranspiration', essentially a form of sweating that has a cooling effect on the surrounding air and contributes to cloud formation, which enhances plants' effectiveness as a living thermostat. The bad news is that, although increased carbon uptake and evapotranspiration has marginally reduced the extent of global heating that otherwise would have occurred due to excess emissions, in other areas drying land is releasing more soil carbon into the atmosphere. The soil holds more carbon than above-ground vegetation, but desiccated land is exposed to erosion while warmer soils also produce greater amounts of carbon dioxide due to increased microbial activity, and these positive feedback effects serve to amplify global heating.

Additionally, the leaf area index has climbed highest in the sub-Arctic boreal region, a northward-creeping line shading in dark green many areas previously covered by snow or ice. The world's polar territories are heating far more rapidly than in other parts of the world – recent studies, for example, indicate that the Arctic has warmed nearly four times faster than the rest of the world over the last 40 years, and on average is 3 degrees Celsius hotter than in 1980 – and, in a reinforcing downward spiral, as the Earth absorbs more solar radiation the amount of sun-reflecting snow and sea ice declines. As a result, permafrost – a wide expanse of frozen soil estimated to sequester more carbon than is presently in the atmosphere – is melting, and as the ground thaws and organic material decomposes these permafrost zones can switch from a carbon sink to a carbon source. Boreal forests encroach poleward in lockstep with melting permafrost, and although these forests can sequester significant quantities of carbon, they are slow-growing and increasingly prone to wildfires and human exploitation.

The boreal woodlands of the far northern latitudes comprise the world's largest intact forest system, and beneath them the cold, damp conditions embalm organic matter and preserve it in carbon-rich peat and bogs. However, less than one-third of these ecosystems remain as virgin forests, and clearing for logging and agriculture is breaking up and drying out soils. Not only are many countries with boreal forests cutting them down for lumber or crops – often resulting in greater carbon loss from soil disturbance than from the initial removal of tree biomass – but these ecosystems are then replaced by forest and farming monocultures that reduce both biodiversity and future carbon storage potential. Most climate models disregard or downplay the potential cascade effects from disrupting high latitude environments – partly because of the remoteness and inaccessibility of the region, partly because some countries are reluctant to share data – but events such as wildfires and permafrost thaw, which liberate vast plumes of greenhouse gases from the carbon-rich soil, are increasing in incidence and severity with each passing year.

Underground ecosystems store the bulk of all terrestrial carbon, but decarbonisation of the soil due to climate change and destructive land management practices creates a self-feeding loop of knock-on effects that limits the Earth's ability to draw down increased levels of atmospheric carbon. Restoring carbon balance in the soil would not only moderate some of the effects of excess emissions, but also improve the land's adaptability to climate change by providing the foundation for a diverse ecosystem that can limit erosion, salinisation, desertification and nutrient depletion. Fritz Haber, in his acceptance speech for the Nobel Prize, commented that

Nitrogen bacteria teach us that Nature, with her sophisticated forms of the chemistry of living matter, still understands and utilizes methods which we do not as yet know how to imitate.

Over the last century, and due to Haber's discovery, soil scientists have focused on chemistry rather than biology – methodically assaying farmland to determine which three elements were scarcest and then applying chemical top-ups as required. But Haber's humility was well placed – over the course of millions of years, Mother Nature has evolved many ingenious strategies, which only now are becoming fully apparent, to ensure not only the health of plants but also the health of those eating them.

Farmaceuticals

Industrial agriculture feeds the plant, rather than the soil, and by cutting out the middleman there is a less compelling need for plants to trade with those soil organisms that provide trace compounds essential for plant health. Fungal networks, the most important plant symbiont, have co-evolved with their green partners to provide crucial nutrients in return for the sugar hit of carbohydrates, and in fact served as a proxy for plant root systems for tens of millions of years until plants could evolve their own roots. A branching web of minuscule fungal tubes known as 'mycelium' entwine with plant roots and provide not just key minerals, but also improve plant robustness by weaving the soil together and preventing erosion, by increasing the soil's water-holding potential, and by stimulating the production of defensive phytochemicals crucial for plant health. In many ways, when it comes to the ancient exchange of minerals for plant sugar these 'mycorrhizal' networks – from the Greek word meaning 'root fungus' – are more sophisticated traders than humans. Recent studies have found that mycorrhizal fungi can modify or withhold the export of minerals to plants that reduce carbohydrate exudation, and even more remarkably seem to engage in arbitrage trading strategies by re-routing nutrient flows to more munificent plant partners.

However, plants – when mainlined with the easy chemical fix of packaged nutrients – spend less energy extracting minerals from the soil, and in consequence root systems become less expansive and the carbohydrate gifts to surrounding organisms more meagre. This, in turn, leads to fewer fungi and microbes in the root zone, and a further reduction in nutrient exchange between soil organisms and plants. Intensive farming practices have compromised the integrity of these plant–fungal partnerships with the application of chemical fertilisers that crowd out the mycorrhizal exchange, and also through practices such as ploughing, irrigation, and the application of fungicides. The imperatives of industrial cropping – which prizes quantity over quality, and seeks to grow grain with the same efficacy as it does a battery broiler chicken – also means that plants are growing faster and larger, and any micronutrients provided by an often diminished soil microbiome are diluted across a larger plant biomass. Like some modern humans, plants subject to intensive agriculture can be fattened but at the same time malnourished.

Couch potato crops now feed couch potato humans, and just as industrial agriculture transforms a landscape's microbiome – turning soil into something approaching the sterile growing medium that Liebig had originally surmised – so too does industrially produced food transform the gut microbiome of those eating it. Each of us is a walking, talking multispecies ecosystem – the human body is colonised by smaller elements of life such as bacteria, parasites and viruses, which in aggregate constitute the majority of our total cell endowment. The human act of eating is the miracle of turning animals and plants into people, a literal reincarnation, with our digestive system the conduit for this transfiguration. Food mixes with gastric juices in the stomach, this soupy material is later combed by millions of tiny worm-like filaments called 'villi' in the small intestine, and the nutrients extracted by the swaying villi are then transported to the bloodstream. Assisting the gastrointestinal tract in this task are trillions of microbial consorts, mainly bacteria, that help break down food, produce vitamins and neurochemicals, repel pathogens and toxins, and condition the immune system. As with soil fungi and plants, human 'gut microbiota' exists in a symbiotic relationship with the collation of cells we think of as the body, each mutually dependent on the other.

Due to the sheer variety and abundance of these microorganisms, it has been impossible until recent years to accurately assess and measure microbial communities in the gut. New technologies such as genetic sequencing now show that, in general, people from more developed countries have less diverse gut microbiota than those from poorer nations. This is due to a number of factors – including more hygienic living conditions, the greater use of antibiotics, and higher consumption of processed foods – that have the effect of selecting out certain species of microbes. The incidence of 'evolutionary mismatch diseases' such as obesity and diabetes is increasing because our bodies are poorly adapted to ultra-processed sugar-laden diets, and the rise in autoimmune and inflammatory disorders has also been associated with shifts towards Western lifestyles. The human immune system is vital in combating infections and eliminating dangerously mutating cells, but an overactive immune system caused by an out-of-kilter gut microbiome can produce antibodies that indiscriminately attack other cells. Like in the wider world, in which variety-rich ecosystems provide balance and bolster overall system resiliency, highly diverse microbial communities appear to be necessary to establish a harmonious and well-functioning immune response.

Industrial agriculture not only contributes to nutrient loss and a reduction in microbial diversity, but it also smuggles novel chemicals into the food chain. Rachel Carson revealed in the early 1960s that DDT could infiltrate the food web, and later studies have demonstrated that other pesticides – a broad category that includes herbicides, insecticides, fungicides and disinfectants – also percolate through to wider systems. Pesticides can reduce crop losses from insects, fight animal-borne diseases, protect grain stores, and prevent food spoilage from fungal infections, and for these reasons the global use of pesticides has increased exponentially over the course of the Great Acceleration. When Carson wrote *Silent Spring* insecticides were the principal pesticide, accounting for approximately 80 per cent of total pesticide use in America, but now herbicides are the dominant biocidal chemical. This is partly because the synthetic inputs used for intensive cropping weaken the symbiotic pact between cultivated plants and the soil microbiome, and as the concentration of protective phytochemicals provided by soil organisms falls then plants become more vulnerable to pathogens, opportunistic invertebrates and invasive weeds. In consequence, cereals that stand in serried ranks, like soldiers in formation, are typically laced with an ever-growing chemical armoury to fend off these predatory assaults.

The world's most widely used herbicide, oil-based glyphosate, was first deployed in the 1970s, but within two decades some plants deemed 'weeds' had outcompeted this synthesised chemical. The emergence of glyphosate-tolerant weeds, in turn, prompted the development and commercialisation of genetically engineered herbicide-resistant seeds. This innovation resulted in more promiscuous spraying of farmland, including the crop itself, and as a result global glyphosate use has increased approximately 15-fold since the introduction of these GMOs in the mid-1990s. Billions of pounds of glyphosate-based herbicide douse farmland and other areas each year, and this water-soluble weedkiller not only accumulates as residue on food but also leaches into surface and groundwater. In addition to ecological impacts, research indicates that glyphosate may trigger epigenetic changes and other human health risks, including possible adverse impacts on neurodevelopment, metabolic processes, and liver and kidney function. Food is the intermediary between planetary health and human health – and in this world where all things are indivisibly linked, substance abuse imposed on the natural world makes all of us co-dependents and potential victims.

Plague animals

The idea of a separate self is an Enlightenment invention, and the rigid division between mind and matter, between humans and the rest of the natural world, has been informed by the low-resolution perspectives of the past. The stories that science tells us now are more about interconnection, interdependency and symbiosis, and humans are increasingly viewed as 'holobionts', each of us an ecological unit comprising the host human body and a multitude of species living in or on it. Just as coral is a hybrid creature, part invertebrate animal and part algae, we too are an assembly of human cells and non-human cells that together constitute an emergent whole. The human gastrointestinal tract alone houses many trillions of microorganisms comprising thousands of species, and these gut microbes influence cognition, emotions, and physiological and mental health. Exploiting the resources provided by the host human body, and driven by the Darwinian imperative to survive and multiply, microbial colonies pursue their own interests with a single-mindedness that would endear them to the most extreme individualists. These microbes can be either helpful or harmful to the complex adaptive system known as the individual, and every now and then they remind us that what is visited on the planet is ultimately also visited on ourselves.

Farming, urbanisation and trade have always been closely linked to disease – influenza, measles and smallpox, for example, all arose after the Agricultural Revolution and thrive in densely settled populations. Around 1.7 million undescribed viruses are estimated to reside in mammals and birds, up to half of which have the potential to spill over into humans, and many 'zoonotic' diseases – those springing from a pathogen that jumps from an animal to a human – were initially transmitted by farm animals kept in close proximity to their human captors. These diseases then hitch a ride on human-created networks to spread and multiply – the plague that felled Pericles during the Golden Age of Athens arrived via its shipping lanes; malaria-carrying mosquitos piggy-backed on humans shuttling along the famous Roman roads; and the Black Death advanced west across the various merchant thoroughfares collectively known as the Silk Road. More recently, human incursions into wilderness areas, combined with the even greater mobility conferred by modern transport systems, have spawned new diseases – including one particular virus that sparked what has been called 'the first economic crisis of the Anthropocene'.

Covid-19, caused by a strain of coronavirus, was first identified in the Chinese city of Wuhan in late 2019. The best guess of health authorities is that transmission to humans occurred at Wuhan's wet market – a sprawling emporium concentrating livestock, wild animals and humans in one place, and acting as a potential mixing pot for the incubation of zoonotic strains. Due to a shared evolutionary path, other mammals are the principal vector for zoonotic infections in humans, and it is thought that one of the market's wild-caught mammals was the intermediary for the virus. Covid Patient Zero was probably a horseshoe bat somewhere in southern China – like humans, bats are social creatures living in dense aggregations, but uniquely among mammals they can also fly. The higher metabolism required for flight results in increased body temperature that mimics the effects of a fever, and in consequence bats have evolved an immune system that is far more tolerant to external stressors. Because of their lack of social distancing, their sturdy immune system and their unrivalled mobility, bats are the ideal brewery, reservoir and broadcaster of viruses.

From the initial spillover infection in Wuhan the virus moved rapidly along the same global arteries that carried people and goods, seeding a pandemic that infected well over a billion humans, claimed tens of millions of lives, and reduced global output more than any event since the Great Depression. Mortality rates were highest among the elderly and people with pre-existing conditions, especially the lifestyle diseases of our industrial era such as obesity and diabetes, and those exposed to significant air pollution also suffered disproportionately. Many globalised supply networks failed as key links in the chain were shut down, and difficulties in sourcing medical and personal protective equipment highlighted the downside of offshoring manufacturing to other countries. Food production in many advanced nations faltered when large processing facilities were closed, bottlenecking the supply chain and sometimes requiring primary producers to dispose of millions of 'slaughter-ready' animals that had outgrown their cramped cages. Covid attacked the weaknesses in our globalised, just-in-time, efficient-but-fragile economic system with the same ruthlessness that it colonised and overpowered those human victims with pre-existing health conditions, and demolished the fiction that humans somehow sit outside the natural world.

This type of 'zoonotic spillover' is not an uncommon event. It is estimated that up to three-quarters of human viruses are zoonotic in origin, with almost all recent infectious diseases – including AIDS, SARS, Zika and Lyme disease – originally coming from animals. As humankind encroaches further into biodiversity-rich habitats, and climate change forces the migration and concentration of wild animal species into particular areas, the virus Venn diagram between animals and humans will intersect ever more widely. A 2022 article in the scientific journal *Nature* predicts that, due to changes in climate and land use, 'species will aggregate in new combinations at high elevations, in biodiversity hotspots, and in areas of high human population density in Asia and Africa, causing the cross-species transmission of their associated viruses an estimated 4,000 times'. Ironically, it has been humankind's success in parasitising the Earth – clearing land for agriculture, cutting down forests, quarrying minerals from remote locales, living in conurbations that congeal and spread into what was previously wilderness – that has also made us obligingly available hosts for novel parasites.

The Great Pandemic demonstrated once again that short-term efficiencies can be inordinately expensive over the long run. A recent scientific paper suggests that annual global spending in the range of $20 billion to $30 billion on measures such as reducing deforestation and regulating wildlife trade would likely provide a return on investment many hundreds of times more than the initial sum spent – in 2020 alone, the first full year of Covid, it is estimated that the pandemic resulted in a $5 trillion shortfall in global GDP, without even accounting for all the other unmeasurable impacts on human wellbeing. Covid proved a boon to what has been called the 'health-industrial complex', but except for a handful of entities – such as pharmaceutical companies providing much-needed vaccines – prevention does not pay in our market system. Just as enormous externalities arising from climate change, land-clearing and declining biodiversity are not captured in market prices or GDP, so too the benefits of pre-emptive action are severely undervalued or not valued at all. Covid showed that we are just another animal to viruses – an opportune site for residence and reproduction, reinforcing the fact that we share our fate with the rest of the living world – but it was also a reminder that governments and the private sector could still work together symbiotically to solve urgent communal problems.

24

WOOD WIDE WEB

Humans as ecosystem engineers

A chaos of delight

For Charles Darwin, who suffered intense bouts of seasickness on the voyage of the *Beagle*, disembarkation at the Brazilian city of Salvador came as a welcome relief. Soon after landing he was venturing into the forests of the hinterland, carried on 'transports of pleasure' as he discovered 'this new & grander world'. Wandering enraptured through the rainforest, Darwin noted that

> if the eye attempts to follow the flight of a gaudy butter-fly, it is arrested
> by some strange tree or fruit; if watching an insect one forgets it in the
> stranger flower it is crawling over ... The mind is a chaos of delight.

'Brazilian scenery', with its thick forests filled with bright colours, is, as he wrote in his diary, 'nothing more nor less than a view in the Arabian Nights, with the advantage of reality'. But despite these enchantments, Darwin, the hard-headed scientist, recognised that in the Amazon brutality also existed alongside beauty.

Darwin identified a species of South American wasp that laid eggs inside live caterpillars, which would then be eaten from the inside out by hatched wasp larvae. Writing later to a fellow naturalist, he explained that:

> I cannot persuade myself that a beneficent and omnipotent God would
> have designedly created [this wasp] with the express intention of their
> feeding within the living bodies of Caterpillars.

In South America he also witnessed another form of barbaric parasitism,
but this time in respect of his own species. Darwin, who came from a
long line of abolitionists, observed humans leeching off the captive living
bodies of slaves in Brazil, while later in Argentina he was repelled by
gauchos boasting about the extermination of 'Pampas Indians'. Darwin's
experience in South America, and later in other newly occupied countries,
strengthened his conviction that the stories of an omniscient Creator, with
Man as His divinely sanctioned deputy, were nothing more than a form of
self-aggrandising make-believe.

South America lay at the bleeding edge of 'the Columbian exchange' –
the intercontinental cross-flow of people, food, microbes and ideologies
that, starting with Columbus in 1492, heralded a truly globalised world.
This transaction proved to be extremely one-sided – Europe gained
valuable new foods such as potatoes and corn, virgin land that yielded
heavy harvests of Old World crops due to the absence of co-evolved
pests, and treasure in the form of precious metals. The New World, in
return, was visited with the destruction of ecosystems, the arrival of other
invasive species in the wake of Western colonists, deadly epidemics such as
smallpox and measles, and the conquest and subjugation of its indigenous
populations. The Four Horsemen of the Apocalypse – pestilence, war,
famine and death – came in Spanish galleons, Portuguese caravels and
British trading ships, and it is estimated that within a century-and-a-half
of Columbus's landing in Hispaniola the number of native Americans
across both continents had declined by 90 per cent, falling from
approximately 60 million to around 6 million. And to offset this lack of
manpower, 12 million men, women and children were brutally abducted
and transported from Africa over almost four centuries to sate Western
hunger for goods and gold.

Writing a few years after the *Beagle*'s voyage, Darwin reflected that:

> Wherever the European has trod, death seems to pursue the aboriginal ...
> The varieties of man seem to act on each other; in the same way as
> different species of animals – the stronger always extirpating the weaker.

Seemingly supporting this grim and shameful observation, the Great
Dying among indigenous Americans was at the same time accompanied
by a population explosion in Europe. Plants such as potatoes produced far
more calories per acre than traditional European crops, and this energy
bonanza eased the way for further urbanisation and industrialisation. A
massive increase in sugar, coffee and tea imports from the colonies helped
fuel the growing army of domestic factory workers, while another gift from
the New World, the anti-malarial compound quinine, later permitted the
exploration and exploitation of yet more lands in Asia and Africa. With
these tools of Empire, the industrial capitalist dynamic – the extraction
of raw materials from all corners of the world, and the processing and
consumption of finished products in home markets – could now be
conducted on a planetary scale.

The yoking together of continents through trade not only altered
European diets, now more reliant on just a handful of high-energy foods,
but it also entrenched the global ascendancy of the West. That shrewd and
unsparing inquisitor of the West, Alexis de Tocqueville, commented that:

> We should almost say that the European is to the other races what man
> himself is to the lower animals; he makes them subservient to his use,
> and when he cannot subdue, he destroys.

One of the consequences of the near-destruction of the indigenous
population of the Americas was extensive forest regrowth in the New
World. Traditional land management techniques – such as small-
scale farming and the controlled burning of patches of forest to create
grasslands – largely perished along with their practitioners, and it has been
estimated that over 50 million hectares of untended land was naturally
reforested within the first two centuries of European conquest. Partly as
a result of this reforestation in the New World, atmospheric carbon levels

fell to multi-millennia lows in the seventeenth century, contributing to a period of global cooling through to the nineteenth century. 'The Little Ice Age', as it is now called, demonstrated in the most macabre way possible that tree regrowth could sequester enough carbon to meaningfully alter the global climate.

Loot

Trees have been venerated in many cultures, including indigenous peoples in the pre-Industrial West. The ancient Celts and their Druid lore-keepers gathered in forest groves to worship the sacred oak and its resident spirits, and 'the world tree' – symbolising the interconnectedness of all life, with branches stretching towards the heavens, a trunk anchored to the earth, and roots reaching down into the underworld – was a common motif in many Indo-European religions. Two trees – one of Life, the other of Knowledge – reputedly stood in the Garden of Eden, and in Asia Siddhartha Gautama became the Buddha beneath the Tree of Enlightenment. But despite this seemingly instinctive reverence, humans have been burning and cutting down trees for millennia. Forests provide fuel, building materials and land that can be converted to farms or settlements – and, as a result, it is estimated that the world has lost a third of its forests since the Agricultural Revolution. Deforestation is an age-old human practice, but one that grew exponentially during the fossil fuelled modern era and climaxed in the early decades of the Great Acceleration.

It is thought that approximately half of all global forest loss occurred in the period from the dawn of the Agricultural Revolution until 1900, with the rest occurring in the twentieth century alone. The majority of this land-clearing was for agricultural purposes – when *The Wealth of Nations* was published towards the end of the eighteenth century, forest covered approximately half of all habitable land with around 10 per cent given over to farming, the remainder comprising wild grasslands and scrub, but today agriculture occupies almost half the world's habitable land. Until the 1920s the logging and clearing of temperate and boreal woodlands in the northern hemisphere was the principal contributor to global forest loss, but for the last century the overwhelming majority of deforestation has been inflicted on tropical systems. The exploitation of tropical forests escalated markedly from the mid-twentieth century, culminating in the 1980s when 150 million hectares of land – the equivalent of over 200 million football fields – was cleared of trees. In this peak deforestation decade, nearly all forest loss comprised tropical and subtropical woodlands, and this trend continues today with approximately 95 per cent of the world's deforestation occurring in areas around the Equator.

The razing of rainforests in Brazil and Indonesia for crops and pastures has been the principal driver of forest loss since the Great Acceleration. As a result of land conversion and degradation, the Amazonian rainforest – the world's largest tropical forest, responsible for around one-sixth of all carbon dioxide removed from the atmosphere through the action of photosynthesis – is believed to have switched from a carbon sink to a carbon source, while Indonesian forests passed this inflection point decades before. Only the Congo Basin rainforest in central Africa – the world's other great tropical forest system, comprising a quarter of the world's remaining tropical forest – now absorbs more carbon than is emitted, but it too is threatened by commercial logging, encroaching plantations and increased mining activity. Although the rate of tropical forest loss has fallen in successive decades since peak deforestation in the 1980s – with net tropical forest loss in the period 2010 to 2020 estimated at around 50 million hectares, a third of the area lost thirty years before – these ecosystems will continue to be exploited for as long as they are worth more dead than alive.

As the biologist and writer EO Wilson observed, 'destroying rainforest for economic gain is like burning a Renaissance painting to cook a meal'. Species richness generally increases the closer an ecosystem is to the Equator, and tropical forests are biodiversity hotspots, holding more species than any other terrestrial habitat, and because of the warm and moist environment they foster explosive growth in plant life. As a result, these ecosystems draw down carbon dioxide more effectively than any other wholly terrestrial forest type, while also providing other vital benefits such as the cooling and watering of areas well beyond the rainforest itself. But in an ever-spiralling cycle, tropical deforestation increases global greenhouse gas emissions, reduces carbon sequestration, and diminishes beneficial biophysical effects such as evapotranspiration and cloud creation – all of which lead to increasingly frequent droughts and changing rainfall patterns, further stressing these ecosystems and making them less biodiverse and more prone to extreme weather events. In the Amazon, for example, some studies estimate that should present trends continue, up to 60 per cent of the Amazonian rainforest could disappear by 2050, to be replaced by drier and more biologically impoverished grassland savannas.

In contrast to the dire situation in tropical rainforest areas, high-latitude temperate and boreal regions have recorded a net gain in forest area since 1990 due to forest regrowth outweighing forest loss. This is partly due to wealthy northern countries generally having more productive agricultural sectors and a low reliance on wood for fuel, but also because much of the deforestation is outsourced to developing nations. Around 30 per cent of tropical deforestation is driven by the production of commodities that are then exported – goods such as beef, soybean, palm oil, paper and lumber. Most Western countries are, in effect, net importers of deforestation, with demand pull from these richer nations driving the burning, felling and clearing of forests in poorer countries. In another permutation of capitalism's program of globalisation and resource exploitation, which began in earnest with the Columbian exchange, this virtual occupation channels enormously undervalued natural wealth to more affluent nations while systematically dismantling one of the planet's most efficient carbon vaults and climate stabilisers.

Origin of the specious

For those focused on short-term profits, or the exigencies of survival, it can be difficult to see the forest for the timber. And because forests and the ecosystem services they provide – including carbon sequestration, climate regulation and biodiversity preservation – are not assigned any value in national accounts, old-growth forests are being liquidated at an unsustainable rate while the longer-term costs of this destruction are largely ignored. The catastrophic 1998 floods in China's Yangtze basin – threaded by the world's third-longest river and home to 400 million people – starkly illustrates the dangers of failing to properly value the natural world. The Yangtze region is one of the cradles of urban civilisation, and for thousands of years its river has provided water for human consumption, irrigation and industry, as well as being a major transport thoroughfare between megacities such as Wuhan and Shanghai. Despite, or perhaps because of, its importance, the river has suffered increasing levels of chemical and plastics pollution, sedimentation from land erosion, the extinction of several iconic endemic species, and, not least, extensive forest and wetlands loss.

In the summer of 1998, above average rainfall in the Yangtze catchment, combined with excessive runoff due to deforestation, led to a flood that killed thousands, left 15 million homeless and resulted in many tens of billions of dollars of economic loss. This tragedy prompted the Chinese government to implement the world's largest publicly funded effort to account and pay for ecosystem services, and studies undertaken as part of this program determined that flood mitigation arising from surrounding forests provided around three times more economic value than the market price achieved from a one-off conversion of trees to lumber. The Chinese leadership – perhaps less wedded to the dogma of market supremacy than some of its more rigidly neoliberal peers in the West – recognised that failing to properly price ecosystem service benefits could generate immense longer-term costs, and acted accordingly. In a broad-based policy response, the government imposed logging bans, restored degraded forests, and converted large swathes of farmland previously devoted to annual crops to tree reforestation.

As the Chinese government belatedly recognised, reforestation or avoided deforestation provides many benefits to humans – not just flood, erosion and sedimentation control, but other positive knock-on effects such as the prevention of disease spillovers. It is, however, the role of trees as a storehouse of carbon that has recently captured the most attention. Those advocates for net zero – the idea that human-sponsored initiatives can absorb and cancel human-created greenhouse gas emissions – note that trees have the great virtue of being a nature-based 'technology', honed over hundreds of millions of years of evolution, that efficiently stores carbon. Forests also, in theory, can be scaled up in size relatively economically – a feat that some other proposals, such as carbon capture and storage, are yet to achieve. As a result, many governments and companies have promised to allocate land for 'biological carbon removal' in the quest for carbon neutrality, with over 600 million hectares – equivalent to almost two-thirds the landmass of the United States – already pledged for reforestation.

Putting to one side the fact that these pledges are likely to go the way of most climate promises – largely aspirational and unenforceable, pitched to take place at some indeterminate time in the future, and therefore another potential mechanism for diversion and delay on emissions reduction – there is another major problem with this proclaimed nature-based solution. Despite Darwin's pessimistic forecast almost two centuries ago, indigenous and other traditional peoples managed to survive the Western onslaught, and their territories, although often lacking secure land rights, are thought to cover around a third of the Earth's terrestrial surface. Much of the land earmarked for forest protection and tree-planting is already occupied by indigenous people, and if a material proportion of the land-based decarbonisation pledges were to be implemented these already marginal communities would once again be subject to an ecological shadow economy in which offshore acres are exploited to sustain Western lifestyles.

In addition to shifting the mitigation burden on to communities abroad and away from reducing fossil fuel emissions, this exercise also founders on the myth of market fungibility – the idea that all carbon stocks are roughly the same in terms of stability and longevity. Living carbon in the form of tree growth is accumulated over decades, sometimes centuries, whereas dead carbon in the form of fossil fuels is burned and instantaneously released as carbon dioxide. Reforested areas are often just another monoculture, and this lack of diversity can lead to less resilient ecosystems. Recent research indicates that primary forests are in fact social networks built on reciprocity and nutrient exchange, with old growth 'Mother Trees' nourishing saplings through fungal connections. A single-species stand of trees all of the same vintage may, in contrast, be as vulnerable to pests and diseases as Irish potato plots were in the mid-nineteenth century, and therefore at much greater risk of giving up the carbon sequestered within.

Healthy forests are a key contributor to climate regulation and provide many other co-benefits, but in this crowded world the solution to accelerating greenhouse gases cannot be utilising even more land to absorb these emissions, or usurping those indigenous communities that have proven effective environmental stewards. Studies show that traditional communities with secure land rights tend to outperform both governments and private landholders in terms of conserving primary ecosystems and maintaining biodiversity, and this land care ethic was observed firsthand by Charles Darwin. In 1836, towards the end of his great circumnavigation, he noted that in eastern Australia:

> The woodland is generally so open that a person on horseback can gallop through it. It is traversed by a few flat-bottomed valleys, which are green and free from trees: in such spots the scenery was like that of a park, and pretty.

He added that 'in the whole country I scarcely saw a place without the marks of fire' – across the entire continent, for tens of thousands of years, the First Nations people of what is now called Australia had employed fire and land management regimes to generate an abundance of wildlife, plants and food. This place-based knowledge was diametrically opposed to the approach of newer settlers, who inexpertly imposed European crops and animals on to the ancient soils of Australia and other 'unimproved' lands, denuding much of the country within the space of a few generations.

The experience of indigenous people around the world is a reminder that humans have filled crucial ecological roles for millennia – and that in many ways the idea of 'the environment', separate from human societies, merely reinforces the artificial distinction between humankind and the rest of nature. Humans have engineered landscapes throughout history, actively shaping them in an effort to obtain optimal biological productivity. And in that other great hope for land-based decarbonisation – the ancient art of agriculture – there is also a growing realisation among Western nations that working with rather than against nature may be one of the best solutions for our planet. Uniquely, agriculture, unlike other major polluting sectors, not only generates carbon dioxide but can also store it – and, unlike the ocean, actually benefits from increased carbon levels. Practised in the right way, agriculture can pivot from being a climate change problem to becoming part of the climate change solution.

25

GROUNDED

Decarbonising the atmosphere by recarbonising the Earth

Dirt cheap

The biblical injunction to be fruitful and multiply, and to subdue the Earth, has been observed by humankind, but the bit about replenishing the planet has been less faithfully followed. Humans have almost completely succeeded in securing 'dominion over the fish of the sea, and over the fowl of the air, and over every living thing that moveth upon the Earth', as God is said to have commanded in the Book of Genesis. More than half of all seafood consumed by humankind now comes from captive sources, caged poultry comprises just over 70 per cent of all bird life, and people and their livestock account for well over nine-tenths of the world's mammal biomass. But this conquest has come at a huge cost. Modern industrial agriculture is responsible for a significant proportion of human-caused greenhouse gases, is the largest contributor to global habitat and biodiversity loss, and pollutes the world's waterways with excess nutrients. Its high-input, high-output model has generated impressive yield returns and reduced the amount of land required to feed an individual, but long-term sustainability has been sacrificed for short-term efficiency. Fuelled by hydrocarbon-derived synthetic fertilisers, and reliant on just a few commodities, intensive agricultural practices degrade the soil and disrupt important global nutrient cycles that have an impact well beyond the terrestrial domain.

The Food and Agriculture Organization projects that global food demand will rise by 70 per cent by 2050, and if present production systems are maintained then demand for fertiliser is expected to increase by a similar amount. Globally, annual use of fertiliser has already climbed approximately 10-fold since the start of the Great Acceleration, with more than 100 million tonnes of synthetic nitrogen fertiliser, around 50 million tonnes of phosphate and more than 40 million tonnes of potassium applied to crops and pastures every year. Fritz Haber achieved what economists call 'technological substitution' when he found a way to convert atmospheric nitrogen to plant-accessible nitrogen, but, unlike nitrogen, phosphorus and potassium are locked in the Earth's crust in limited quantities and cannot be simply manufactured. Almost 90 per cent of global phosphorus deposits are found in just five countries, with 70 per cent located in Morocco and the disputed territory of Western Sahara alone, while 85 per cent of potash deposits are found in six countries, with nearly half of all global potash reserves lying in Canada and Belarus.

Due to this extreme geographic concentration, industrial agriculture's dependency on just a handful of suppliers for its phosphorus and potassium needs is even greater than the wider world's dependency on the 12 oil-producing OPEC nations that together hold three-quarters of global oil reserves, and this supply bottleneck sometimes leads to large price spikes and supply irregularities. Of greater concern than this volatility, however, is the fact that Liebig's law of the minimum – which states that plant growth is determined by the scarcest available single key nutrient – may eventually be applicable at a global level. Some studies predict that 'peak phosphorus' – the point of maximum phosphorus production – will be reached by around 2030, and that the Earth's economic reserves of phosphorus may be entirely consumed within the next century. As with almost all extractable minerals, the more accessible and highest quality reserves of phosphorus were the first to be exhausted, and, as with hydrocarbon production or fishing, an increasing amount of effort is required to obtain further stocks. As a result, phosphorus – which along with nitrogen fertiliser is the most commonly applied crop nutrient – is expected to become far more costly as global reserves are depleted.

But although some synthetic farm inputs are likely to become significantly more expensive in coming decades, they will still be far cheaper than if there was a proper accounting for their ecological costs. The impacts of nitrogen and phosphorus pollution on waterways are not captured in market prices, and in fact many of the countries that have benefitted most from the Green Revolution continue to subsidise rather than tax synthetic fertilisers, reducing the financial incentives for farmers to use these inputs more judiciously. For pesticides, too, the externalities from their use are not recognised in prices, and with herbicides there can be a type of Tragedy of the Commons arising from the excessive application of these chemicals. Because herbicide resistance is mobile across property boundaries, due for example to pollen or seed movement, there is no strong incentive for individual farmers to adopt more expensive and time-consuming practices that would prevent or delay tolerance. As with overfishing in the open ocean or overgrazing on a commons or the draining of an aquifer, management decisions that may be rational from an individual perspective can lead to collectively irrational outcomes – in this case, a race to the bottom in which farmers apply ever-higher quantities of underpriced herbicide and thereby speed up overall weed resistance.

Although industrially produced food is cheap in terms of what is paid at the supermarket checkout, ultimately all of us, including future generations, are picking up the tab for the unrecorded costs inflicted on the environment. By utilising excessive amounts of polluting chemical fertilisers, the Green Revolution on land has also seeded a malign green revolution in some of the world's waters, pesticides and herbicides have increased environmental toxic load and promoted pest resistance, while near-term performance is prioritised over longer-term soil fertility and plant health. However, there is an alternative to the destructive and industrialised agriculture typical of our modern era – that is, farming practices that replenish the soil, help to rebalance the carbon cycle, restore biodiversity, increase the resilience of the land, while providing cleaner and more nutrient-rich food to the general population. If the true costs of modern food production were internalised in market prices, industrial farming would become far less affordable, while this more ecologically produced food would emerge as a relative bargain.

Turf wars

Lawns – another type of domesticated grass, like wheat, rice and corn – may perhaps be the ultimate emblem of modern middle-class aspiration. Lovingly tended by an army of suburban Sisyphuses on weekends, these closely clipped carpets of green are evidence of membership into the club of the conforming, and a visible agreement to its rules. Since the Victorian period, they have been the platform for feats of competition on football fields and golf courses, and turfed parks provide a pastoral respite for those in the cities. They are a form of superfluous consumption, primarily serving an aesthetic purpose, and are also a playground for modern masculinity – a place for men to congregate around a bloody piece of steak at a backyard barbeque, and perhaps a vestigial reminder of the open savannas of hunter-gatherer days. And lawns are also industrial agriculture writ small – a domestic form of monoculture, thirstier for fertilisers and water than the average farm, and a biological desert other than for the favoured cultivated species.

The lawn-loving middle class also has a taste for animal products, and this has largely been serviced by burgeoning intensive animal production. Broadly speaking, meat and dairy consumption increases in line with growing affluence, and, as a result, global meat production has more than tripled and global milk production more than doubled over the last 50 years. Over three-quarters of the world's agricultural land is now used for livestock production and the growing of fodder – an area almost equivalent to the remaining area of global forest – but using animal intermediaries as a human food source appears, on the face of things, to be remarkably inefficient. For grain-fed livestock, every 100 calories of grain provides only 40 new calories of milk, 12 calories of chicken meat, 10 calories of pork, and a miserly 3 calories of beef. Mindful of the huge growth in the livestock industry, together with animal welfare concerns, many have very reasonably noted that land needed for agriculture could be even further reduced if the world adopted a plant-based diet.

It is estimated that if the world's human population did not consume animal products then global agricultural land use would fall from approximately 4 billion to 1 billion hectares. Although problems relating to fertiliser and pesticide use for cropping would remain, a shift towards a meat-light diet would yield significant additional benefits. The use of antibiotics in intensive animal production creates a negative externality in the form of antimicrobial resistance in both humans and livestock, while a diet heavy in primary animal products and processed meats is believed to materially increase the risk of heart disease, stroke and diabetes – in turn, generating another negative externality through higher public health costs. But the most commonly cited reason today for reducing humankind's reliance on meat and dairy products is because of their high embedded carbon levels – greenhouse gas emissions for some forms of beef production, for example, can be well over 50 times greater on a carbon dioxide–equivalent basis than for the same weight of grains, vegetables or fruit. This hefty carbon footprint is partly because methane – a relatively short-lived gas that nevertheless has a warming potential around 25 times greater than carbon dioxide – is belched prodigiously by certain ruminant animals, including cattle, sheep and goats.

In another miracle of symbiosis, these ruminants rely on gut microbes to digest cellulose that is then released to the host animal as absorbable nutrients, while in return these microorganisms are provided with food and a home. A byproduct of this mutual nourishment, however, is the generation of methane from the microbes living inside the grazing animal. The ever-increasing hoofprint of the global livestock industry – since the early 1960s the global cattle herd has increased almost two-thirds to 1.5 billion, and in aggregate there is now a greater mass of cattle than people on Earth – has been the principal factor in the agriculture sector becoming the largest human-caused emitter of methane. Because ruminants are one of the main methane culprits other high-protein options have been suggested as substitutes for red meat, including tank-brewed bacterial yeast and 'cell-based meat' cultured in bio-reactors. These forms of meatamorphosis – in many ways the logical next step in the industrialisation of food production – are, however, yet to be proven at scale, and, in any case, some arguments for eliminating livestock may rest on flimsy foundations.

Methane is indeed a powerful greenhouse gas, but its lifespan in the atmosphere is generally only around 12 years. Carbon dioxide, in contrast, can last for many centuries – remnants of the first puffs of black smoke from James Watt's steam engine may still be circulating in the air we breathe. Carbon dioxide from fossil fuels is a net addition to the stock of greenhouse gases because it is exhumed from the Earth's crust in an extremely stable form and then vaporised when burned for energy, accumulating over time. Methane emitted by animals, on the other hand, is recycled carbon – carbon dioxide is drawn down into grass and other vegetation through the action of photosynthesis, converted to carbohydrates that are consumed by ruminants, and then burped back as carbon dioxide which relatively quickly breaks down into carbon dioxide once again. Because methane production from animals is a circular process, in general terms the net level of methane from livestock production only increases when ruminant herd sizes increase – and although the composition of ruminants has changed over the modern period, the aggregate numbers have not shifted markedly.

Prior to the arrival of Columbus, for example, in addition to millions of other wild ruminant animals such as elk and deer there were at least 50 million bison in the United States – and this single species, up to twice the size of their domesticated bovine cousins, is estimated to have emitted almost as much methane each year as America's entire herd of farmed livestock now releases annually. But more importantly, healthy ecosystems need herbivores. In the looping trophic cascades of nature, just as grasslands rely on carnivores to keep plant-eaters in check, they also depend on those very same plant-eaters for defoliation-driven growth spurts and the recycling of nutrients through manure and urine. Aside from the reality that approximately two-thirds of global agricultural land cannot be used to grow regular crops because of soil or water deficiencies, and that much of this pastoral land is located in poorer countries where livestock is an important source of both nutrition and income, herbivores and the grasslands on which they feed have co-evolved into tight mutual dependencies. Taking a lead from these complex biological systems with their continuous cycles of exchange, a new form of farming has emerged in recent decades – one that works with nature rather than in opposition to it, that seeks to adapt agricultural practices to the land rather than adapting the land to industrialised processes.

Radical

In the same way that microbes inside a cow or a human gut work symbiotically with the host body, the soil acts as an external digestive system for plants. Soil organic matter – comprising living creatures such as microorganisms and earthworms, fresh plant and animal detritus, and humus in the form of fully decayed biological remains – is broken down by microbes into nutrients that are absorbed by plant root systems, and in exchange plants provide carbohydrates and protein to their microscopic partners. Filaments of fungi range widely through the soil as they forage for nutrients, including among humus where these fungal networks produce glue-like compounds that facilitate soil aggregation. This not only results in porous soils that enhance moisture retention, but – because soil aggregates encase organic matter and shield it from microbial activity and further decomposition – humus is a particularly stable form of carbon. Due to this subterranean collation of carbon, both living and dead, it is believed that the Earth's soils contain more than three times the amount of carbon in the atmosphere and four times the quantity of carbon stored in all living plants and animals.

Modern agricultural practices have, however, upset this vast carbon store. The UN Food and Agriculture Organization estimates that around 40 per cent of farmland soils have been degraded, and that up to 70 per cent of soil organic carbon has been lost from cultivated land – initially through the conversion of native ecosystems such as forests and grasslands to farmland, and then by practices such as the ploughing of fields which exposes soil organic matter to oxidation. Soil carbon losses have been greatest in major cropping regions and semi-arid pastoral environments, and this in turn has resulted in a decline in soil structure and higher erosion, reduced water retention, and an overall decline in natural nutrient supply. Global heating is projected to result in soils releasing ever-higher amounts of carbon – due mainly to increased microbial activity which boosts the respiration of carbon dioxide from soil organisms – and some studies predict that, unless agricultural practices change, much of the world's farmland will switch from a carbon sink to a carbon source.

Recarbonising the soil is one of the lowest-hanging fruits on the path to decarbonising the atmosphere. Recent studies suggest that, under a management regime that actively promotes soil health, croplands have the potential to store as much carbon dioxide as is emitted by the global transportation sector annually. Although soils would eventually reach carbon equilibrium after a few decades, increasing soil carbon levels has many advantages over other 'negative emissions' options such as carbon capture and storage or planting new forests – these alternative proposals usually require significant amounts of energy or land, or are simply too expensive to be conducted at scale, whereas soil carbon sequestration is a natural mechanism for removing carbon from the atmosphere and would use only existing farmland. Additionally, land management practices that increase soil carbon provide many other co-benefits – including higher levels of soil fertility and moisture, biodiversity and pest resistance, lower rates of erosion and desertification, and an overall greater resilience to the impacts of climate change.

Industrial agriculture – which relies on high application rates of pesticides and the agricultural steroids otherwise known as fertilisers, while at the same time turning over the ground through deep ploughing and often leaving it bare – has devastated soil food webs in many parts of the world. Fertilisers stifle the give-and-take between plants and their microbial partners, while pesticides lay waste to diverse communities of soil organisms. Reduced plant uptake of key nutrients provided by microbes and fungi, in turn, sets off a vicious cycle in which even greater amounts of artificial inputs must be ladled on to farmland. To address this problem, 'precision farming' techniques – which measure variables such as nutrient levels, soil moisture and topography in a particular area, and co-opts new technology such as GPS, drones and satellite imagery – have been increasingly deployed to allow a more finely calibrated application of inputs such as irrigated water, fertilisers and pesticides. By understanding the variability of landscapes and their different requirements, this agriculture technology increases farm efficiency by producing more 'crop per drop', while also reducing externalities in the form of polluting and potentially dangerous synthetic inputs.

A similar ethos – understanding a particular piece of land and responding to its needs – is favoured by those practising 'regenerative agriculture'. But whereas precision agriculture relies almost entirely on the latest technology, regenerative agriculture seeks to mimic age-old natural processes. As the writer and ecologist Aldo Leopold commented in the depths of the Dustbowl era:

> Civilization is not … the enslavement of a stable and constant earth.
> It is a state of mutual and interdependent cooperation between human
> animals, other animals, plants, and soils, which may be disrupted at
> any moment by the failure of any of them.

By nurturing interlocking symbiotic relationships regenerative agriculture seeks to produce more life than is taken, and employs a range of management techniques – including reduced or zero tillage, the sowing of cover crops and the rotational grazing of livestock to prevent overgrazing – to conserve and restore soil carbon levels, the foundation of all terrestrial life.

Regeneration – 're-generation' – also implies the re-use of resources, and regenerative agriculture seeks to close the metabolic rift cleaved by industrial agriculture. It is a low-input, but high-knowledge approach that, like indigenous communities that have effectively stewarded the land for millennia, understands and honours the particular ecosystem. Studies suggest that regenerative farming practices tend to not only generate significantly higher soil carbon levels, but because of increased soil fertility over time they can also produce yields comparable to or better than conventional farming techniques. Additionally, both regeneratively farmed crops and pasture-fed livestock raised on low-input grassland also tend to record higher levels of minerals, vitamins and other nutrients important for human health. And the benefits of ecological farming can also extend into the world of money – although regenerative agriculture is usually more labour intensive, the cost of external inputs is substantially lower, and on balance many farmers practising this form of 'natural systems agriculture' often enjoy greater overall profit margins.

Regenerative agriculture is, in some ways, like Adam Smith's original conception of capitalism – a bottom-up system that, with some human steering, permits the natural world to perform its triumphs of self-organisation and self-regulation. It moves away from the simplistic idea that increases in volume and efficiency are the only solution to global food challenges, while also focusing on system resilience, improved food quality and reduced food waste. The act of eating is humankind's most intimate and regular communion with nature, and in our entangled world what we eat and how that food is produced influences the carbon cycle, the health of the wider world, and ultimately our own wellbeing. Agriculture was responsible for the birth of civilisation, and good land management practices could help to save it – industrial farming practices set in motion by the Green Revolution have yielded huge increases in food production, but we now need what has been called a 'doubly green revolution' to ensure the continued fertility of the Earth. Just as in regenerative farm systems long-dormant seeds will germinate under the right environmental conditions, a new way of thinking will help transform agriculture into perhaps the single best solution to the crisis in human and planetary health.

THE ELEMENTS

26

THE ILLTH OF NATIONS

Outgrowing the idea of growth

Reign of error

We live on a star-powered planet – a superorganism that for billions of years has fed off the distant fire of the Sun, a self-regulating network in which life is not merely a passive recipient but is also an active agent in creating the conditions for its own flourishing. The living world has been subject to mass extinction events in the past – caused by often interlinked factors, such as extraterrestrial visitations in the form of asteroid impacts, gamma-ray bursts from the implosion of other stars, or the eruption of giant volcanoes – and the most recent, 66 million years ago when a 10-kilometre-wide space rock hurtled into Central America, marked the near-complete demise of the dinosaurs and an eventual explosion in mammal diversity. One beneficiary of this evolutionary Big Bang was the upright ape Homo sapiens – at a mere 300,000 years old as a species, a relative newcomer to the sprawling family of life on Earth, which until very recently boasted a greater variety of organisms than at any other time in the planet's history.

Humankind has endured significant climatic changes during its time on Earth, but for the last twelve millennia has basked in the temperate conditions of the Holocene epoch – a period that scientists say could last another 50,000 years in the absence of any 'climate forcing' that materially unbalances the Earth's net energy budget. This climate stability, in turn, sparked the Agricultural Revolution and the rise of urban civilisations, with city-dwelling humans kept in their place by stories about wrathful gods, divinely appointed leaders and immutable social hierarchies. Around 500 years ago a new story, one that dared to question the older self-serving tales, took hold in certain parts of the world – a narrative celebrating human agency, rationality and ingenuity, but carrying with it the accompanying conviction that humans could subjugate nature as completely as some people controlled others. Then, halfway between the start of the Scientific Revolution and the present day, another chapter in the story of human exceptionalism was written. In 1776, the world's first modern democracy enshrined the rights of liberty and the pursuit of happiness for certain of its citizens, while over in the Old World *The Wealth of Nations* provided a theoretical superstructure that seemed to justify individuals prioritising their own interests above others.

Adam Smith asserted that those who seek to enrich themselves will also enrich broader society by generating a 'universal opulence' that percolates down and benefits all – an example of what today might be called a positive externality. But while popularising this particular story, Smith also planted the seed for what would become a gigantic negative externality by failing to properly value the natural world. In Smith's day, natural assets – including British coal seams sitting just beneath the ground – were plentiful, and the price of primary resources was considered to be only their extraction cost as measured by expenditure on scarce machinery and labour. Smith argued that 'The real price of every thing … is the toil and trouble of acquiring it', and he therefore focused on human effort and manufactured capital as the primary 'factors of production' – that is, those inputs needed to produce final goods and services. Prosperity was measured by what could be generated by human hands, the bounty of the natural world was treated as a given, and nowhere in *The Wealth of Nations* was the word 'energy' mentioned. This last omission is not surprising, as Smith's book was completed before coal had been harnessed to efficiently drive machines, but fossil fuels have been a crucial contributor to the spectacular economic growth seen during the industrial age.

Prior to the modern era, almost all organisms lived off – either directly or indirectly – the immediate energy provided by the Sun, but by tapping into a buried hoard of hydrocarbons humankind has burst through what Herman Daly called 'the solar income budget constraint'. Fossil fuels are the cheap labour of the natural world – each barrel of oil, for example, provides the energy equivalent of between 10,000 and 20,000 hours of human effort – and our carbon-fired growth spurt has powered much of humanity to unprecedented wealth, while permitting the proliferation of our species and its menagerie of domesticated animals. But the burning of hydrocarbons has also resulted in the transfer of tremendous quantities of heat-trapping gases into the atmosphere, and the exploitation of this particular natural resource has enabled the overexploitation of many other natural assets. As a result, humankind's long retreat from the natural world – thousands of years in the making, but reaching escape velocity only during this Anthropocene age – is now breaching the boundaries of a liveable Earth.

In addition to the Anthropocene, there have been other names suggested for the epoch humanity has engineered – 'the Pyrocene', the Age of Fire, in recognition of the fossil fuels that launched us into the Great Acceleration; 'the Homogenocene', the Age of Sameness, reflecting our culture of monocultures and plummeting global biodiversity; and 'the Myxocene', the Age of Slime, signalling our possible regression, as more complex forms of life die off, to the primeval organisms that marked Earth's early days. Whatever the label, the choice of alternative names for this current geological period is a suggestive signpost to our ultimate destination unless we tread a radically different path. The Anthropocene age arguably began with the testing of atomic bombs in the mid-1940s, and the atomising of the atom was perhaps the logical final step in humankind's dismembering of the natural world. However, unless we value and protect nature then what started with a bang may well end with a whimper – for the Earth is now subject to a sixth 'extinction spasm', the first to be experienced by Homo sapiens.

Destructive creation

The IPCC's latest Assessment Report, released in instalments over 2021 and 2022, is couched in the dry language of science, but even with its carefully constructed scenarios and qualifications based on levels of confidence it is a frightening read. The IPCC notes that annual net human-caused global greenhouse gas emissions have increased by more than 50 per cent since its first report was issued in 1990, that each of the last four decades has been successively warmer than any preceding decade since temperatures have been recorded, and that in 2019 'atmospheric carbon dioxide concentrations were higher than at any time in at least 2 million years'. It is an onslaught, a relentless rollcall of woe, setting out the likely consequences of the scorched Earth policy wrought by excessive fossil use and rapacious industrialism – the 'loss and degradation of much of the world's forests, coral reefs and low-lying coastal wetlands', an 'increased ... chance of compound extreme events' such as concurrent heatwaves and droughts, and 'increased malnutrition in many communities'. Pressure on ecosystems and unsustainable agricultural practices will lead to 'competition for land and/or water resources', 'violent intrastate conflict', and what the IPCC coyly terms 'involuntary migration' from regions with high exposure to climate change.

This Mad Max dystopian vision is in many ways a return to the dark forebodings of Thomas Malthus. The world's first professional economist and the original 'dismal scientist', Malthus thought that population growth would outstrip 'the power in the earth to produce subsistence for man' and that the ultimate result would be famine, disease and widespread death. Malthus's concern was that human populations increased in what he called 'a geometrical ratio' – that is, exponentially, such that incremental changes become ever wider each period – but in his time food production tended to only increase in a linear or 'arithmetical' fashion, with incremental changes relatively constant. His timing, however, could not have been worse – Malthus had the misfortune of proffering his prediction at the beginning of the Industrial Revolution, just as the Western world was deploying fossil fuelled energy and opening up wide new vistas of exploitation. Globalisation and the superhuman power granted by hydrocarbons has allowed the world to evade the 'Malthusian trap' for the time being, but at the cost of an ever-expanding ecological deficit that takes more from the planet's ecosystems than can be renewed.

Malthus was broadly correct in relation to population growth – when he wrote *An Essay on the Principle of Population* in 1798, the world contained around 1 billion people, and it would take another 130 years for the population to double by the late 1920s. In the time since, the rate of population growth has indeed increased exponentially – in 1960 the number of people in the world passed the 3 billion threshold, in 1974 the 4 billion mark was recorded, and since that time it has doubled again. But Malthus's predicted cataclysm has not eventuated – in fact, over the course of the Great Acceleration the quantity of calories available per person globally has increased by around a third although the world population has more than tripled. And in addition to greater food security, world output as measured by GDP – the amount of goods and services consumed globally and transacted in markets – has increased more than 10-fold, rising from just under $10 trillion in 1950 to more than $100 trillion today. This material abundance has, however, been bought at a significant cost – since the start of the Great Acceleration, for example, annual energy consumption and carbon dioxide emissions have increased more than six-fold, annual freshwater withdrawals have more than tripled, and the consumption of synthetic nitrogen has increased more than 30-fold.

The flipside to this ever-growing exploitation of natural resources is an intensifying pace in materials transformation as nature is turned into objects. Recent studies suggest that the dry mass of the Earth's living organisms – microbes, plants, fungi and all animals, including humans – is now less than the weight of human-made products. At the start of the twentieth century, human-created 'anthropogenic mass' was equivalent to around 3 per cent of the world's aggregate biomass, but a paper published in 2020 suggests that the weight of manmade material – such as concrete, metals and plastic – has now overtaken the world's total biological mass. Anthropogenic mass is exhibiting its own form of geometric progression, doubling roughly every 20 years, and it is projected that if present trends continue then the weight of human-made objects will be almost triple that of living organisms by 2040. Modern industrialism's linear production system – moving from raw materials to finished goods, with expanding reservoirs of waste as a byproduct – has induced a globe-spanning metabolic rift and remade the planet.

But although our particular story of capitalism largely disregards the natural world, matter matters. Mainstream economics suffers from a bad case of physics envy, aspiring to the flinty mathematical certainty of some of the hard sciences, but its scientific pretensions do not extend to taking account of the biggest physical limit on the continued viability of our economic system – the goods and services provided by nature. Indicators such as GDP measure only flows of money, not changes in natural capital stocks, but money is a mere token of wealth – a human fiction that is expected to grow at compound interest over time, and whose supply can be expanded at will. Money, like other forms of debt, is a claim on future production, but economic productivity is ultimately constrained by the planet's natural resource endowment. As boundless human desire collides with the hard limits of our finite world, and the natural asset base continues to be depleted, we are racking up an escalating ecological debt and writing cheques that cannot be cashed.

Capital punishment

Capitalism celebrates disruption, moving fast and breaking things, and the standard response from apologists for capitalism's creative destruction is that 'you need to break a few eggs to make an omelette'. But much of our apparent wealth is illusory – the omelette may in fact be more of a soufflé – because our economic system does not value natural capital and its services to humans, fails to capture those social costs dismissed as externalities, and has proven ineffective at solving collective action problems. Capitalism is predicated on wealth creation through the accumulation of capital, but natural capital – the ultimate foundation for all material prosperity and the provider of ecosystem services far more valuable than market-generated GDP – has been in freefall in recent decades. Instead, our present form of capitalism focuses on 'manufactured capital' such as machines, buildings and infrastructure, and 'human capital' in the form of knowledge, skills and education, and fixates on the quantity of human-produced goods and services as measured by GDP.

GDP is a metric of its time – valuable in the 1930s when spending flows needed to be shocked back into life by the defibrillator of government spending, in the 1940s to manage economies mobilised for war, and in the early decades of the Great Acceleration when the Western world was rebuilding – but it has transmuted from being a means to an end to becoming an end in itself. Simon Kuznets, who introduced GDP to the world in the 1930s, warned that:

> Distinctions must be kept in mind between quantity and quality of growth, between its costs and return, and between the short and the long term. Goals for more growth should specify more growth of what and for what.

As Kuznets noted, GDP – although a useful short-term policy tool – measures only the quantity of market transactions rather than the overall quality of life, does not net out the additional costs of economic expansion against the additional benefits, and fails to account for parasitic growth that depletes the underlying capital base and compromises future prosperity.

For these reasons, those challenging the orthodoxy argue that GDP is more an index of the welfare of capitalism than an index of the welfare of society. Mainstream economists justify the furious pursuit of economic growth because they consider material wealth, as measured by lifetime consumption, to be a proxy for human wellbeing. However, the simplistic equation of 'more' with 'better' is becoming increasingly tenuous as the gap between economic activity and human wellbeing widens. In the mid-1970s the American economist Richard Easterlin published a paper that asked in unusually bald language 'Does economic growth improve the human lot?' His verdict was, in broad terms, only up to a point – while there is a positive correlation between income and happiness both within and between nations, after a certain income threshold is passed then the happiness trend flattens. Easterlin concluded that 'the growth process itself engenders ever-growing wants that lead it ever onward', and what is now known as the 'hedonic treadmill' – that is, the tendency for humans to return to a baseline level of happiness, regardless of major life changes – means that people's desires tend to expand in line with increased income.

Not only does GDP merely measure aggregate income and expenditure – taking no account of wealth distribution within a society, or whether this economic activity is being underwritten by an unsustainable drawdown on nature – but 'the Easterlin paradox' suggests that growth in consumption does not necessarily result in a commensurate increase in happiness. As Thorstein Veblen recognised over a century ago, after the needs of subsistence have been met it is relative wealth rather than absolute wealth that is important to most people. The urge to climb higher on the social ladder, and to convey the altitude of our ascent with outward shows of material wealth, results in an arms race for relative affluence, which by definition always recedes before us as societal wealth increases. This form of competitive consumption is something like the never-ending race in Lewis Carroll's *Through the Looking-Glass*, in which, as the Red Queen tells Alice, 'it takes all the running you can do, to keep in the same place … [i]f you want to get somewhere else, you must run at least twice as fast as that!'.

In developed economies, the Red Queen's race of ever-rising consumption results in wants becoming needs, while at the same time the negative impacts of 'off-balance sheet' items such as pollution and a declining natural resource base can increasingly outweigh the positive impacts of 'on-balance sheet' items as measured by GDP. 'Economists' in the original sense of the word – wise and prudent household managers – would halt growth in which additional social and environmental costs exceed benefits, that subtracts from rather than adds to aggregate wealth in a society. Instead, mainstream economics assumes that growth, the very thing that got us into this predicament, will also get us out – that because later generations are projected to be significantly richer, the task of reducing emissions and repairing a broken biosphere can be deferred as it will be relatively cheaper at some future date.

But as we continue to run down the Earth's finite stock of natural resources and the ecosystem services they provide, the assumption of continuing exponential economic growth looks increasingly fragile. Future growth is likely to be compromised not only by the faltering natural systems, but also because of the increasingly arduous effort required to extract a declining quantity of natural resources from the Earth. The UN, for example, estimates that, across a number of key metals, on average three times more material now has to be gouged from the ground to obtain an equivalent quantity of ore compared to a century ago. Likewise, the 'Energy Return on Investment' – a ratio measuring the amount of energy expended to produce a given amount of net energy – for hydrocarbon products has fallen from around 100:1 in the salad days of fossil fuel extraction to approximately 5:1 today. Humans picked the low-hanging fruit, or more correctly the high-sitting energy reserves, first, and are now obliged to employ increasingly damaging and costly methods such as offshore rigs, fracking operations, and enormous oil sand projects to satisfy the accelerating demand for fossil fuels. As with most other instances of resource extraction, hydrocarbon production is another pyramid scheme seeking to withdraw ever-higher returns from a shrinking asset base.

Stories are like a virus – they compete with others, they morph and hybridise, and they can be widely transmitted by influential super-spreaders. And like some viruses in human bodies, our story of consumption-driven capitalism has triggered a condition in which certain rogue cells metastasise at the expense of the larger entity. In conventional economics, the word 'growth' usually carries connotations of improvement and progress, but unchecked growth is a pathology – the manifestation of a system out of balance. The disease of cancer has been defined as a situation in which 'certain cells of the body enhance their fitness at the expense of the organism as a whole', and today's strain of industrial capitalism has triggered a similar malady – by privileging our short-term interests, humankind is imperilling the network of vital Earth systems that some call Gaia. Like the biosphere in which it is embedded, modern human society adapted to a steady climate, but it is cannibalising the superorganism that is our stable, beneficent planet. Rather than defining economic success as the quantum of resources burned through in a given period, we must instead embrace a system as parsimonious and self-sustaining as nature itself.

27

EIGHT BILLION ASTRONAUTS

A Spaceman Economy for Spaceship Earth

It all depends

The words human, humus and humility all derive from the same Latin root, meaning 'from the Earth'. We are Earthlings, beings of the Earth, and we spring forth out of the rocks and plants and animals and air that sustain the entire living world. Each of us is a complex adaptive system, a collation of 30 trillion cells constantly working towards a stable physical state, nestled within a far larger system which is also infinitely intricate and geared such that it tends towards an overall equilibrium. Influenced by the stories told by economics and Newtonian science, we think of ourselves as individuals, but in reality nothing on this planet is an individual. No man or woman is an island – not only is each of us a multispecies ecosystem comprising human cells and countless colonies of symbiotic microbes, but we also only know ourselves in relation to other people and other things. The gaps are just as important as the nodes, and the gaps are not even gaps – it is what lies in between that is most important, factors like love, trust, regard, and the miracles of nature, things that are clinically labelled as 'social capital' and 'natural capital' by the profession of economics and which are not captured in any measurement of GDP.

And despite the words 'human' and 'humility' arising from the same source, modern mankind has largely lost the sense of dependence and embeddedness within the wider world. Fuelled by the four classical elements – by Fire, the eternal energy of the sun; by Air, the winds that whirl turbines; by Water, the rushing currents or heaving tides that produce hydropower; but most importantly by Earth, the distilled and compressed sunlight disinterred in the form of hydrocarbons – humankind has vaulted away from the rest of the planet. Our Earth-shaking experiment has resulted in the Anthropocene age, a period of apparent abundance for much of the world's population, but one in which the webs of life are breaking down into ever simpler structures while human-forged networks become more complex and entangled. The Cowboy Economy enabled by fossil fuels and our particular version of capitalism has fenced off and exploited the pieces of the world that are profitable, heedless of desolated natural systems and the waste left in its wake, while shifting the costs onto others. We flatter ourselves that we have ushered in a new era, but our recently dawned Anthropocene age may ultimately become more epitaph than epoch.

It took a half-millennium of cumulative discoveries, allied with the self-organising wonders of capitalism, to re-orient humankind's idea of its place in the world. The *Apollo 8* mission was the first manned spacecraft to orbit the Moon, and on that journey the astronaut Bill Anders became the first human to see Earth rising above the Moon's horizon. On Christmas Eve 1968 he took what would later become known as the 'Earthrise' photograph – a tiny ball of blue adorned in swirling white clouds, peeking above the barren lunar landscape, spotlit against the black vacuum of outer space. The Earthrise picture became emblematic, considered by many to be the most influential environmental photo ever taken. In a year of unrest and troubles – deepening disillusion in America about the Vietnam War, the assassinations of Robert Kennedy and Martin Luther King, uprisings in Eastern Europe against the Soviet overlords, terrorism in Western Europe, Chairman Mao's re-education camps for urban elites, and student riots across the world – this picture, captioned 'Dawn' on the cover of *Time* magazine's final edition for 1968, provided both optimism and a radically new perspective. As Anders commented upon his return home, 'We came all this way to explore the Moon, and the most important thing is that we discovered the Earth'.

The following year, in July 1969, man took his first steps on the Moon, our most audacious conquest so far in humankind's long adventure in opening up new frontiers. But in many ways, the *Apollo 8* journey seven months prior was the more consequential event in the Space Race between the duelling empires of capitalism and communism. Rather than gazing out at the stars, the Earthrise picture allowed us for the first time to see what many of us knew in our bones – the unity of everything, the deep networks of mutuality co-evolved over countless aeons, Earth as a finite and interdependent entity. On the night of Christmas Eve, celebrated as a time of renewal and hope across the Western world, the crew of the *Apollo 8* sent a message back to the Earthlings almost 400,000 kilometres away. In the most listened to Bible lesson ever, around one billion people heard the three astronauts read from the Book of Genesis. 'In the beginning God created the heaven and the Earth', Bill Anders intoned, 'And the Earth was without form, and void'. Other verses were recited and another crew member then closed the reading: 'And God called the dry land Earth; and the gathering together of the waters called He Seas: and God saw that it was good'.

Despite this sermon from space, the Scientific Revolution had largely displaced God from the story of Creation, with the theories of Copernicus and Darwin and others overturning the tale that humankind was divinely decreed to rule a planet around which the rest of the cosmos turns. The decentring of humanity has continued with more recent discoveries, but although science teaches that we are but one thread in the fabric of life, in modern economics Man is still the paragon of animals. Within our economic system, only those things produced by humankind are assigned any formal value in national accounts, and economic storytellers propagate the fairytale that the natural world can be relegated to the sidelines – a mere resource rather than a life source. The failure to register the destruction of natural capital enables our variant of capitalism to methodically eat the Earth and leaves an impoverished planet to future generations.

The promise of nature's continual replenishment is in danger of being broken, as the 'grand oasis' first viewed by astronauts orbiting the Moon is overconsumed in a cycle of eat, deplete, and repeat. Rather than acting like those spacemen in their capsule – constrained by finite supplies requiring careful stewardship and conservation – we have instead embraced the ethos of the cowboy, rolling onward to the next frontier of exploitation under the banner of capitalism's Manifest Destiny. Mainstream economics has abetted this smash-and-grab operation by telling a particular story – one that treats the natural world as little more than a raw input and a waste dump, attributes no significant value to natural capital or its life-giving benefits, and which focuses on the market-ordained price of goods and services consumed in a given period. Now, almost 500 years after the theories of Copernicus, we need another Copernican Revolution – this time in economics – that moves on from the egocentric idea that everything revolves around us.

Counter culture

One definition of economics is the study of choice under conditions of scarcity – a comparison of the relative costs and benefits arising from a particular course of action, an evaluation of any resulting trade-offs, and an allocation of resources based on this assessment. Freely operating markets – comprising highly motivated agents, and marshalling crowdsourced wisdom to efficiently discover, collate and transmit information – can be extremely effective in allocating resources, but only those that are counted. If scarcity is not priced – if, for example, natural capital and the services it provides are in effect valued at zero by the market – then the balancing act that is allocative efficiency topples, and market failure can be the result. Because our present economic system does not properly value natural capital and ecosystem services, and instead focuses on manufactured and human capital, there is an economic incentive to overharvest the bounty of the natural world, to overpollute ecosystems, and to underinvest in natural assets.

Some have argued that pricing nature – reducing it to the common denominator of money – is a wildly imprecise exercise, and that any attempt to do so could result in the natural world becoming even more of a pawn and plaything of market forces. But a proper accounting of the natural world would not only make the unavoidable trade-offs between growth in material wealth and the loss of natural wealth far more apparent, but could actually insulate parts of the non-human world from the predations of the market. In the 1990s, for example, New York City was confronted with a choice to either build a water filtration system for a total outlay in the order of $10 billion, or instead protect the upstate watersheds that fed naturally purified water into reservoirs. A cost-benefit study determined that safeguarding the watersheds would provide similar filtration services for a far lower capital outlay, and rather than undertaking a huge infrastructure project a program to preserve the catchment area was instead enacted. As also demonstrated in the Yangtze basin, where ongoing flood mitigation services from forests yielded far more long-term economic value than a one-off conversion of trees to lumber, putting nature on the balance sheet can provide economic incentives to maintain or enhance a given stock of natural capital.

And as natural assets become more depleted, the need to price nature becomes more urgent. Adam Smith observed that in a market economy:

> The things which have the greatest value in use have frequently little or no value in exchange; and ... those which have the greatest value in exchange have frequently little or no value in use. Nothing is more useful than water; but ... scarce any thing can be had in exchange for it. A diamond, on the contrary, has scarce any value in use; but a very great quantity of other goods may frequently be had in exchange for it.

This 'paradox of value' – the difference between the 'use value' and 'exchange value' of a good or service, between its utility to humans and the market price – is essentially a function of scarcity. Although the use value of water is infinite because it is absolutely vital to our survival, its exchange value is low because it is usually readily available. As natural resources become scarce, the case for pricing them becomes increasingly acute – especially because compromised ecosystems are liable to abrupt failure, there is generally no substitute for degraded systems, and it is usually far cheaper to prevent environmental destruction rather than attempt to remedy it.

The focus on prices as determined in market transactions means that unpriced natural capital is consumed profligately and without regard to its true value. If, instead, natural capital was to be treated in national accounts in the same way that manufactured capital is recorded on company books – with any depletion in the asset base debited as a cost against income – then a better picture of sustainable scale would be given. In the jargon of accounting, in addition to backward-looking income statements in the form of GDP we also need to have forward-looking balance sheets that measure stocks of capital and their ability to provide goods and services in the future. Accounting for the natural world in this way would not only give a more accurate representation of real economic performance – as the absence of a depreciation charge for impairments to natural capital means that historic GDP growth rates have been overstated – but would also provide incentives to preserve the natural world.

Unhinged

Many economists argue, however, that their assumptions are becoming reality – that the human construct known as the economy is becoming less dependent on the bounty of the natural world. They contend that as economies and technologies mature they will reach a stage of 'decoupling', in which the link between economic growth and raw material consumption is broken. Decoupling can be either relative – that is, while there is still a positive correlation between economic growth and material use, the rate of growth in inputs is less than the growth in GDP – or absolute, in which economic growth continues while the quantity of throughput stabilises or falls. But although a number of advanced economies have achieved relative decoupling in recent decades, this is largely due to the outsourcing of heavy industry to emerging economies and the increasing strength of the service sector as a component of GDP. Worldwide, however, the rate of material efficiency use – broadly speaking, the proportion of primary resources converted into marketable products – has in fact decreased over the last three decades as much of the global manufacturing base has shifted to less input-efficient economies.

Combined with the consumption effects seen under the Jevons

paradox – in which greater efficiency in materials use sparks a 'rebound effect' due to lower prices, leading to increased consumption of the underlying input – humankind is in fact doubling down, rather than slowing down, on the exploitation of natural resources. The UN Environment Programme notes that a true decoupling of escalating material use from economic growth is 'essential for the prosperity of human society and a healthy natural environment' – but it adds, however, that any such decoupling would require huge changes to how goods are produced and consumed, how technologies are used, and also to the financial system. In a phenomenon known as 'path dependence' – in which past events and decisions influence later outcomes – the bulk of the productive capacity of the modern industrial economy has been built around access to carbon-based energy, and a transition to a decarbonised economy will be a gargantuan undertaking.

The scientist Vaclav Smil notes that Project Apollo, the US space program which achieved its ultimate goal of a Moon landing in 1969, cost just over $200 billion in today's money – averaged out over the 12 years of its existence, this comprised around 0.2 per cent of total American expenditure each year. For all its mythic power, the Apollo program was a relatively contained exercise – costing a sliver of national income and directly affecting only a small number of people – but transitioning away from our fossil fuel dependency will be a far more involved and expensive task. At present, our fossil fuelled civilisation is absolutely reliant on hydrocarbons – fossil fuels still account for well over 80 per cent of all global primary energy consumption, and although wind and solar power have recorded strong growth rates over the last decade, they currently only produce a little over 3 per cent of the world's energy. The McKinsey Global Institute has conservatively estimated that the costs of global decarbonisation over the three decades from 2021 to 2050 is likely to be in the order of $275 trillion – around $9 trillion each year, or almost 10 per cent of the world's total annual expenditure.

The challenge of decarbonisation is therefore huge, but even if a transition to clean energy can be achieved in coming decades, this will not necessarily halt the destruction of other natural systems. Climate change is a colossal global problem, and the one that garners the most public attention – a recent study, for example, determined that media coverage of the effects of global warming was around eight times higher than biodiversity loss. But climate change is just one symptom of a broader malady caused by the overextraction of natural resources and the overpollution of ecosystems. Electrification using renewable energy will also require significant resources in the form of raw materials and any embedded carbon used in the production process, and merely consuming differently – rather than consuming less – will not be enough. To switch the world's billion or so internal combustion vehicles to electric, for example, is projected to require huge quantities of metals such as cobalt, lithium and nickel, some of which may need to be damagingly dredged from seabed floors if projected demand for these elements is to be satisfied. The road to 'clean' technologies is often a dirty one – relatively low carbon, but high in metals and other materials – which, in turn, necessitates even greater resource extraction and requires the opening up of new areas of exploitation.

Path dependence occurs not only in the physical realm but also in the discipline of economics. The most pervasive story of our time, the idea of increasing material progress achieved through the magic of the market, is impossible in a finite world – in the same way that we cannot borrow our way out of debt, we cannot continue to unsustainably exploit the Earth in a quest for ever-greater material riches. 'Sustainable growth' is a contradiction in terms – up there with other venerable financial oxymorons such as 'toxic assets' and 'sub-prime' – but mainstream economics is still wedded to a growth-driven model. Deluded by the idea of limitless abundance, the modern industrial world is acting like an aristocratic household in decline – selling off the family silver to support an unsustainable lifestyle, outsourcing unpleasant tasks, and leaving it to others to clean up the mess. Our material riches have been won at a huge and unrecorded cost to the natural world, but Mother Nature is now presenting the bill.

28

GREENPRINT

A natural capitalism to curb parasitic growth

Eco-economics

In addition to failing to properly value the natural world, Adam Smith's other great error may have been in overestimating human rationality. By all accounts, Smith was an odd individual – seemingly undisturbed by the gusts of emotion that affect most of us, never having any known romantic dalliances, while one of his contemporaries noted that 'He knew nothing of characters'. The classic absent-minded professor, Smith was like an anthropologist from another planet, equipped with the objectivity of one observing from the edges, but the Spock-like Scot projected too much good sense and prudence on to his fellow humans. He observed that:

> The qualities most useful to ourselves are ... superior reason and understanding, by which we are capable of discerning the remote consequences of all our actions ... and ... self-command, by which we are enabled to abstain from present pleasure or to endure present pain, in order to obtain a greater pleasure or to avoid a greater pain in some future time.

Smith thought that one of the defining markers of humans was the ability to take the long view, the deferral of near-term gratification in return for rewards in the future, but he failed to take into account the tremendous power of stories to subvert reason.

Our particular economic story tells us that self-interest leads to society-wide benefits, that the price mechanism permits the efficient allocation of resources, and therefore that freely operating markets will produce optimal results for the humans they are meant to serve. However, despite these assurances, markets are not always omniscient and infallible – they allow failings such as unpriced externalities, foster an economic accounting system that permits a Ponzi scheme on the natural world, and are subject to feedback effects in the financial realm that can destabilise wider society. And while complex biological systems rely on enforcement mechanisms to suppress selfish behaviour by their constituent units, our current form of capitalism does the exact opposite – indiscriminately celebrating and licensing self-interest, and permitting parasitic gains in which certain economic actors gain at the expense of the whole.

For a new form of capitalism to prosper it must be, like all reasonably stable complex systems, largely self-correcting. The challenge for humanity is to reach the global homeostasis seen in the natural world, a point of equilibrium in which returns extracted today do not compromise returns available in the future. The simplest way to build self-correction into the human invention that is the market is to re-enfranchise national govern-ments so that, rather than being mere first responders in times of economic crises, they instead reclaim one of their essential functions as a proactive counterbalance to market failure. Although governments are in theory tasked with setting policies to ensure the long-term wellbeing of their population, much of this responsibility has been outsourced to unelected private interests, especially fossil fuel companies that have polluted politics as well as the atmosphere. Neoliberalism has been called 'a program for destroying collective structures which may impede pure market logic', and it has been largely successful in this mission. But at its best, democratic capitalism is a symbiotic system separating political power from wealth – and accordingly markets should be subservient to societal needs, not the other way around, and governments should be re-empowered to set policies that promote a closer alignment between individual and collective welfare.

A multidimensional solution requires a multidimensional approach, but the most significant, and in some ways the most straightforward, initiative from governments would be the taxing of hydrocarbons to reflect the social costs of their use. An additional loading on the price of fossil fuels is easy to calculate and administer, would provide a more concise snapshot of the relative costs and benefits of hydrocarbon use, and is a light-touch form of regulation that allows the market to do what it does best – achieve allocational efficiency through the operation of the price mechanism. Although a carbon tax will not place a hard cap on greenhouse gas emissions, it should have the effect of directing demand and dollars to less carbon-intensive goods, while at the same time rewarding those producers and consumers transitioning to a lower-carbon future. The problem of free-riding by individual countries, which has afflicted international negotiations in the past, can be addressed by the formation of a 'climate club' which provides strong financial incentives to members in the form of tariffs or trade bans on non-complying nations.

Governments should also actively assume the role as custodians for the protection of natural capital, in the same way that unions and business owners have an active interest in ensuring that human capital and manufactured capital are properly valued. For an economy to be truly sustainable it should not extract more from natural systems than can be regenerated or substituted, nor pollute these systems more than can be safely assimilated, and by setting the right incentives governments can stimulate the redirection of capital towards solutions that restore rather than deplete natural capital. Perverse subsidies, such as those paid to fossil fuel producers or fishing fleets, should be abandoned, while subsidies and research funding that speed the transition to renewable energy and reduce the advantages of incumbency held by fossil fuel companies could be introduced. In addition to encouraging economic actors to protect rather than exploit the biosphere, governments should curb the lobbying power of corporations and other vested interests, and make these parties' efforts at policy influence more transparent. Adam Smith, despite the best efforts of some to argue otherwise, wanted competitive markets rather than unregulated markets, and was well aware of the pernicious dangers of state capture by powerful business interests.

Governments also have an essential role to play in guarding the interests of future generations, for the problems of resource overexploitation are not only international, but also intergenerational. Governments can provide 'patient capital' to effect transformative social projects that are expected to provide benefits for decades to come, and perhaps more importantly they can also ensure a fairer distribution of resources to future society members. Future generations cannot participate in market transactions or reciprocate actions made today, and so strictly 'rational' individuals seeking to optimise their pay-off have an incentive to maximise the immediate extraction of natural resources and the exploitation of ecosystems. Social experiments seeking to determine the distribution of intergenerational goods indicate that a particular resource is almost always exhausted if extraction decisions are made individually, and that this 'failure to co-operate with the future' tends to be driven by a minority who extract more than is sustainable over the long term. However, resource use tends to be sustainable when extraction decisions are democratically decided by vote – because there is an effective mechanism allowing the majority inclined towards co-operation to restrain the overconsuming minority, while also reassuring 'conditional co-operators' that their efforts will not be futile.

Earthshot

A new form of capitalism would also take lessons from the longest lived, most stable, most sustainable emergent system ever known – the natural world itself. Humans are already edging into the realm of photosynthetic organisms through the utilisation of solar power, increasingly accessing the immediate energy of the Sun rather than relying solely on fossil fuels that pollute the atmosphere and ocean. But even if renewable forms of power are used, the net throughput of materials must fall and so measures to increase the recycling of materials are required. Although some inputs cannot be recycled – energy, for example, is effectively a single-use product, and plastic can be reprocessed only a limited number of times before degrading – better efforts can be made towards approximating the completely closed system that is nature. In-built obsolescence, for example, can be combated through compulsory extended warranties, or through a leasing rather than ownership model, for certain products. When ownership of the underlying good remains with the manufacturer, and the product is rented to individuals as a service, there is a strong economic incentive to maintain and repair these assets.

As part of the polluter-pays ethos behind a carbon tax, governments should also impose rules and incentives discouraging the disposal of other waste products, thereby ensuring that ecological costs from economic activity are internalised as business costs. By putting nature on the balance sheet – that is, factoring in the environmental costs of production and consumption alongside the monetary returns from natural resources exploitation – 'bads' arising from pollution and resource depletion would be a cost against revenue from produced goods, which would provide a more honest overview of the net economic effects of production while encouraging the minimisation of waste. As part of this move to a more inclusive measure of wealth, GDP should revert to its original role – as a measure of broad macroeconomic flows, just one instrument in the economic toolkit. GDP is a proxy for the metabolism of the markets – how quickly the economic machine is running, how much throughput is expended – and gives increasingly misleading signals as ever-greater quantities of natural wealth are liquidated and converted into material wealth.

In the private sector, ESG measures should focus on the most important and easily quantifiable metric – greenhouse gas emissions – rather than amorphous social and governance yardsticks that tend to be more amenable to skilfully told tales and selective narratives. Carbon offsets should be subject to more rigorous common standards, with benefits only recognised as carbon is drawn down or substituted. 'Biological carbon sequestration' in the form of forestry or agricultural practices can be a useful bridge on the path to a decarbonised economy, and has the considerable benefit of utilising the Sun's free energy, but they are at best short-term solutions. The carbon locked away in plants or the soil remains part of the carbon cycle – exposed to reversals such as forest fires, changes in land management techniques and climate and ecosystem instability – and there is also only a finite capacity for these natural systems to absorb carbon. As with other areas, nature shows the way – coal, oil and natural gas locked in the Earth's crust remains the best form of carbon capture and storage, and in the longer term, any scheme awarding carbon credits should ideally be able to demonstrate enduring geological carbon sequestration.

Solar radiation management, currently the most popular geoengineering suggestion among techno-optimists, does nothing to address other harmful effects of carbon pollution such as increasing ocean acidification, and will require the emission of a steady stream of light-reflecting aerosols into the air to achieve the required level of dimming. Carbon dioxide removal technologies, although in theory reducing atmospheric pollution, similarly do not address the core problem of excess resource use. More pragmatically, and as the IPCC comments, they 'are unable, or not yet ready, to achieve the scale of removal that would be required to compensate for current levels of emissions, and most have undesired side effects'. These proffered 'solutions' are at present a fantasy technology, unable to be rolled out cost effectively at scale – currently they exist only as a hopeful entry on financial model spreadsheets, serving mainly as a smokescreen for businesses arguing that there is no need for external regulation to limit emissions.

For farming, forestry and other forms of land use, the path ahead lies in realising that our global crises in the natural world all tend to have carbon, that shapeshifting element, in common – the problem is essentially one of carbon imbalances, with too much carbon entering the atmosphere and oceans, too much leaving the land, and not enough animating living beings. Problems such as global heating and ocean acidification are caused by excessive carbon emissions, while compromised soil health is largely due to a loss of carbon from the ground – these consequences are two sides of the same coin, and implementing regenerative farming practices and other forms of sustainable land management will assist in decarbonising the air while recarbonising the earth. There is a debate about whether 'land-sparing' or 'land-sharing' is best – that is, adopting intensive agriculture or an ecological farming approach – but the solution is most likely a mix. Intensive farming tends to have severe negative effects on local biodiversity, but low-input regenerative agriculture methods usually require more land, and the right balance will be guided by existing land use practices and the relevant landscape.

In addition to adverse human health and animal welfare impacts, it is estimated that over half of global biodiversity loss is attributable to meat-based diets, and it follows that the consumption of meat should be significantly reduced in most developed countries. A recent study found that less than 3 per cent of the Earth's land surface area can be considered to be 'faunally intact', and eating lower on the food chain and where possible restoring ecosystems to their previous vitality is therefore essential. Healthy ecosystems are not only more resilient to climate extremes, but they also absorb and sequester greater amounts of carbon, while providing important ecosystem services to the human world. In the oceans, underwater and often overlooked, marine reserves starkly demonstrate that market-based solutions are not always the best approach, and that 'investing' in nature can in fact be a passive exercise. Unlike greenhouse gas emissions, biodiversity loss cannot be easily quantified, and often the best solution is for humans to let nature take its course and simply do nothing.

Enough

But perhaps the biggest change that can be made in the transition to a more sustainable economy lies not in the vast expanses of the planet, but in the minds of humans. We are hypersocial creatures, taking our cues from others, and research has found that the desire for emulation and social approbation – so deleterious in the pursuit of positional goods – can also instil positive behaviours. Adam Smith noted that we 'view ourselves ... with the eyes of other people', and changing social norms around consumption can drive positive feedback effects that can eventually produce a tipping point in community behaviour. Individuals can still make a difference – as Darwin observed, incremental and cumulative changes can have an enormous impact over time, and by reclaiming our role as citizens rather than mere consumers we can do our best to ensure that governments faithfully execute their role as agents for the collective.

Transitioning to a system that seeks to maximise wellbeing for a given level of sustainable consumption should be seen for what it is – a recognition of abundance rather than scarcity, and an acceptance that in developed economies we have the capacity to satisfy all citizens' absolute needs, although this will entail policies that ensure a more equitable distribution of resources and wealth. More egalitarian societies generally have stronger bonds of solidarity and greater levels of social capital, and therefore a greater willingness to tackle difficult communal challenges, while research suggests that members of unequal societies devote a greater proportion of their resources to competitive consumption on positional goods. Conspicuous consumption, another negative externality, could be moderated by a progressive consumption tax on luxury goods, and the findings of Richard Easterlin suggest that a redistribution of income will result in greater overall wellbeing for a society as increased incomes have the greatest impact when starting incomes are low.

The arc of human history is about humankind coming together – from foraging bands to the sprawling conurbations of today – into ever-expanding collectives and degrees of complexity, like nature itself. However, as Adam Smith noted, human 'sympathy' – love and concern for others – is usually bound by a tight radius, rapidly petering out in concentric circles from the bullseye that is the individual. In *The Theory of Moral Sentiments* Smith surmised that if 'the great empire of China ... was suddenly swallowed up by an earthquake' a European would express the regulation 'humane sentiments', but soon enough 'would pursue his business or his pleasure, take his repose or his diversion, with the same ease and tranquillity, as if no such accident had happened'. As Smith implied, the impartial spectator is myopic and focused on immediate kith and kin, but in our globalised world of niche specialisations and world-encompassing supply chains our flourishing also depends on the flourishing of others. Confronted with a planetary-level problem, we must widen our conception of community both in space and time – if only for the sake of self-interest.

29

EVERY MAN FOR HIMSELF?

A final story

All aboard

James Hansen alerted the wider world to the dangers of excessive fossil fuel use 35 years ago, but he has since lamented that he was not 'able to make this story clear enough for the public'. Charts, numbers, high levels of scientific confidence and empirical validation have proven to be no match against vested interests peddling alternative tales, the inertia of an economic system still overwhelmingly reliant on hydrocarbons, the complexity and interrelatedness of the problems arising from consumption-driven capitalism, and the cognitive dissonance produced by material prosperity amid collapsing ecosystems. Humans are story-making and story-consuming animals, comprehending the world through narratives, and so a final allegory is offered – an almost too perfect metaphor for our modern era, one illustrating the dangers of overweening human confidence, the folly of disregarding the natural world, and the fact that ultimately we all voyage on the same vessel.

The RMS *Titanic*, when launched in April 1912, was the largest moving object ever constructed, almost a thousand feet long and a temporary abode for 2,200 denizens. The social stratification of the passengers was reflected in the layout of the ship, with the upper classes having dominion over the upper decks; the butchers, bakers, butlers and other assorted crew occupying the mid-levels; and emigrants drawn by the siren song of the American Dream lodging in the depths of steerage. The boat was famed not only for its size, but its luxury – for those with enough money it was a floating Ritz, with a swimming pool, gymnasium, squash court and Turkish baths. For all its grandeur, however, the *Titanic*'s biggest boast was that it was unsinkable – although weighing more than 50,000 tonnes when fully laden, it was protected by apparently watertight compartments that could be sealed off with the flick of a switch.

Driven by engines burning 600 tonnes of coal every day, the *Titanic* powered west from England towards New York. On the fifth day of the journey, and only two days from port, some passengers noticed drifting ice on the horizon and alerted the crew. Despite the warnings and radio messages from other ships in the vicinity, the *Titanic* continued to steam along just shy of maximum speed – punctuality was prized by the owners of the vessel, especially for a flagship on its heavily publicised maiden voyage. Later that same day, just before midnight, a sharp-peaked pyramid of ice loomed in the darkness a quarter of a mile ahead. Engines were frantically reversed and the vessel attempted to swerve, but it was too late – the ship was travelling much too quickly and momentum carried the *Titanic* towards the iceberg, which sheared into the starboard side of the boat, holing it below the waterline. The seams of the hull buckled and separated, the allegedly impervious compartments were breached, cataracts of water just a couple of degrees above freezing point rushed into the *Titanic*, and almost immediately the ship began to sink bow-first into the sea.

The captain of the *Titanic*, Edward Smith, was initially decisive, displaying the British sangfroid and stiff upper lip so esteemed by his compatriots. He co-ordinated the muster of passengers through a megaphone, and attempted to direct women and children to the lifeboats. But after a certain point, it seems that he became immobilised by indecision, or perhaps by the realisation of the sheer hopelessness of the task at hand. Some reported that, just prior to his ship going down, Captain Smith walked around the deck muttering to his crew: 'Now it's every man for himself'. The *Titanic* was equipped with only 20 lifeboats – they were merely designed to relay people to nearby rescue vessels, and they took up deck space that could be used for the leisure of paying passengers – and this was sufficient for less than half of the ship's total complement. In any case, many lifeboats were launched half-full, as the crew – perhaps lulled into complacency by claims of the *Titanic*'s indestructibility – had not been adequately drilled in evacuation procedures.

Less than three hours after hitting the iceberg, the *Titanic* slipped into the sea, barely creating a ripple, the silence pierced for just a moment by the sound of boilers ripping from their footings and crashing headlong through the plunging vessel. There were two large steamships in the area at the time of the sinking, the SS *Californian* and the RMS *Carpathia*. Some of the crew of the *Californian*, only 10 miles away from the *Titanic*, saw flares light up in the distance, but inexplicably the boat failed to respond to these distress signals. The *Carpathia*, much further away than the *Californian*, received a radio message that the *Titanic* had struck an iceberg, and the ship's captain turned his ship around and steamed towards the stricken vessel. Threading through the treacherous ice fields, it took the *Carpathia* over three hours to finally reach the 705 survivors of the *Titanic*, with the other 1,500 passengers and crew having already perished in the cold northern sea. Despite Captain Smith's exhortations that women and children file first into the lifeboats, the proportional survival rate of men in First Class was higher than that of children in Third Class, and overall around 60 per cent of First Class passengers were rescued compared to only a quarter of those in Third Class.

Full steam ahead

The *Titanic* story is mythical in dimension, one of hubris and pathos, privilege and poverty, action and inaction, heroes and villains, mistakes and missed opportunities. It is a vivid, visceral tale distilling so many aspects of the modern world into a neat narrative whole. Climate change and other impacts arising from humankind's carbon-fired journey are far less amenable to an easily encapsulated story, but there are parallels. Like an iceberg, the dangerous bulk of which is out of sight, the monolith that is industrial capitalism is proudly crowned with gleaming abundance while the damaging downside from all that material wealth is largely hidden from view. Astounding GDP growth since the Great Acceleration is testimony to the ability of the economic machine to convert nature into merchandise, but humankind is exploiting natural systems far quicker than they can be regenerated while waste accumulates faster than can be safely absorbed. The *Titanic*, like all commercial ships, was required to have a Plimsoll line marking its maximum load limit – but no such indicator or threshold exists for the global economy, and GDP has never pretended to be a measure of the scale of sustainable resource extraction or waste pollution.

Like with the *Titanic*, frequent hazard warnings are largely ignored, rather than treated as a firm instruction to slow down or change direction. In 1992 a majority of Nobel science laureates sounded a 'Warning to Humanity', asserting that 'Human beings and the natural world are on a collision course'. Thirty years later a group of scientists issued a '"code red" on planet Earth', and noted that extreme risks such as 'simultaneous global failure of crop yields across multiple major food producing regions' were becoming more likely. But despite rising levels of alarm, the dismal science of economics has not caught up with the dismal science of climate change. In the early 1990s the pioneering climate economist William Nordhaus claimed with pinpoint precision that 87 per cent of the US economy would be 'negligibly affected by climate change', and today many of his peers remain just as sanguine. They argue that, because the sectors that contribute most to GDP tend to be indoors or in controlled environments, then extreme weather events should only have a marginal impact on economic output. Food production, for example, comprises less than 1 per cent of GDP in many developed economies – roughly one-tenth the figure for the finance industry – but this metric is based on market-determined prices, reflecting only the exchange value of food rather than its use value. Although humans cannot eat financial services, most conventional economists still insist on viewing things through the distorting lens of GDP, which values only market-determined transactions rather than underlying natural wealth.

As with the *Titanic*, our consumption-driven economic system continues to steam ahead far too quickly, shortening reaction times and making any sudden course correction difficult. Propelled by a relentless growth imperative, and with no steady hands controlling the tiller or easing the throttle, industrial capitalism has its own tremendous momentum – as does its best-known byproduct, global heating arising from excess greenhouse gas emissions. The iceberg that sank the *Titanic* is thought to have been calved in Greenland, which lies almost entirely within the Arctic Circle – an area that has warmed nearly four times faster than the rest of the world over the past 40 years due to interrelated and reinforcing factors such as rising air temperatures, the loss of light-reflecting ice, and warmer ocean currents. The IPCC believes that due to this 'Arctic amplification', the Greenland ice sheet may pass a tipping point somewhere within an average global warming range of 1.5 to 2 degrees Celsius, and once this happens a self-perpetuating dynamic will be triggered – one that may not fully take effect until a few decades after the threshold has been crossed, but which would then set in motion changes that would be 'irreversible for millennia'. Both the climate system and the global economy are emergent entities in which small movements in component parts can spark a step change in the whole, but most economic models do not factor in the potential impacts of rapid climate destabilisation or the sudden loss of other vital ecosystem services.

As with Captain Smith – who, five years before the *Titanic*'s sinking, casually observed that 'I have never been in … any predicament that threatened to end in disaster of any sort' – many today look backward and are seduced into a false sense of security. Most economists complacently assume that GDP growth seen over recent decades will continue, but much of this explosion in material wealth has been obtained by eating into natural capital, and a depleted natural asset base will provide fewer goods and services to humans in the future. By overconsuming nature's yield, long-term prosperity has been traded for short-term growth – and unprecedented levels of financial debt serves to bring forward even more consumption, further swelling the titanic overdraft on the natural world. Dwindling reserves of raw materials are becoming more expensive to extract while economic damage from adverse weather events accelerate, acting as a further drag on future growth, and economic models tend to underplay the potential for a compounding chain reaction of adverse effects as the planetary shock absorbers wear thin.

And, finally, like with the sinking of the *Titanic*, it will be the poor who suffer most in the event of a calamity. Ice core samples from Greenland and Antarctica indicate that both the rate of increase in greenhouse gas emissions and the absolute magnitude of these gases are higher than at any other time over the last 800,000 years. When analysed alongside other sources of paleoclimatic data – such as lake and ocean sediments, tree rings, and fossils – these ice archives demonstrate that the global climate is capable of large and abrupt shifts, sometimes within the span of a human lifetime, in response to changes in atmospheric composition. Climate disruption will exacerbate many of the inequalities already created by capitalism, further deepening the divide between the Global North and the Global South. Although colder parts of the world may on balance benefit from the effects of climate change – Greenland, for example, may yet fulfil Erik the Red's thousand-year-old promise of a green and pleasant land, one of history's more brazen instances of real estate puffery – for most of the planet global heating and fragmenting ecosystems will result in less food and usher in ever-expanding zones of inhabitability. Low-income nations tend to be located in tropical and subtropical regions where the adverse effects of global heating will be most pronounced, and these countries are not only far more dependent on natural capital than richer industrialised nations, but they also have fewer resources to combat the fallout from faltering natural systems.

A minute to midnight

Sigmund Freud remarked that the perfect crime thriller would be one in which the detective discovers that he is in fact the culprit, and our story is similar to that hall of mirrors scenario. Anger is justifiably directed at fossil fuel companies prosecuting campaigns of deflection and delay, governments in thrall to corporate interests, and authoritarian leaders waving through the ruination of rainforests. Alarm is rightly expressed as kaleidoscopic coral reefs fade to white, the Arctic turns green, and verdant tropical forests dull a dusty brown. Hope sometimes flares with the possibility that speculative technologies or vast revegetation schemes could one day absorb the exhaust from the modern world's carbon conflagration, and perhaps slam shut Pandora's box. But in many ways these are just diverting stories – a form of displacement that transfers attention on to other people, places and panaceas, and away from the root cause. The truth is that – despite the cavalier use of the words 'humankind', 'humanity' and 'the Anthropocene' – the problems of resource depletion, climate change and ecosystems breakdown are largely attributable to overconsumption by a relatively small cohort of super-consumers.

As a recent scientific paper bluntly concluded, 'the affluent citizens of the world are responsible for most environmental impacts and are central to any future prospect of retreating to safer environmental conditions'. Spaceship Earth, an increasingly crowded ark swinging around the sun, is listing partly because of an unbalanced distribution of passengers and possessions. The top 1 per cent of global emitters are estimated to have a carbon footprint more than 1,000 times greater than the bottom 1 per cent, while it is thought that the emissions of the richest 0.001 per cent – a mere 50,000 or so individuals worldwide, each of whom has wealth well in excess of $100 million – are so large that the individual consumption choices of this elite 'can have the same impact as nationwide policy interventions'. The enormous resource footprint of the super affluent is largely attributable to cliched billionaire baubles such as mansions, private jets and superyachts, while in contrast the emissions of the world's poor are almost entirely attributable to non-discretionary household energy use.

Fairness dictates that the world's apex consumers, the majority of whom still reside in the West, should do most of the heavy lifting in terms of curbing emissions. Not only is there an asymmetry between responsibility and repercussions – the US and the European Union, for example, together comprise approximately 10 per cent of the global population, but account for just over half of all cumulative carbon dioxide emissions since 1750 – but the affluent have much greater scope to reduce non-essential consumption, as well as the ability to adopt energy-saving measures that may be costly in the near term. In addition to these moral considerations, there is also a supremely pragmatic argument – because the problems caused by overconsumption are so tightly confined to just a small portion of global society, much could be done to right the planetary ship by curbing the consumption patterns of the global one-percenters.

But instead of embracing an all hands to the deck response, some prefer an every man for himself approach. Rather than Captain Smith stoically going down with his ship, certain billionaire runaways from a runaway climate change scenario see settling on other worlds as a potential lifeboat from the sinking ship that is planet Earth. These space cowboys are indulging in escapist fantasies in the most literal sense by fleeing our living planet and seeking sanctuary on dead planets, the most extreme example of human separation from nature. Gaia was fashioned out of chaos, an event so improbable as to be a miracle, and there is an arrogant madness in the idea of leaving a planet that still – despite everything – is life-giving and potentially abundant, and instead trying to terraform one that has never been alive. We already have a world that can provide everything we need, and the only reason we might need a Planet B is because there are cowboys seduced by promise of human ingenuity and confident that there will always be new frontiers to exploit.

Prometheus was a Titan in the Greek pantheon, but his titanic feat of gifting fire to humankind unleashed both wonders and curses. In 1776, two stories and a technology birthed industrial capitalism – and during this period of less than a quarter of a millennium, equivalent to the last minute before midnight in terms of humankind's existence on Earth, tremendous wealth has been bought by burning through carbon and other irreplaceable natural resources. But much of this wealth is quite literally fabulous – based on the fable of a limitless natural world. This is the biggest story of our time, and it is time for a new story – one that returns to some of the old stories of our embeddedness within the wider world, which recognises that everything is connected, that we are all in this together, and that our wellbeing is inextricably connected to the prosperity of the planet.

FURTHER READING

Perhaps the best source of up-to-date information regarding some of the world's most pressing problems is the *Our World in Data* website (ourworldindata.org). Guided by a research team at Oxford University, *Our World in Data* draws on the work of a global community of academics and distils this research into highly accessible charts, maps and explanatory narratives.

For more detailed information on human-induced climate change, the UN-sponsored Intergovernmental Panel on Climate Change produces assessment reports reviewing the latest climate science. The IPCC's Sixth Assessment Report (ipcc.ch/assessment-report/ar6/), released in three instalments over 2021 and 2022, totals many thousands of pages, but key findings can be found in the more user-friendly 'Summary for Policymakers' sections.

Paul Strathern's *Dr Strangelove's Game: A Brief History of Economic Genius* (Penguin, 2001) provides an entertaining overview of key figures in the development of modern economics, and *A History of Economic Thought* (Penguin, first published in 1967) by William J Barber traces the evolution of economic theory from Adam Smith through to John Maynard Keynes.

Many of the issues addressed in Part 2, 'Air', are covered in detail in *The*

Climate Book (Penguin / Allen Lane, 2022), created by Greta Thunberg and comprising contributions from over 100 experts on the climate and related global crises.

The Ocean of Life (Penguin, 2012) by marine scientist Callum Roberts is perhaps the best overall guide to humankind's relationship with the sea, from prehistory through to the present, and explains how the state of the world's aquatic environments is intimately interrelated with other human-caused impacts on the natural world.

Three books – *Dirt: The Erosion of Civilizations* (University of California Press, 2007) by David Montgomery, *Call of the Reed Warbler: A New Agriculture, A New Earth* (University of Queensland Press, 2017) by Charles Massy, and *Entangled Life: How Fungi Make Our Worlds, Change Our Minds & Shape Our Futures* (Random House, 2020) by Merlin Sheldrake – together give an excellent overview of the role of soil health on agriculture and wider society.

Drawdown (Penguin, 2017), edited by Paul Hawken, provides a comprehensive summary of potential decarbonisation solutions, and is regularly supplemented by additional information on the website drawdown.org/.

NOTES

Monetary values

All monetary values are given in United States dollars, unless otherwise noted.

References

Writers in an earlier age had a predilection for the prolix, and, accordingly, in the notes that follow:

- '*The Theory of Moral Sentiments*' refers to *The Theory of Moral Sentiments; or, An Essay Towards an Analysis of the Principles by which Men Naturally Judge Concerning the Conduct and Character, First of their Neighbours, and afterwards of Themselves* (first published in 1759);

- '*The Wealth of Nations*' refers to *An Inquiry into the Nature and Causes of the Wealth of Nations* (first published in 1776);

- '*The Communist Manifesto*' refers to *Manifest der kommunistischen Partei* (first published in German in 1848);

- '*On the Origin of Species*' refers to *On the Origin of Species by Means of Natural Selection, or the Preservation of Favoured Races in the Struggle for Life* (first published in 1859); and

- '*The Descent of Man*' refers to *The Descent of Man and Selection in Relation to Sex* (first published in 1871).

Additionally:

- 'FAO' refers to the Food and Agriculture Organization of the United Nations;

- 'IEA' refers to the International Energy Agency;

- 'IPCC AR6' refers to the IPCC's Sixth Assessment Report, with the three separate Working Groups abbreviated as WGI, WGII and WGIII; and

- '*OWID*' refers to the *Our World in Data* website.

PREFACE

Page x   *has ruled over us rather by hereditary right* ... Keynes, 'The End of Laissez-Faire' (originally published in 1926), *Essays in Persuasion* (1931).

Page xiv   *the ideas of the ruling class* ... Marx, *The German Ideology* (written in 1846, first published in 1932).

Page xv   *scientists issuing increasingly urgent warnings about the intensifying climate crisis* ... See, eg, Ripple et al., 'World Scientists' Warning of a Climate Emergency 2022' (2022), *BioScience*, Volume 72, Issue 12.

CHAPTER 1: THE BIRTH OF EGO-NOMICS

Page 4   *universal opulence which extends* ... Smith, *The Wealth of Nations* (1776), Book I, Chapter I.

Page 4   *propensity to truck, barter, and exchange* ... Smith, *The Wealth of Nations*, Book I, Chapter II.

Page 4   *nobody ever saw a dog* ... Smith, *The Wealth of Nations*, Book I, Chapter II.

Page 4   *It is not from the benevolence* ... Smith, *The Wealth of Nations*, Book I, Chapter II.

Page 4   *encourages every man to* ... Smith, *The Wealth of Nations*, Book I, Chapter II.

Page 4   *led by an invisible hand* ... Smith, *The Wealth of Nations*, Book IV, Chapter II.

Page 6   *almost two-thirds of all economic output is generated by the country's private sector* ... See, eg, Cunningham, 'What is the future of China's private sector?', Harvard Kennedy School (2022, https://www.hks.harvard.edu/faculty-research/policy-topics/international-relations-security/what-future-chinas-private-sector), who notes that in China '[p]rivate firms contribute approximately 60% of China's GDP, 70% of its innovative capacity, 80% of urban employment and 90% of new jobs'.

Page 7   *People of the same trade* ... Smith, *The Wealth of Nations*, Book I, Chapter X.

Page 7   *who have generally an interest* ... Smith, *The Wealth of Nations*, Book I, Chapter XI.

Page 8   *sparked by the economist Thomas Robert Malthus's* ... Malthus's book was first published anonymously in 1798, and then updated in subsequent editions over the next three decades.

Page 8   *during his lifetime, more commercially successful book* ... See, eg, Buchan, *Adam Smith and the Pursuit of Perfect Liberty* (2006), Chapter 3.

Page 8   *How selfish soever man* ... Smith, *The Theory of Moral Sentiments* (1759), Part I, Section I, Chapter I.

Page 9   *Smith likening individual conscience to an 'impartial spectator'* ... See, eg, Smith, *The Theory of Moral Sentiments*, Part I, Section I, Chapter V.

Page 9   *As some have noted, there is an inherent contradiction* ... See, eg, Bell, *The Cultural Contradictions of Capitalism* (1976), who argues that there is a tension between stories told in the consumerist sphere that encourage instant gratification and stories told in the productive sphere that encourage hard work and deferred gratification.

Page 10   *Allowing every man to* ... Smith, *The Wealth of Nations*, Book IV, Chapter IX.

CHAPTER 2: REVOLUTIONARY ROADS

Page 12   *wealth inequality widening as property ownership narrowed* ... As Adam Smith would later note in *The Wealth of Nations*, 'Wherever there is great property there is great inequality' (Book V, Chapter I).

Page 12   *possibly a Sumerian beer baron* ... The name 'Kushim' – which may refer to either an individual, an officeholder, or an institution – was appended to a number of clay tablets from the Uruk period between 5,500 and 5,000 years ago (see, eg, Krulwich, 'Who's the first person in history whose name we know?', *National Geographic*, 19 August 2015).

Page 13   *farmland occupies around half the planet's habitable area* ... Ritchie and Roser, 'Land use', *OWID* (https://ourworldindata.org/land-use). See also Ellis et al., 'Anthropogenic transformation of the biomes, 1700 to 2000', *Global Ecology and Biogeography* (2010), Volume 19, Number 5, who estimate that 55 per cent of ice-free land has been converted to agricultural or urban purposes.

Page 13   *humans and their subject animals comprising* ... Bar-On et al., 'The biomass distribution on Earth', *Proceedings of the National Academy of Sciences* (2018), Volume 115, Number 25. The authors conclude that livestock accounts for 62 per cent of global mammal biomass, humans 34 per cent, and wild mammals only 4 per cent.

Page 14   *the power to conquer and subdue her* ... Bacon, 'Description of the intellectual globe', in Robertson (ed.), *The Philosophical Works of Francis Bacon* (1905).

Page 14   *The Scientific Revolution was an almost entirely European phenomenon* ... Although prior to Copernicus's book imperial China was arguably the global leader in terms of technological advances – boasting inventions such as gunpowder, the compass and the printing press – the monolithic Chinese state then largely turned inward, electing to trade stability for innovation.

Page 14   *the grand secret of the whole Machine* ... Arbuthnot, *An Essay on the Usefulness of Mathematical Learning* (1745).

Page 14   *His* Principia *became the new bible for the Age of Enlightenment* ... Newton's *Philosophiae Naturalis Principia Mathematica* ('The Mathematical Principles of Natural Philosophy') was published in London in 1687. In expounding his Laws of Motion and Law of Universal Gravitation, Newton used a form of calculus that focused on infinitesimally small quantities.

Page 15   *innovations such as the selective breeding of higher-yielding plants* ... Other developments boosting agricultural productivity included land drainage and reclamation, improved transportation infrastructure such as roads and canals, and the introduction of crop rotation to increase productivity and soil fertility.

Page 15   *progressively fewer farmhands were required* ... See, eg, Bernstein, *The Birth of Plenty: How the Prosperity of the Modern World Was Created* (2004), who notes that in 1776 just under half of the British workforce was engaged in agriculture, compared to around 30 per cent by 1850 (Figure 7-1).

Page 15   *resulting in the centralisation of land ownership into relatively few hands* ... The number of individual landowners in Britain is estimated to have fallen from around 250,000 at the time *The Wealth of Nations* was first published to just over 30,000 only 30 years later, with the politically influential generally helping themselves to the best opportunities (see, eg, Lasica, 'This land is your land', *Idler*, 16 February 2023).

Page 15   *civil government, so far as it is instituted* ... Smith, *The Wealth of Nations*, Book V, Chapter I.

Page 16   *through other means such as tariffs* ... The British 'Corn Laws' promulgated between 1815 and 1846, for example, imposed tariffs on grain imports, which had the effect of protecting the monopoly profits of landowners while increasing scarcity – and therefore costs – to consumers.

Page 16 *obliged to become tradeable commodities themselves* ... As the contemporary modern philosopher Michael Sandel notes, 'The more things money can buy, the harder it is to be poor'. See video from *The Guardian* website (7 January 2015, https://www.theguardian.com/commentisfree/video/2015/jan/07/michael-sandel-more-things-money-can-buy-harder-to-be-poor-video).

Page 16 *ten persons ... could make among them* ... Smith, *The Wealth of Nations*, Book I, Chapter I.

Page 17 *natural effort of every individual to better his own condition* ... Smith, *The Wealth of Nations*, Book IV, Chapter V.

Page 18 *obvious and simple system* ... Smith, *The Wealth of Nations*, Book IV, Chapter IX.

CHAPTER 3: *DAS JUGGERNAUT*

Page 19 *during its rule of scarce one hundred years* ... Engels & Marx, *The Communist Manifesto* (1848), Part I.

Page 19 *accomplished wonders far surpassing* ... Engels & Marx, *The Communist Manifesto*, Part I.

Page 19 *capital comes dripping from head to toe* ... Marx, *Capital* (1867), Volume 1, Chapter 31.

Page 20 *I don't suppose anyone has ever written* ... quoted in Mehring, *Karl Marx: The Story of His Life* (1918), Chapter 9. Marx also occasionally indulged in stock market speculation, commenting in a letter to his uncle in 1864 that 'it's worthwhile running some risk in order to relieve the enemy of his money'.

Page 20 *A sort of black smoke* ... Tocqueville, *Journeys to England and Ireland* (1835).

Page 20 *the highest and most unconcealed* ... Engels, *The Condition of the Working Class in England* (1845), Preface.

Page 21 *lay bare the economic law* ... Marx, *Capital*, Volume 1, Preface.

Page 21 *must nestle everywhere* ... Engels & Marx, *The Communist Manifesto*, Part I.

Page 21 *reduction to a machine* ... Marx, *Economic and Philosophic Manuscripts of 1844*.

Page 21 *by the very mechanism of the process* ... Marx, *Capital*, Volume 1, Chapter 32.

Page 21 *the Juggernaut of capital* ... Marx, *Capital*, Volume 1, Chapter 25.

Page 21 *agitators like Marx provoked a type of immune response in the body politic* ... For example, the various 'Factory Acts' introduced by British Parliament from the early nineteenth century through to the mid-nineteenth century imposed steadily higher employment standards, beginning with early legislation regulating hours of work for children and later women, and culminating in the 'Ten Hour Act' that fixed a maximum daily shift for millworkers.

Page 22 *The mills that enriched the Engels family* ... The cotton industry had been transformed by the mechanisation of the cleaning and processing of raw cotton, but the harvest of the original fibre remained labour-intensive. Around three-quarters of raw cotton imported by British mills in the mid-nineteenth century came from American plantations.

Page 22 *need of a constantly expanding* ... Engels & Marx, *The Communist Manifesto*, Part I.

Page 23 *intercourse in every direction* ... Engels & Marx, *The Communist Manifesto*, Part I.

Page 23   *All old-established national industries* ... Engels & Marx, *The Communist Manifesto*, Part I.

Page 23   *callous 'cash payment'* ... Engels & Marx, *The Communist Manifesto*, Part I.

Page 23   *deprived the whole world* ... Marx, *On the Jewish Question* (1843).

Page 23   *Philosophers have previously* ... Marx, *Eleven Theses on Feuerbach* (1845).

Page 24   *complicated hocus-pocus ... detective story* ... Keynes quoted in Straight, *After Long Silence* (1983).

Page 25   *We are faced at every turn* ... Keynes, 'Francis Ysidro Edgeworth, 1845–1926', *The Economic Journal*, March 1926.

Page 25   *seems to imagine that* ... Smith, *The Theory of Moral Sentiments*, Part VI, Section II, Chapter II.

Page 26   *The whole magic of a well-ordered society is that each man works for others* ... Mirabeau, *Philosophie rurale* (1763).

Page 26   *the important social decisions* ... Galbraith, 'The affluent society after ten years', *The Atlantic* (May 1969).

Page 27   *It is better that a man* ... Keynes, *The General Theory of Employment, Interest and Money* (1936), Chapter 24.

Page 27   *creates a world after its own image* ... Engels & Marx, *The Communist Manifesto*, Part I.

Page 27   *perennial gale of creative destruction* ... Schumpeter, *Capitalism, Socialism and Democracy* (1942), Chapter 7.

CHAPTER 4: THE RECKONING

Page 28   *the proportion of the global population living in extreme poverty* ... The World Bank estimates that extreme poverty fell from 37 per cent in 1990 to just under 10 per cent (656 million people) in 2018 (see Serajuddin and Yoshida, 'What does it mean to "eradicate extreme poverty" and "halve national poverty" by 2030?', World Bank, 30 June 2016; for more recent data, see 2018 figures at https://www.worldbank.org/en/understanding-poverty).

Page 28   *broadly defined as a daily income of around $2 or less* ... In late 2022, the World Bank set the 'extreme poverty' line at $2.15 per person per day, replacing the former poverty threshold of $1.90 per person per day (see 'Fact sheet: an adjustment to global poverty lines', World Bank, 14 September 2022).

Page 28   *Cross-border trade comprises more than half* ... The World Bank estimates that international trade as a proportion of global output was 57 per cent in 2021, compared to 25 per cent in 1970 (see https://data.worldbank.org/indicator/NE.TRD.GNFS.ZS).

Page 29   *It is hardly possible* ... Mill, *The Principles of Political Economy: With Some of Their Applications to Social Philosophy* (1848), Book V, Ch XVII.

Page 29   *The bold claim that trade not only promotes prosocial behaviour* ... A more modern variation of the idea that trade ties should encourage peace rather than belligerence was advanced by the journalist Thomas Friedman in the mid-1990s, when he proposed the 'Golden Arches theory' – the observation that 'no two countries that both have a McDonald's have ever fought a war against each other' (see Friedman, 'Foreign Affairs Big Mac I', *The New York Times*, 8 December 1996). Sadly, the Golden Arches theory has been falsified by more recent events including the Russian invasion of Ukraine.

Page 29 *two nations that negotiate between themselves become reciprocally dependent…* Montesquieu, *The Spirit of Laws* (1748), Book XX.

Page 29 *The inhabitant of London …* Keynes, *The Economic Consequences of the Peace* (1919), Chapter II.

Page 29 *a thin and precarious crust …* Keynes, 'My early beliefs', *Two Memoirs* (1949).

Page 30 *the 'Carthaginian peace' of punitive reparations …* In June 1919 Keynes resigned as economic adviser to the British delegation at the Paris Peace Conference, criticising the war guilt clause imposed on Germany as 'the shifting by the victors of their unbearable financial burdens on to the shoulders of the defeated'. In the bestselling *The Economic Consequences of the Peace*, published at the end of 1919, Keynes criticised the Conference terms as short-sighted and potentially destabilising, predicting that:

> vengeance … will not limp. Nothing can then delay for very long that final civil war between the forces of reaction and the despairing convulsions of revolution, before which the horrors of the late German war will fade into nothing, and which will destroy, whoever is victor, the civilization and the progress of our generation.

Page 30 *traced an almost vertical ascent …* The Dow Jones Industrial Average, an index of 30 prominent US-listed companies, more than quadrupled from mid-1924 until its peak in August 1929.

Page 30 *like a weather-vane …* See Chancellor, *Devil Take the Hindmost* (2000), p. 200.

Page 31 *suckers' rallies …* A 'suckers' rally' occurs when temporarily increasing share prices encourage investors to re-enter an overall downward-trending market.

Page 31 *some twenty-four thousand families …* Heilbroner, *The Worldly Philosophers: the Great Economic Thinkers* (1969), p. 242.

Page 32 *in the long run we are all dead …* Keynes, *A Tract on Monetary Reform* (1923).

Page 33 *Modern capitalism is absolutely irreligious …* Keynes, 'A short view of Russia', *Essays in Persuasion* (1925).

Page 33 *deliver the goods …* Keynes, 'National Self-Sufficiency', *Yale Review* (June 1933), Volume 22, Number 4. Keynes noted that:

> The decadent international but individualistic capitalism in the hands of which we found ourselves after the war is not a success. It is not intelligent. It is not beautiful. It is not just. It is not virtuous. And it doesn't deliver the goods.

Page 34 *Euclidean geometers in a non-Euclidean world …* Keynes, *The General Theory of Employment, Interest and Money*, Chapter 2.

Page 34 *largely revolutionise … the way the world thinks about economic problems …* Letter from Keynes to George Bernard Shaw, 1 January 1935.

Page 34 *asserted that just as in hard times a household should exercise strict financial discipline …* Adam Smith made a similar error, reasoning in *The Wealth of Nations* that 'What is prudence in the conduct of every private family, can scarce be folly in that of a great kingdom' (Book IV, Chapter II).

Page 35 *an impulse, a jolt, an acceleration …* Keynes, *Collected Works*, Volume 19 ('Activities 1922–29).

Page 35 *it is surprising that his ideas took so long to be accepted by policymakers …* Note, however, that some countries had already taken the first steps towards a form of managed capitalism prior to the publication of *The General Theory*. In the US, for example, the *National Industrial Recovery Act* of 1933 granted federal authorities the power to fix prices and wages, establish production quotas, and restrain corporate alliances deemed to be uncompetitive.

Page 36   *the tax burden on the developed world's richest citizens often exceeding* ... In 1944, for example, the US taxed its richest citizens at a marginal rate of 94 per cent and inheritance taxes averaged 40 per cent during this period (see Hopkin, 'Thirty glorious years', *Aeon*, 2 October 2020, https://aeon.co/essays/postwar-prosperity-depended-on-a-truce-between-capitalism-and-democracy). Adam Smith was an early supporter of progressive taxes, remarking in *The Wealth of Nations* that 'it is not very unreasonable that the rich should contribute to the public expense, not only in proportion to their revenue, but something more than in that proportion' (Book V, Chapter I).

Page 36   *reluctantly conceding that 'we are all Keynesians now'* ... Milton Friedman, quoted in 'We are all Keynesians now', *Time*, 31 December 1965.

Page 37   *Practical men, who believe themselves* ... Keynes, *The General Theory of Employment, Interest and Money*, Chapter 24.

Page 37   *served to entrench the idea that increased spending was the go-to solution* ... In addition to recommending 'a somewhat comprehensive socialisation of investment' at the government level, Keynes also encouraged retail consumer spending. In a 1931 BBC radio broadcast, for example, he urged: 'O patriotic housewives, sally out tomorrow early into the streets and go to the wonderful sales which are everywhere advertised' (Keynes, 'The Problem of Unemployment II', *The Listener*, 14 January 1931).

CHAPTER 5: THE SORCERER'S APPRENTICE

Page 38   *out of the tunnel of economic necessity* ... Keynes, 'Economic possibilities for our grandchildren' (originally published in 1930), *Essays in Persuasion*.

Page 38   *wisely managed ... it can probably* ... Keynes, 'The end of laissez-faire', *Essays in Persuasion*.

Page 38   *a means to the enjoyment* ... Keynes, 'Economic possibilities for our grandchildren', *Essays in Persuasion*.

Page 38   *strenuous purposeful money-makers* ... Keynes, 'Economic possibilities for our grandchildren', *Essays in Persuasion*.

Page 39   *to live wisely and agreeably and well* ... Keynes, 'Economic possibilities for our grandchildren', *Essays in Persuasion*.

Page 39   *as humble, competent people* ... Keynes, 'Economic possibilities for our grandchildren', *Essays in Persuasion*.

Page 39   *when the accumulation of wealth is no longer* ... Keynes, 'Economic possibilities for our grandchildren', *Essays in Persuasion*.

Page 39   *Through the whole of his life* ... Smith, *The Theory of Moral Sentiments*, Part IV, Chapter I.

Page 39   *wealth and greatness are mere trinkets* ... Smith, *The Theory of Moral Sentiments*, Part IV, Chapter I.

Page 40   *works with all its force against* ... Weber, *The Protestant Ethic and the 'Spirit' of Capitalism* (1905).

Page 40   *Modern bourgeois society* ... Engels & Marx, *The Communist Manifesto*, Chapter I.

Page 41 *With the greater part of rich people* ... Smith, *The Wealth of Nations*, Book I, Chapter XI.

Page 41 *a substantial and patent waste of time* ... Veblen, *The Theory of the Leisure Class* (1899), Chapter 3.

Page 42 *with the exception of the instinct* ... Veblen, *The Theory of the Leisure Class*, Chapter 5.

Page 42 *When we consider the condition of the great* ... Smith, *The Theory of Moral Sentiments*, Part I, Section II, Chapter II.

Page 42 *the key to economic prosperity is the organized creation of dissatisfaction* ... Charles Kettering, Head of Research at General Motors (1929).

Page 42 *transformed five of the seven deadly sins* ... Mumford, *Technics and Human Development* (1967).

Page 43 *the share of high-income workers who averaged more* ... See, eg, Markovits, *The Meritocracy Trap* (2019). Markovits notes that over the same period the share of the lowest wage earners working more than 50 hours each week fell by almost a third.

Page 43 *to widen the market* ... Smith, *The Wealth of Nations*, Book I, Chapter XI.

Page 43 *there's no such thing as society* ... Thatcher, interview for *Woman's Own* (1987).

Page 43 *It doesn't matter whether the cat is black or white* ... Attributed to Deng Xiaoping.

Page 44 *the Chinese economy has more than doubled in each full decade* ... Rebasing GDP figures to 2015 US dollars, China GDP was $422 billion in 1980, $1.03 trillion in 1990, $2.77 trillion in 2000, $7.55 trillion in 2010, and $14.62 trillion in Covid-affected 2020. In 2021, Chinese aggregate GDP was $15.8 trillion (World Bank data, https://data.worldbank.org/indicator/NY.GDP.MKTP.KD?locations=CN). As a result of this growth, China – which Adam Smith noted was 'a much richer country than any part of Europe' in his time – is now on some measures the largest economy in the world, restoring the nation to the pre-eminence it has enjoyed for much of the last 2000 years.

Page 44 *the Soviet bloc finally disintegrated in the early 1990s* ... From the late 1980s the Soviet Union experimented with its own form of economic liberalisation – *perestroika*, or 'restructuring' – which, although introducing a number of market reforms, was less focused on foreign investment and trade. Perestroika was more tentative in scope than the Chinese approach, and ultimately far less successful.

Page 44 *characterised by low inflation and unusually stable markets* ... Although during this period capitalist economies still endured a number of crises, including the Asian financial crisis of 1997, the Russian ruble crisis of 1998, and the dot.com crash of the early 2000s.

Page 44 *premature back-slapping* ... See, eg, the former US Federal Reserve Chair Ben Bernanke's 2004 speech in which he cited improved monetary policy as a key factor in the decline in macroeconomic volatility, and declared his belief that this state of affairs would continue (Bernanke, 'The Great Moderation', speech at the meetings of the Eastern Economic Association, 20 February 2004).

Page 44 *The business cycle was declared dead* ... See, eg, Weber, 'The end of the business cycle?', *Foreign Affairs* (July/August 1997).

Page 45 *global debt now sits at roughly 50 per cent higher in real terms than in the mid-1990s* ... Global debt – the aggregate borrowings by governments, businesses and individuals – now stands at over $300 trillion (see https://www.weforum.org/agenda/2022/05/what-is-global-debt-why-high/).

Page 45 *the future is purchased by the present* ... Johnson, *The Rambler* (1751).

CHAPTER 6: THE BUCK STOPS HERE

Page 47   *a recording, registering, and measuring machine* … Scott, *Against the Grain: A Deep History of the Earliest States* (2017).

Page 48   *The criminal produces not only crimes* … Marx, *Economic Manuscripts of 1861–1863* (Part 3). Marx goes on to remark tongue-in-cheek that:

> This brings with it augmentation of national wealth … The criminal moreover produces the whole of the police and of criminal justice, constables, judges, hangmen, juries, etc.; and all these different lines of business, which form just as many categories of the social division of labour, develop different capacities of the human mind, create new needs and new ways of satisfying them. Torture alone has given rise to the most ingenious mechanical inventions, and employed many honourable craftsmen in the production of its instruments. The criminal produces an impression, partly moral and partly tragic, as the case may be, and in this way renders a 'service' by arousing the moral and aesthetic feelings of the public.

Page 48   *illegal activities … are often included in GDP calculations* … For example, since 2014 European Union member states have been encouraged to include activities such as prostitution and tobacco smuggling in GDP calculations.

Page 48   *does not allow for the health of our children* … Robert F Kennedy, transcript from an address at the University of Kansas, 18 March 1968.

Page 49   *the welfare of a nation can* … Kuznets, 1934 report to the US Congress (see also Vanham, 'A brief history of GDP – and what could come next', World Economic Forum, 13 December 2021).

Page 49   *Every inch of the existence of mankind* … Dickens, *Hard Times* (1854), Chapter VIII.

Page 49   *after a certain income threshold is reached* … See the 2021 *Social Progress Index: Executive Summary*, Social Progress Imperative (https://www.socialprogress.org/), which notes that:

> The relationship between economic development and social progress is not linear. At lower income levels, small differences in GDP per capita are associated with large improvements in social progress. As countries reach high levels of income, however, the rate of change slows.

Page 49   *the average pre-tax income of the top 10 per cent of earners has doubled* … See, eg, Ashkenas, 'Nine new findings about inequality in the United States', *The New York Times* (16 December 2016), and Giridharadas, 'The new elite's phoney crusade to change the world – without changing anything', *The Guardian* (22 January 2019).

Page 49   *material wealth would eventually trickle down* … In *The Culture of Contentment* (1992), John Kenneth Galbraith described trickle-down theory as 'the less than elegant metaphor that if one feeds the horse enough oats, some will pass through to the road for the sparrows'.

Page 51   *while the world's manufactured capital* … See Dasgupta, *The Economics of Biodiversity* (February 2021). This British Government–backed review concluded that 'Estimates show that between 1992 and 2014, produced capital per person doubled, and human capital per person increased by about 13% globally; but the stock of natural capital per person declined by nearly 40%'.

Page 51   *The economist Robert Costanza estimated* ... Costanza, 'Changes in the global value of ecosystem services', *Global Environmental Change* (May 2014), Volume 26.

Page 51   *the economy is a wholly owned subsidiary of the environment* ... Daly, *Steady-State Economics* (1977).

Page 52   *totalitarian capitalism* ... See, eg, comments from the British environmental writer George Monbiot, who describes 'totalitarian capitalism' as a situation in which 'everything must now be commodified and brought within the system. It extends the capitalist revolution even into our relations with the living world'.

CHAPTER 7: COWBOYS & ASTRONAUTS

Page 56   *the only natural economy* ... Quoted in Wolf, *Why Globalization Works* (2004).

Page 57   *economics students ... tend to become more self-interested and less altruistic than others over time* ... See, eg, Frank et al., 'Does studying economics inhibit cooperation?' *Journal of Economic Perspectives* (Spring 1993), Volume 7, Issue 2. The authors note that empirical studies tend to demonstrate that economists behave in more self-interested ways compared to the broader population, but this evidence alone 'does not demonstrate that exposure to the self-interest model causes more self-interested behavior, since it may be that economists were simply more self-interested to begin with, and this difference was one reason they chose to study economics'. The second part of the paper, however, provides 'preliminary evidence that exposure to the self-interest model does in fact encourage self-interested behavior'.

Page 57   *the majority of citizens in industrialised countries have shown marked increases in individualistic attitudes in recent decades* ... See, eg, Santos et al., 'Global increases in individualism', *Psychological Science* (July 2017), Volume 28, Issue 9.

Page 57   *economics is the most male-dominated academic discipline* ... See, eg, Dolar, 'The gender gap in economics is huge – it's even worse than tech', *The Conversation* (13 March 2021).

Page 57   *consumption is regarded as a good thing* ... Boulding, 'The economics of the coming Spaceship Earth' (paper presented at the Sixth Resources for the Future Forum on Environmental Quality in a Growing Economy in Washington DC, 8 March 1966).

Page 58   *the doctrine of Malthus* ... Darwin, *On the Origin of Species* (1859), Chapter III.

Page 58   *from the war of nature* ... (and following quotes in this paragraph) Darwin, *On the Origin of Species*, Chapter XIV.

Page 58   *those communities, which included the greatest number* ... Darwin, *The Descent of Man* (1871), Chapter IV.

Page 59   *The essential measure of the success of the economy* ... Boulding, 'The economics of the coming Spaceship Earth'.

Page 60   *Although opinions vary as to the start date of the Anthropocene* ... See, eg, Steffen et al., 'The Anthropocene: are humans now overwhelming the great forces of nature?', *Ambio* (December 2007), Volume 36, Number 8, who suggest that the Anthropocene epoch started in 1800 with the onset of industrialisation. Others have dated the beginning of the Anthropocene with to-the-second precision – it has been suggested by some that 11:29:21 Greenwich Mean Time on 16 July 1945, when the first nuclear bomb was detonated in New Mexico and produced a worldwide spike of artificial radionuclides, marked the start of the Anthropocene age.

Page 62   *species die-offs estimated to be occurring at a speed thousands of times higher than the historic background rate* ... Ceballos et al., 'The sixth extinction crisis loss of animal populations and species', *Journal of Cosmology* (June 2010), Volume 8.

Page 62   *an average 69 per cent decline in the abundance of monitored wildlife populations* ... Almond et al., *Living Planet Report 2022: Building a Nature Positive Society*, WWF (formerly the World Wide Fund for Nature) in collaboration with the Zoological Society of London's Institute of Zoology (2002).

Page 62   *around one million plant and animal species may vanish within the next few decades* ... Diaz et al., *The Global Assessment Report on Biodiversity and Ecosystem Services*, The Intergovernmental Science-Policy Platform on Biodiversity and Ecosystem Services (IPBES), 2019. Note that the IPBES report estimates that there are eight million animal and plant species on Earth, although other papers suggest that the total is likely to be far higher (eg, Ceballos et al., 'The sixth extinction crisis loss of animal populations and species', which estimates that the number of species, including microorganisms, could be anywhere between 5 and 100 million). Since adopting the Linnaean classification system, around 2 million species have been formally described, and on average around 50 new species are identified each day (see, eg, Ceballos et al.).

Page 62   *90 per cent of the world's topsoil is likely to be at risk by 2050* ... United Nations News, 'FAO warns 90 per cent of Earth's topsoil at risk by 2050' (27 July 2022, https://news.un.org/en/story/2022/07/1123462).

Page 63   *the purpose of studying economics is not to* ... Robinson, *Contributions to Modern Economics* (1978), Chapter 7.

CHAPTER 8: EMISSION POSSIBLE

Page 67   *the greenhouse effect has been detected* ... Hansen was invited before the US Senate Energy and Natural Resources Committee to provide an overview of the papers he had published on climate change earlier in the decade.

Page 68   *What now remains, compared with what existed* ... Plato, *Critias* (c. fourth century BCE).

Page 72   *after the last great extinction event 66 million years ago it is estimated that ... atmospheric carbon levels* ... See, eg, Le Page, 'Asteroid that killed the dinosaurs caused massive global warming', *New Scientist* (24 May 2018).

Page 73   *it's become a religion* ... Vaughan, 'James Lovelock: environmentalism has become a religion', *The Guardian*, 31 March 2014.

Page 74   *a complex entity involving the Earth's biosphere* ... Lovelock, *Gaia: A New Look at Life on Earth* (1979), Introduction.

Page 74   *Lovelock took the advice of a neighbouring novelist* ... Lovelock's neighbour was William Golding, author of *The Lord of the Flies*. There is no little irony in the fact that the writer of one of the most famously Social Darwinist novels suggested 'Gaia' as the tag for the complex symbiotic organism that is planet Earth.

Page 74   *not living, but like a cat's fur* ... Lovelock, *Gaia*, Introduction.

Page 75   *no more serious ... 'than the thoughts of a sailor who refers to his ship as "she"'* ... Lovelock, *The Revenge of Gaia* (2006), Chapter 1.

Page 75   *The biologist Lynn Margulis contributed her expertise* ... James Lovelock and Lynn Margulis began collaborating on the Gaia hypothesis in 1972, and in 1974 published their first joint paper ('Atmospheric homeostasis by and for the biosphere: the Gaia Hypothesis').

Page 75   *symbiosis seen from space* … Margulis and Sagan, *What is Life?* (1993).

Page 75   *Gaia is a tough bitch* … Margulis, quoted in *Edge* magazine (1 May 1996).

Page 75   *the froth on top of a glass of beer* … Lovelock, *The Man Who Named the World* (documentary film, 1990).

CHAPTER 9: THE EFFLUENT SOCIETY

Page 77   *a planet changing before our eyes is more interesting and important* … Hansen, TED talk (2012, https://www.ted.com/talks/james_hansen_why_i_must_speak_out_about_climate_change).

Page 77   *comprise around half the world's commercial tonnage* … Bernstein, *A Splendid Exchange: How Trade Shaped the World* (2008), Chapter 14.

Page 78   *concentrations of carbon dioxide increasing by around 50 per cent and methane by more than 150 per cent* … At the end of the eighteenth century atmospheric carbon dioxide levels were around 280 parts per million, and today are approximately 420 ppm. Methane levels are estimated to have been around 715 parts per billion in 1800, and now exist in a concentration of around 1,900 ppb (see Forster et al., 'Changes in atmospheric constituents and in radiative forcing', IPCC, 2007; and the US National Oceanic and Atmospheric Administration, 'Increase in atmospheric methane set another record during 2021', 7 April 2022).

Page 78   *on track to lift global average temperatures by at least 3 degrees Celsius by 2100* … See, eg, the IPCC AR6 Synthesis Report, which notes that 'Without a strengthening of policies, global warming of 3.2°C is projected by 2100 (medium confidence)' (paragraph A.4.4). See also comments from the UN World Meteorological Organization (see, eg, 'Global temperatures on track for 3–5 degree rise by 2100: UN', *Reuters*, 29 November 2018).

Page 79   *now in our own lifetime we are witnessing a startling alteration of climate* … Carson, *The Sea Around Us* (1951), Chapter 12.

Page 79   *projections by the UN and other bodies predict that carbon dioxide concentrations of 600 parts per million* … See, eg, Le Page, 'CO$_2$ set to hit levels not seen in 50 million years by 2050', *New Scientist* (4 April 2017).

Page 79   *a study published in 2019 showing that the overwhelming majority of climate models had correctly forecast* … See Hausfather et al., 'Evaluating the performance of past climate model projections', *Geophysical Research Letters* (4 December 2019), Volume 47, Issue 1. The paper reviewed the performance of 17 climate models published between 1970 and 2007 in projecting future global mean surface temperature changes, finding that '14 of the 17 model projections were consistent with observations', with two overshooting and one undershooting these observations.

Page 79   *what the Germans call* Heisszeit … In 2018 'Heisszeit' was voted as the German Word of the Year by the Association for the German Language.

Page 80   *since the first IPCC report was released in 1990, annual global emissions have increased by more than 40 per cent* … Annual global greenhouse gas emissions – measured in 'carbon dioxide-equivalents' which takes into account the 'global warming potential' of the various gases – increased from approximately 35 billion tonnes in 1990 to 50 billion tonnes in 2019 (see Ritchie and Roser, 'Greenhouse gas emissions', *OWID*).

Page 81   *scientists are biased not toward alarmism but rather the reverse* … Oreskes et al., 'Climate change prediction: erring on the least side of drama?', *Global Environmental*

Change (1 February 2013), Volume 23, Issue 1.

Page 81   *a rather sudden and uncontrollable decline* ... Meadows et al., *The Limits to Growth* (1972).

Page 82   *There is general scientific agreement* ... See Banerjee et al., 'Exxon's Own Research Confirmed Fossil Fuels' Role in Global Warming Decades Ago', *Inside Climate News* (16 September 2015).

Page 82   *Man has a time window of five to ten years* ... Banerjee et al., 'Exxon's Own Research Confirmed Fossil Fuels' Role in Global Warming Decades Ago' (2015).

Page 83   *so-called global climate change* ... Speech by Lee Raymond, then Chairman of Exxon Corporation, at the Annual Meeting of the American Petroleum Institute (Washington DC, 1996).

Page 83   *sponsored editorials in newspapers* ... Mann, *The New Climate War: The Fight to Take Back Our Planet* (2021), Chapter 4.

Page 83   *inventing the concept of a 'carbon footprint'* ... First popularised, with assistance from the advertising agency Ogilvy, in the early 2000s by the oil and gas company BP.

Page 83   *over 99 per cent of published scientific literature now accepts the reality of human-caused climate change* ... Lynas et al., 'Greater than 99% consensus on human caused climate change in the peer-reviewed scientific literature', *Environmental Research Letters* (19 October 2021), Volume 16, Number 11. The study concludes with high statistical confidence that 'the scientific consensus on human-caused contemporary climate change – expressed as a proportion of the total publications – exceeds 99% in the peer reviewed scientific literature'.

Page 83   *neither the most acknowledged probity* ... Smith, *The Wealth of Nations*, Book IV, Chapter II.

Page 84   *corporations have not been averse to playing the man or woman rather than the ball* ... Rachel Carson, for example, was accused of being a front for the Communist Party following the release of *Silent Spring*, while the president of a chemical company that produced DDT said that Carson wrote 'not as a scientist, but as a fanatic of the cult of the balance of nature'.

Page 84   *Great is the power of steady misrepresentation* ... Darwin, *On the Origin of Species* (1872 edition), Chapter XIV.

Page 84   *their thoughts ... are commonly exercised rather about the interest of their own particular branch of business* ... Smith, *The Wealth of Nations*, Book I, Chapter IX.

CHAPTER 10: POLLUTOCRATS

Page 85   *CEOs of fossil energy companies know* ... Dr James E Hansen, Briefing to the House Select Committee on Energy Independence & Global Warming (23 June 2008, http://www.columbia.edu/~jeh1/2008/TwentyYearsLater_20080623.pdf).

Page 85   *liken the corporation to a type of licensed psychopath* ... For an example of this perspective, see Bakan, *The Corporation: The Pathological Pursuit of Profit and Power* (2003).

Page 85   *they have become the key players in our global economic system* ... In 2022, for example, the Fortune 500 companies (the 500 largest US corporations by revenue) recorded aggregate sales of $37.8 trillion, comprising more than a third of world GDP over the same period (https://fortune.com/ranking/global500/2022/).

Page 86   *the average holding period for a security ... has fallen* ... See, eg, Lu, 'The Decline of

Long-Term Investing', Visual Capitalist (8 December 2021, https://www.visualcapitalist. com/the-decline-of-long-term-investing/).

Page 86   *The threat of 'capital flight'* ... Capital flight refers to a situation in which money and other assets rapidly exit a nation due to adverse political or economic developments.

Page 87   *It is wholly a confusion of ideas* ... Jevons, *The Coal Question* (1865), Chapter VII.

Page 87   *appendage of the machine* ... Engels & Marx, *The Communist Manifesto* (1848), Part I.

Page 88   *just as importantly they can disperse overall risk* ... An early example of the value of risk dispersion is seen in the biblical injunction to go forth and diversify in the Book of Ecclesiastes:

> Send your grain across the seas, and in time you will get a return. Divide your merchandise among seven ventures, eight maybe, since you do not know what calamities may occur on earth.

Page 89   *it was not until the early nineteenth century that the British Government again permitted the formation* ... Another reason for the resurrection of joint-stock companies in the early nineteenth century was the rise of capital-intensive heavy industries such as steelmaking and railroads, which required large corporate combinations.

Page 90   *the monopolizing spirit of merchants and manufacturers* ... Smith, *The Wealth of Nations*, Book IV, Chapter III.

Page 90   *Want, famine, and mortality* ... Smith, *The Wealth of Nations*, Book I, Chapter VIII.

Page 90   *by raising their profits above what they naturally would be* ... Smith, *The Wealth of Nations*, Book I, Chapter XI.

Page 90   *The proposal of any new law or regulation* ... Smith, *The Wealth of Nations*, Book I, Chapter XI.

Page 90   *Smith's book was ... an argument against state capture by powerful corporate interests* ... Smith was resolutely focused on consumer, rather than producer, welfare – commenting in *The Wealth of Nations* that 'the interest of the producer ought to be attended to only so far as it may be necessary for promoting that of the consumer' (Book IV, Chapter VIII).

Page 92   *first popularised by the American ecologist Garrett Hardin* ... Hardin, 'The Tragedy of the Commons', *Science* (13 December 1968), Volume 162.

Page 92   *the greatest example of market failure we have ever seen* ... Nicholas Stern, *The Economics of Climate Change: The Stern Review* (2007).

CHAPTER 11: COSTING THE EARTH

Page 93   *Emissions aren't going to go down if* ... Milman, 'Ex-Nasa scientist: 30 years on, world is failing "miserably" to address climate change', *The Guardian* (19 June 2018).

Page 94   *being extravagant with your carbon footprint costs the same* ... Fitch, 'The price is wrong: talking to William D Nordhaus', *Los Angeles Review of Books* (28 May 2021).

Page 95   *The average age of coal plants in Asia* ... Rogoff, 'The Case for a World Carbon Bank', *Project Syndicate* (8 July 2019). Rogoff notes that:

> In advanced economies, where the average age of coal plants is 42 years, many are reaching the natural end of their lifespan, and it is not a great burden to phase

them out. But in Asia, where one new coal plant a week is being built, the average age is only 11 years, and most will be running for decades to come.

Page 95   *climate change is what economists term a 'wicked problem'* ... As William Nordhaus summarised in his Nobel Prize Lecture (8 December 2018):

> Global warming is the most significant of all environmental externalities. It menaces our planet and looms over our future like a Colossus ... It is particularly pernicious because it involves so many activities of daily life, affects the entire planet, does so for decades and even centuries, and, most of all, because none of us acting individually can do anything to slow the changes.

Page 96   *'the Tragedy of the Horizon'* ... See, eg, Carney, 'Breaking the Tragedy of the Horizon – climate change and financial stability', speech by the Governor of the Bank of England to Lloyd's of London (29 September 2015).

Page 96   *that arrogant oligarchy* ... Chesterton, *Orthodoxy* (1908), Chapter IV.

Page 97   *The proprietor of stock is properly a citizen of the world* ... Smith, *The Wealth of Nations*, Book V, Chapter II.

Page 98   *Economists have suggested a carrot-and-stick solution* ... See, eg, 'Economists' Statement on Carbon Dividends', *The Wall Street Journal* (17 January 2019). This declaration was the largest public statement by economists in history, supported by 28 Nobel Laureate economists, four former Chairs of the US Federal Reserve, and over 3,000 other economists.

Page 98   *Club members could impose sanctions on non-participants in the form of tariffs or trade bans* ... Some economists have suggested a 'carbon border tax adjustment' that would reflect the embodied carbon in imports. However, due to the complexity in calculating carbon content in goods, others have suggested that a simple broad-based tariff is preferable (see, eg, Nordhaus, 'How to fix a failing global effort', *Foreign Affairs* (10 April 2020)). In either case, from a government perspective it would be preferable to receive additional domestic revenue in the form of tax receipts rather than let another country take revenue in the form of tariffs imposed at the border.

Page 99   *the wealthiest 1 per cent of the global population is estimated* ... Gore, 'Confronting carbon inequality', Oxfam and the Stockholm Environment Institute (21 September 2020). The report notes that

> [t]he richest 10 percent accounted for over half (52 percent) of the emissions added to the atmosphere between 1990 and 2015. The richest one percent were responsible for 15 percent of emissions during this time – more than all the citizens of the EU and more than twice that of the poorest half of humanity (7 percent).

Page 100   *An additional 3 degrees of heating above pre-industrial levels is predicted to result in* ... See, eg, *The Economist*, 'This is what 3°C of global warming looks like' (30 October 2021).

Page 101   *the desire of persuading* ... Smith, *The Theory of Moral Sentiments*, Part VII, Section IV, Conclusion.

Page 102   *the preferences of the average American appear to have only a minuscule* ... Gillens and Page, 'Testing theories of American politics: elites, interest groups, and average citizens, *Perspectives on Politics* (2014), Volume 12, Number 3.

CHAPTER 12: HOT AIR

Page 103 *some economists edge into parody* ... Gary Becker, a Nobel Prize winner in Economics in 1992, was perhaps the best known exponent of this relentlessly market-based perspective. In addition to making an analogy between children and consumer durables, he also suggested that criminals are rational actors who weigh the costs of crime (the probability of apprehension, conviction and punishment) against the potential benefits, and Becker therefore concluded that the optimal policy response would be to maximise fines and minimise surveillance; that discriminatory employers might be dissuaded from their bigoted ways due to higher costs arising from a smaller potential worker pool; and that a free market in organ donation (pricing a kidney at $15,000 and a liver at just over $30,000) would solve the problem of organ scarcity.

Page 104 *an ideology to end ideologies* ... Robinson, *Economic Philosophy* (1962).

Page 104 *the institutionalization of individualism and non-responsibility* ... Schumacher, *Small Is Beautiful: Economics as if People Mattered* (1973).

Page 105 *a corporation does not age* ... Berry, *What Matters? Economics for a Renewed Commonwealth* (2010).

Page 105 *The celebrated* Homo economicus *of neoclassical economics is an outlier, the sociopathic exception rather than the rule* ... Although note that, perhaps responding to adaptive pressures in the corporate environment, some studies suggest that company CEOs have significantly higher rates of diagnosable sociopathy compared to the general population. See, eg, McCullough, 'The Psychopathic CEO', *Forbes* magazine (9 December 2019), who notes that:

> Roughly 4% to as high as 12% of CEOs exhibit psychopathic traits, according to some expert estimates, many times more than the 1% rate found in the general population and more in line with the 15% rate found in prisons.

Page 106 *one of the few organisations in our modern economy that thinks 20 years ahead* ... See James Lovelock obituary, *The Times* (27 July 2022).

Page 106 *business is the only mechanism on the planet today* ... Hawken, speech to the Commonwealth Club of San Francisco (1992); see also Epstein-Reeves and Weinraub, 'Paul Hawken: programming a new operating system for civilization', *The Guardian* (24 September 2013).

Page 106 *as these managers become 'universal owners'* ... Although note that these investment managers are not the true owners of the underlying assets – rather, these assets are held and managed in trust for clients, although investment managers exert substantial effective power through the exercise of shareholder voting rights and also the ability to buy and sell significant parcels of stock.

Page 107 *global profit enforcement agency* ... See, eg, Austin, 'Can ESG grasp what ecology says?', *Responsible Investor* (23 February 2021).

Page 107 *many past studies ... concluded that high-rating ESG companies tend to outperform* ... See, eg, Eccles et al., 'Is sustainability now the key to corporate success?', *The Guardian* (7 January 2012), which argued that '[o]ver an 18-year period, the high-sustainability companies dramatically outperformed the low-sustainability ones in terms of both stock market and accounting measures'.

Page 108 *such arguments are at odds with the 'efficient markets hypothesis'* ... This theory states that financial exchanges incorporate all public information which could possibly affect the price of a financial asset. Eugene Fama, the founder of the efficient markets theory, explained the hypothesis as follows:

> In an efficient market, competition among the many intelligent participants leads to a situation where, at any point in time, actual prices of individual securities already reflect the effects of information based both on events that have already occurred and on events which, as of now, the market expects to take place in the future.

(Fama, 'Random Walks in Stock Market Prices' (1965), *Financial Analysts Journal*, Volume 21, Number 5.)

Page 108 *there is little to no evidence that funds labelled 'high sustainability' outperform conventional funds* ... See, eg, Hartzmark and Sussman, 'Do investors value sustainability? A natural experiment examining ranking and fund flows', *The Journal of Finance* (December 2019), Volume 74, Issue 6.

Page 108 *the quantity of disclosure is ... not correlated with the relevant firms' levels of ESG compliance* ... Raghunandan and Rajgopal, 'Do ESG funds make stakeholder-friendly investments?', *Review of Accounting Studies* (27 May 2022). The authors note that, based on a sample of self-labelled ESG mutual funds in the US from 2010 to 2018, those 'funds hold portfolio firms with worse track records for compliance with labor and environmental laws, relative to portfolio firms held by non-ESG funds managed by the same financial institutions in the same years'. They bluntly conclude that '[o]ur findings suggest that socially responsible funds do not appear to follow through on proclamations of concerns for stakeholders'.

Page 109 *it is estimated ... that some major brands have over 100,000 suppliers and sub-contractors* ... See, eg, Hilgers, 'The Alarming Human Toll of Cheap Stuff "Made in China"', *The New York Times* (2 February 2021), which quotes Amelia Pang:

> It is common for a major brand to have over 100,000 suppliers at the first level ... But when 100,000 suppliers are subcontracting to factories that are subcontracting to other factories, even the cheapest audits can quickly become expensive.

Page 111 *the Haifa daycare experiment* ... See, eg, Levitt and Dubner, *Freakonomics* (2005), Chapter 1.

Page 112 *significantly less than half the money spent on some carbon offset schemes is directed to the actual offset project* ... See, eg, 'The Efficiency of Carbon Offsetting Through the Clean Development Mechanism', *Carbon Retirement* (7 December 2009), which found that 'for every £10 a buyer spends with a carbon offsetting retailer using CERs, £2.76 typically goes to setting up and running the project. For a statutory buyer dealing direct with brokers, £3.06 from every £10 typically goes to the environmental project.' See also Kahya, '"30% of carbon offsets" spent on reducing emissions', *BBC News* (7 December 2009).

Page 112 *while spawning new markets that do not always address the root problem* ... A now defunct website called 'Cheat Neutral' parodied the concept of offsetting by claiming to have thousands of 'faithful people ready to neutralise your misdemeanours', and offering those who wish to cheat on their partner the ability to pay someone else to refrain from an act of infidelity.

CHAPTER 13: PANDORA'S BOX

Page 114 *the poorest half of the global population owns just 2 per cent of total global wealth* ... Chancel et al., *World Inequality Report 2022*, World Inequality Lab (https://wir2022.wid.world/executive-summary/).

Page 115 *we would need approximately three Earths* ... See, eg, Buchholz, 'The staggering figures for this year's Earth Overshoot Day', World Economic Forum (6 August 2021).

Page 115 *the US alone consumes around a quarter of global resources* ... See, eg, Scheer and Moss, 'Use it and lose it: the outsize effect of US consumption on the environment', *Scientific American* (14 September 2012), which notes that 'the U.S. uses one-third of the world's paper, a quarter of the world's oil, 23 percent of the coal, 27 percent of the aluminum, and 19 percent of the copper'.

Page 115 *The 10 per cent of households with the heaviest carbon footprints discharge around four times more emissions* ... See Chancel et al., *World Inequality Report 2022*, World Inequality Lab, which estimates that 'the top 10% of emitters are responsible for close to 50% of all emissions, while the bottom 50% make 12% of the total' (https://wir2022.wid.world/chapter-6/).

Page 115 *would require ever-increasing amounts of chemicals* ... And note that if a program of solar radiation management were to be stopped, then this would result in what scientists call 'termination shock' – a rapid and damaging spike in temperatures.

Page 116 *we are but one of the multitude* ... Smith, *The Theory of Moral Sentiments*, Part III, Chapter II.

Page 116 *The latest IPCC report estimates that almost half the world's population* ... IPCC AR6 WGII, 'Summary for policymakers headline statements' (28 February 2022).

Page 117 *pressure on food production and access ... leading to malnutrition and micro-nutrient deficiencies* ... IPCC AR6 WGII, 'Summary for policymakers'.

Page 118 *the health of the economy and the health of our environment are totally dependent upon each other* ... Thatcher, Speech to the Royal Society (27 September 1988).

Page 118 *manufacturers did not have the political sway* ... See, eg, Maxwell and Briscoe, 'There's money in the air: the CFC ban and DuPont's regulatory strategy' (December 1998), *Business Strategy and the Environment*, Volume 6, Issue 5. The authors argue that the pursuit of economic interests also played a significant role in the development of the Montreal Protocol, offering manufacturers such as DuPont 'the possibility of new and more profitable chemical markets at a time when CFC production was losing its profitability'.

Page 118 *hydrocarbon subsidies amounted to around $1 trillion* ... IEA, *Fossil Fuels Consumption Subsidies 2022* (February 2023). This report notes that global fossil fuel consumption subsidies in 2022 'doubled from the previous year to an all-time high of USD 1 trillion', largely due to geopolitical factors. In recent years, global hydrocarbon subsidies have been in the order of $500–600 billion annually.

Page 120 *in the decade beginning in 2010 unit costs of solar energy fell by 85 per cent* ... IPCC AR6 WGIII, 'Summary for Policymakers'.

Page 120 *hydrocarbons still account for over 80 per cent of all global energy consumption* ... See Ritchie and Roser, 'Energy mix', *OWID*, which notes that 84 per cent of global energy still comes from fossil fuels, and that this proportion has reduced only marginally from levels seen in 2000 (when hydrocarbons comprised 86 per cent of the energy mix). Of the remaining energy sources, 11.4 per cent was attributable to renewables and 4.3 per cent to nuclear, but wind produces just 2.2 per cent and solar just 1.1 per cent of total energy at present – hydropower comprises 6.4 per cent of all primary energy, almost double the combined total of wind and solar. Other renewable sources – such as biofuels, geothermal and tidal power – together constitute 1.6 per cent of global energy consumption.

Page 120 *global carbon dioxide emissions fell by only 5.8 per cent* ... IEA, *Global Energy Review: Global Energy and CO₂ Emissions in 2020* (2 March 2021). This report notes that the pandemic 'drove down fossil fuel consumption for much of the year, whereas renewables and electric vehicles, two of the main building blocks of clean energy transitions, were largely immune'. Although the pandemic triggered a 4 per cent decline in primary energy demand in 2020 – the largest annual percentage fall in energy consumption since the Second World War – energy-related carbon dioxide emissions only fell by 5.8 per cent.

Page 120 *battery storage, which itself has fallen in cost by almost 90 per cent over the last decade* ... See IPCC AR6 WGIII, 'Summary for Policymakers', which notes that from 2010 to 2019 the unit cost of lithium-ion batteries fell by 85 per cent.

Page 120 *by 2050 renewable energy technologies could provide just over half of the world's energy needs* ... IEA, World Energy Outlook 2022: An updated roadmap to Net Zero Emissions by 2050 (https://www.iea.org/reports/world-energy-outlook-2022/an-updated-roadmap-to-net-zero-emissions-by-2050).

Page 121 *in mid-2019 ... Britain ... generated more electricity from renewables than hydro-carbons* ... Ambrose, 'Renewable electricity overtakes fossil fuels in UK for first time', *The Guardian* (14 October 2019).

Page 121 *the IPCC estimates that green investment requirements for the decade from 2020 to 2030 will be up to six times greater than current levels* ... IPCC, 'The evidence is clear: the time for action is now. We can halve emissions by 2030' (4 April 2022).

Page 122 *around 70 per cent of Americans believe that the 'political system seems to only be working for the insiders ...'* ... Henderson, 'The Business Case for Saving Democracy', *Harvard Business Review* (10 March 2020). See also Wike et al., 'Many Across the Globe Are Dissatisfied With How Democracy Is Working', Pew Research Center (29 April 2019).

CHAPTER 14: LIQUID ASSETS

Page 128 *murmuring noise, which is heard from afar* ... Oliver Goldsmith, *A History of the Earth and Animated Nature* (1774).

Page 130 *more than 3.3 billion people obtaining at least 20 per cent of their protein intake* ... FAO, *The State of World Fisheries and Aquaculture 2022*, Executive Summary. The FAO further notes that in a number of African, Asian and small island states, aquatic foods contribute half or more of total animal protein intake.

Page 130 *estimated to support the livelihoods of around 600 million people globally* ... FAO, *The State of World Fisheries and Aquaculture 2022*, Executive Summary. The FAO estimates that in 2021 58.5 million people were employed in the primary fisheries and aquaculture production sector, but when subsistence and secondary sector workers (and their dependants) are included then 'about 600 million livelihoods depend at least partially on fisheries and aquaculture'.

Page 130 *these ... 'phytoplankton' – supply at least half the Earth's free oxygen* ... See, eg, the US National Ocean Service–National Oceanic and Atmospheric Administration, 'How much oxygen comes from the ocean?'

Page 131 *The ocean also soaks up over 90 per cent of excess heat* … The IPCC's *Climate Change 2021: The Physical Science Basis* (Summary for Policymakers) notes that 'Ocean warming accounted for 91% of the heating in the climate system, with land warming, ice loss and atmospheric warming accounting for about 5%, 3% and 1%, respectively (high confidence)'.

Page 131 *by 2100 it is likely that the ocean will warm by between five and seven times faster* … The IPCC's *Special Report on the Ocean and Cryosphere in a Changing Climate*, Technical Summary (2019) notes that 'By 2100 the ocean is very likely to warm by 2 to 4 times as much for low emissions … and 5 to 7 times as much for the high emissions scenario … compared with the observed changes since 1970'.

Page 131 *Ten thousand fleets sweep over thee in vain* … George Gordon Byron, *Childe Harold's Pilgrimage* (1812).

Page 132 *flags of convenience* … A 'flag of convenience' describes a situation in which a commercial vessel is registered in a country other than its owner's residence, thereby usually benefitting from the less rigorous governance standards in the registering country.

Page 132 *it has, I am afraid, been too common* … Smith, *The Wealth of Nations*, Book IV, Chapter V.

Page 132 *global fishing subsidies estimated to total around $35 billion a year* … See Sumaila et al., 'Updated estimates and analysis of global fisheries subsidies', *Marine Policy* (November 2019), Volume 109.

Page 133 *The world's wild fish catch plateaued in the mid-1990s* … For the last two decades, the global wild fish catch has moved between 90 and 95 million tonnes per annum, which nevertheless is well over double the figure of 35 million tonnes for wild caught fish in 1960 – see, eg, Ritchie and Roser, 'Fish and Overfishing', *OWID* (October 2021).

Page 133 *more than a third of global fish stocks are now fished at biologically unsustainable levels* … Ritchie and Roser, 'Fish and Overfishing', *OWID*. Based on FAO data, the authors estimate that in 2017, 34 per cent of global fish stocks were 'overfished' (ie, fish are caught faster than they can reproduce), and a further 60 per cent were 'maximally fished' (a situation where catch is maximised while attempting to ensure that fish stocks do not fall below the most productive level).

Page 133 *'Fishing effort' … has increased markedly* … See, eg, Roberts, *The Ocean of Life* (Chapter 3), who notes that in southern British waters landings per unit of fishing power fell almost 90 per cent over the course of the last century.

CHAPTER 15: A MOVEABLE FEAST

Page 137 *Japan remains the beating heart of the global bluefin trade* … See Chapman, 'A Tuna's Worth', *Hakai Magazine*, 18 August 2020; Gagern et al., 'Trade-Based Estimation of Bluefin Tuna Catches in the Eastern Atlantic and Mediterranean, 2005–2011', *PLoS ONE* (2013), Volume 8, Number 7; and Dinmore, 'Italy backs ban of bluefin tuna trade', *Financial Times* (26 January 2010).

Page 137 *the creature that accelerates faster than a Porsche can now cost more than one* … In 2019, for example, a near-300 kilogram Pacific bluefin tuna was auctioned for $3.1 million at the Tokyo fish market (see 'Japan sushi tycoon pays record tuna price', BBC, 5 January 2019). A bluefin of this size would typically sell for $60,000 but prices in the first auction of the new year are significantly boosted by publicity and status considerations (see also Telesca, 'How global regulators are selling out the world's largest tuna', Yale School of the Environment, 16 June 2020).

Page 138 *In the year 1238, the inhabitants of Gothia* ... Gibbon, *The History of the Decline and Fall of the Roman Empire* (1788), Volume 6.

Page 138 *bound together by a web of complex relations* ... Darwin, *On the Origin of Species*, Part III.

Page 138 *the global fertility rate has more than halved* ... The World Economic Forum (Alvarez, *What does the global decline of the fertility rate look like?*, 17 July 2002) estimates that the global fertility rate – defined as the total number of births in a year per 1,000 women of reproductive age in a population – has fallen from 5.0 in 1950 to 2.4 in 2020. World Bank data shows that the global fertility rate peaked in 1963 at 5.3 children, and has steadily fallen since this time.

Page 139 *the Brookings Institution estimates that* ... Kharas and Hamel, 'A global tipping point: Half the world is now middle class or wealthier', The Brookings Institution (27 September 2018, https://www.brookings.edu/blog/future-development/2018/09/27/a-global-tipping-point-half-the-world-is-now-middle-class-or-wealthier/).

Page 139 *as recently as 1997 ... just over 40 per cent of the people in China and India* ... Rosling et al., *Factfulness* (2018), Chapter 2. The authors note that 'In 1997, 42 percent of the population of India and China were living in extreme poverty. By 2017, in India, that had dropped to 12 percent. In China, that share dropped to a stunning 0.7 percent over the same period'.

Page 139 *it is expected that by 2030 the middle class in China and India* ... See Kharas, *The Unprecedented Expansion of the Global Middle Class: An Update*, The Brookings Institution (February 2017), which observes that by 2030 'Asians could represent two-thirds of the global middle-class population', although also noting that in 2030 the US is still projected to account for over 50 per cent of rich household spending globally.

Page 139 *Seafood has recorded the highest growth in consumption of any animal protein* ... The FAO notes that 'Global consumption of aquatic foods (excluding algae) has increased at an average annual rate of 3.0 percent since 1961, compared with a population growth rate of 1.6 percent' (*The State of the World Fisheries and Aquaculture 2022*, FAO, Key Messages*).

Page 139 *in China annual consumption has increased 10-fold over the same period* ... Per capita seafood consumption in China increased from 3.8 kilograms in 1970 to 38.5 kilograms in 2019 (Ritchie and Roser, 'Fish and Overfishing', *OWID*, October 2021).

Page 139 *it is thought that in 2017 and 2018 alone China manufactured more cement* ... Smil, 'Concrete facts' (March 2020), *IEEE Spectrum* magazine.

Page 139 *The Chinese leadership has the tiger economy by the tail* ... As Tocqueville commented two hundred years ago, 'the greatest firebrands from revolutionary France were not from regions untouched by progress but from those areas where prosperity was growing'.

Page 140 *China now accounts for around 30 per cent of global manufacturing output ... and emits a commensurate amount of carbon dioxide* ... See, eg, Richter, 'These are the top 10 manufacturing countries in the world', World Economic Forum (25 February 2020), which notes that:

China accounted for 28 percent of global manufacturing output in 2018. That puts the country more than 10 percentage points ahead of the United States, which used to have the world's largest manufacturing sector until China overtook it in 2010.

Page 140 *China ... emits a commensurate amount of carbon dioxide ...* But note that although China contributes around 30 per cent of the annual global total of human-caused carbon dioxide emissions, on a per capita basis it discharges only around half as much as Americans (in 2020, for example, China is estimated to have released 7.4 tonnes of carbon dioxide per person compared to 14.2 tonnes in the US). Moreover, much of the carbon emitted in China is attributable to energy-intensive manufactured products exported to Western markets – Western nations are, in effect, offshoring their emissions to countries such as China.

Page 140 *it is thought that around 17,000 Chinese fishing boats comb the open seas ...* See Gutierrez and Jobbins, 'China's distant-water fishing fleet: scale, impact and governance', ODI (formerly the Overseas Development Institute), 2 June 2020, which estimated that China's distant water fleet comprised 16,966 vessels. Another report (Urbina, 'How China's expanding fishing fleet is depleting the world's oceans', Yale School of the Environment (17 August 2020)) found that in 2015 'the European Union had 289 vessels in its distant water fleet in 2014 and the United States had 225 large vessels outside its waters'.

Page 140 *the world's fastest growing consumer market ...* See, eg, Barnett, 'China: Fastest Growing Consumer Market in the World', International Monetary Fund (2 December 2013).

Page 140 *the world's ... second-largest importer ...* See, eg, Eurostat, *China-EU-international trade in goods statistics*, European Commission (February 2022).

Page 140 *given a cosmopolitan character to production and consumption ...* Engels & Marx, *The Communist Manifesto*, Part I.

Page 140 *Seafood is the world's most traded animal protein ...* See, eg, Sharma and Nikolik, *World Seafood Map 2022: Seafood Trade Keeps Growing From Strength to Strength*, Rabobank (May 2022), which notes that '[i]n 2021, seafood trade was roughly 3.6 times the size of beef trade (the second most traded animal protein), five times the size of global pork trade, and eight times the size of poultry trade'.

Page 141 *Any tendency to overfishing ...* Huxley, Inaugural address to the International Fisheries Exhibition, London (1883). In this address, Huxley also complacently observed that

> I believe ... that the cod fishery ... and probably all the great sea fisheries, are inexhaustible; that is to say, that nothing we do seriously affects the number of the fish. And any attempt to regulate these fisheries seems consequently, from the nature of the case, to be useless.

Page 141 *If any trawling ground be overfished, the trawlers themselves will be the first persons ...* Huxley et al., 'Report from the Commissioners on the Sea Fisheries of the United Kingdom' (1866).

Page 141 *may welcome a reassuringly expensive item as a marker of status ...* In the case of certain luxury products, including bluefin tuna, high prices may actually increase consumer demand as it is a conspicuous demonstration of membership within the elite. These luxury products are sometimes termed 'Veblen goods' by economists because ownership or consumption of these goods confers social status.

Page 142 *some tuna and shark stocks ... are estimated to have fallen by approximately 90 per cent ...* See, eg, Ritchie and Roser, 'Fish and overfishing', *OWID*, which notes that stocks of commercially fished sharks and rays have collapsed by around 90 per cent over the last half century.

Page 142 *almost 10 per cent of creatures caught by humans are thrown back into the ocean ...* Zeller et al., 'Global marine fisheries discards: A synthesis of reconstructed data', *Fish and Fisheries* (January 2018), Volume 19, Issue 1. Only fish 'landings' – those fish brought back to land – are generally recorded, with discards remaining unreported, and the authors employed conservative assumptions in arriving at this figure. The authors further note that there has been an improvement in the discard rate, with discards comprising 'between 10% and 20% of total reconstructed catches per year until the year 2000, after which discards account for slightly less than 10% of total annual catches'. Despite this improvement, the amount of fish and other marine animals thrown back in the ocean is around 10 million tonnes each year.

Page 142 *The overwhelming majority of discards ... come from industrial fishing ...* See, eg, Zeller et al., 'Global marine fisheries discards: A synthesis of reconstructed data', who note that '[t]he vast majority of discards (around 93% averaged over 1950–2014) were made by industrial (i.e. large-scale) fisheries, while small-scale fisheries contributed very little to global discarding'. Bottom trawling, which accounts for a quarter of all fish landed, has the highest discard rate at around 20 per cent, and some forms of this marine dredging, such as shrimp trawls, have considerably higher discard rates.

Page 142 *Japan's inbound Atlantic bluefin tuna supply has exceeded legal quotas by up to 50 per cent ...* See, eg, Klinger and Narita, 'Peak tuna', *Foreign Policy* (12 February 2010), who note that '[i]n recent years, ICCAT scientists estimate that more than half of bluefin catches in the Eastern Atlantic and Mediterranean have been illegal'. As a result of routinely exceeding bluefin quotas, in 2006 Japan voluntarily agreed to cut its Atlantic bluefin allocation, in part to prevent imposed cuts which were likely to be more severe (see McCurry, 'Japan to halve bluefin tuna quota', *The Guardian* (6 October 2006)).

Page 142 *additional thousands of tonnes of bootleg bluefin ...* See, eg, 'How the illegal Bluefin tuna market made over EUR 12 million a year selling fish in Spain', Europol (16 October 2018), which estimated that the volume of the illegally traded Mediterranean bluefin market was double the annual volume of legal trade.

Page 143 *multinational conglomerates have effectively cornered the market by building 'strategic reserves' ...* It is thought that one or more of the Japanese conglomerates involved in fishing have built up multi-thousand tonne supplies of deep-frozen bluefin tuna, and therefore there may be incentives for economically 'rational' actors to encourage a collapse in stocks.

CHAPTER 16: NEXT LEVEL

Page 145 *it is quite credible that the presence of a feline animal ...* Darwin, *On the Origin of Species*, Chapter III.

Page 145 *old maids keep cats ...* Huxley, *Collected Essays* (1892).

Page 147 *due to the narrowness of the area ...* Strabo, *Geographica* (first century BCE). For a more recent overview on the decline of this once biodiverse area, see Yackley, 'Turkey's marine crisis: "death knells are ringing for Sea of Marmara"', *Financial Times* (31 July 2021), which notes that only 'a generation ago, the Marmara's rich fauna included seahorses, poisonous scorpionfish and great white sharks'.

Page 147 *at times comprising around 90 per cent of the total biomass of the Black Sea* ... Grescoe, *Bottomfeeder: How the Fish on Our Plates Is Killing Our Planet* (2008), Chapter 4.

Page 148 *what our grandparents used as bait* ... Attributed to the Canadian fisheries biologist Daniel Pauly, who observed that fishing down the food web meant that 'what our grandparents called fish bait we now call calamari'.

Page 149 *Studies have concluded that declining species diversity is strongly correlated to* ... See, eg, Worm et al., 'Impacts of biodiversity loss on ocean ecosystem services', *Science* (November 2002), Volume 314, Issue 5800, which notes that 'rates of resource collapse increased and recovery potential, stability, and water quality decreased exponentially with declining diversity'.

Page 149 *hundreds of the world's biggest animals were driven to extinction* ... See, eg, Sandom et al., 'Global late Quaternary megafauna extinctions linked to humans, not climate change', *Proceedings of the Royal Society B* (2014), and also Ritchie, 'Wild mammals have declined by 85% since the rise of humans, but there is a possible future where they flourish', *OWID* (April 2021),

Page 149 *to keep every cog and wheel is the first precaution of intelligent tinkering* ... Leopold, 'The Conservation Ethic', *Sand County Almanac* (1949).

Page 149 *The division of labour* ... Smith, *The Wealth of Nations*, Book I, Chapter I.

Page 150 *a richly diverse system is far more efficient at absorbing atmospheric carbon* ... See, eg, Willoughby, 'Can predators have a big impact on carbon emissions calculations?', *Proceedings of the National Academy of Sciences* (March 2018), Volume 115. The author notes that 'Ecologists recently found that the amount of diversity in an ecosystem is itself linked to increased amounts of carbon storage'.

Page 151 *instability is an inherent and inescapable flaw of capitalism* ... Minsky, 'Global consequences of financial deregulation', presented at the Wallenberg Forum, Financial Fragility and Global Growth (2 October 1986).

CHAPTER 17: NET LOSS

Page 152 *the Mediterranean has one of the highest proportions of fish stocks* ... FAO, *The State of the World Fisheries and Aquaculture 2022*. This report notes that, of the areas the FAO monitors, the Mediterranean and Black Sea has the second-highest percentage of stocks (63.4 per cent) fished at unsustainable levels, with only the Southeast Pacific area having a higher proportion (at 66.7 per cent). Even in classical times writers were lamenting the loss of local fisheries – the first-century poet Juvenal, for example, complained that 'in the rage for gluttony our own seas have given out; the nets of the fish market are forever raking our home waters, and prevent Tyrrhenian fish from attaining their full size'.

Page 153 *the Great Pacific Garbage Patch* ... Somewhat appropriately, this giant trash vortex sits between the world's two largest carbon polluters, China and the US. China is estimated to contribute to around 30 per cent of global ocean plastic pollution, while the US is the only rich industrialised country in the top 20 ocean polluting nations (see Dunham, 'World's oceans clogged by millions of tons of plastic trash', *Scientific American* (12 February 2015)).

Page 153 *expanding at a steady rate* ... Some studies suggest that the Great Pacific Garbage Patch has increased 10-fold each decade since the start of the Great Acceleration (see, eg, Maser, *Interactions of Land, Ocean and Humans: A Global Perspective* (2014)).

Page 154 *less than 10 per cent of all plastic is recycled while around 14 per cent is incinerated* ... UN Environment Programme, *Drowning in Plastics* (21 October 2021).

Page 154 *The remaining mass of plastics, around 5 billion tonnes in total* ... See UN Environment Programme, *Drowning in Plastics*, which notes that in aggregate 'around 6.9 billion tonnes of primary plastic waste have been generated and hundreds of millions of tonnes are added each year'.

Page 154 *the volume of plastic pouring into the oceans* ... Although estimates vary widely, it is thought that somewhere between 8 million and 14 million tons of plastic waste ends up in the ocean each year (see, eg, IUCN Issues Brief, 'Marine plastic pollution', International Union for Conservation of Nature (November 2021) and Parker, 'The world's plastic pollution crisis explained', *National Geographic* (7 June 2019)).

Page 154 *Annual global production of plastics has soared from around 2 million tonnes* ... Ritchie and Roser, 'Plastic pollution', *OWID* (April 2022), note that since 1950 'annual [plastic] production has increased nearly 230-fold, reaching 460 million tonnes in 2019'.

Page 154 *the rate of plastics pollution into the ocean will double by 2030* ... United Nations Environment Programme, *From Pollution to Solution: A global assessment of marine litter and plastic pollution* (October 2021).

Page 154 *if trends in plastic consumption continue then by 2050 there will be a greater mass of plastic than fish in the planet's oceans* ... A paper by the World Economic Forum, 'The new plastics economy: rethinking the future of plastics' (January 2016), stated that '[i]n a business-as-usual scenario, the ocean is expected to contain 1 tonne of plastic for every 3 tonnes of fish by 2025, and by 2050, more plastics than fish (by weight)'. Note, however, that more recent studies suggest that '[t]he amount of plastic alone is greater than the overall mass of all terrestrial and marine animals left on the planet today' (Elhacham et al., 'Global human-made mass exceeds all living biomass', *Nature* (December 2020), Volume 588.

Page 154 *Microplastics are believed to interfere with animals' metabolic and reproductive systems* ... See, eg, D'Angelo, 'Microplastics: a threat for male fertility', *International Journal of Environmental Research and Public Health* (March 2021), Volume 18; Yuan et al., 'Human health concerns regarding microplastics in the aquatic environment – from marine to food systems', *Science of the Total Environment* (June 2022), Volume 823; and Demeneix, 'How fossil fuel-derived pesticides and plastics harm health, biodiversity, and the climate', *Lancet Diabetes Endocrinology* (June 2020), Volume 8, Number 6. The author of the last article notes that:

> The massive increase in chemical production since 1950 corresponds to a steep rise in the incidence of non-infectious diseases including obesity, diabetes ..., fertility problems, reproductive cancers ..., thyroid disease, neurodevelopmental disorders ..., and IQ loss. These disorders are certainly multifactorial; however, both epidemiology and experimentation has linked all these disorders to EDCs [endocrine-disrupting chemicals].

Page 154 *when washed ashore they are treated as toxic waste* ... See, eg, Hoare, 'Plastic pollution surfaces as whale killer', *The Times* (25 June 2017) which noted that '[t]he pristine white beluga whales of the St Lawrence river in Canada are now so contaminated that dead whales have to be disposed of as toxic waste'.

Page 155 *coral bleaching is a result of polyps expelling algae from their safe harbour* ... Coral bleaching typically occurs when a rise in water temperature causes symbiotic algae to overproduce reactive oxygen from photosynthesis, harming the coral hosts. As a result, corals expel algae from their bodies, but over the longer term the corals will starve without the energy generated by their algal symbionts.

Page 156 *it is likely that the rate of ocean warming has more than doubled over the last 30 years* … the IPCC *Special Report on the Ocean and Cryosphere in a Changing Climate*, Summary for Policymakers (2019) notes that '[s]ince 1993, the rate of ocean warming has more than doubled (likely)'.

Page 156 *Marine heatwaves … have become more frequent, more intense and more pervasive* … the IPCC *Special Report on the Ocean and Cryosphere in a Changing Climate*, 'Summary for Policymakers' (2019), notes that marine heatwaves 'over the period 1982 to 2016, have doubled in frequency and have become longer-lasting, more intense and more extensive (very likely)'.

Page 156 *up to 90 per cent of marine heatwaves in the period from 2006 to 2015 were attributable to human-caused global warming* … the IPCC *Special Report on the Ocean and Cryosphere in a Changing Climate*, 'Summary for Policymakers' (2019), notes that '[i]t is *very likely* that between 84–90% of marine heatwaves that occurred between 2006 and 2015 are attributable to the anthropogenic temperature increase'.

Page 156 *Some studies predict that the Great Barrier Reef will be largely dead by as soon as 2050* … Hughes et al., *Lethal Consequences: Climate Change Impacts on the Great Barrier Reef*, Climate Council of Australia (2018). The authors note that '[u]nder a business-as-usual scenario, where greenhouse gas pollution continues unabated and local stressors remain constant, mean coral cover is projected to decline to approximately 5 percent by 2050, with 72 percent of the decline attributable to climate change'.

Page 157 *An island in the Great Barrier Reef has already recorded the first known mammal extinction as a result of sea level rise* … In February 2019 the Bramble Cay melomys, a small nocturnal rodent, was declared extinct due to inundation from sea level rises.

Page 157 *the rate of sea level rise is very likely to exceed that of reef growth by 2050* … IPCC AR6 WGII, Chapter 3. The report notes that due to marine heatwaves, coral reefs 'are at risk of widespread decline, loss of structural integrity and transitioning to net erosion by mid-century due to increasing intensity and frequency of marine heatwaves', and that because of these impacts 'the rate of sea level rise is *very likely* to exceed that of reef growth by 2050, absent adaptation'.

Page 157 *Some studies predict that a combination of these feedback loops could lead to the sea level increasing by more than two metres by 2100* … See, eg, IPCC AR6 Synthesis Report (March 2023) which notes that '[d]ue to deep uncertainty linked to ice-sheet processes, global mean sea level rise above the likely range – approaching 2 m by 2100 and in excess of 15 m by 2300 under the very high GHG emissions scenario … cannot be excluded' (paragraph B.3.3).

Page 157 *around two-thirds of the world's cities with five million or more people are located in low-lying coastal areas* … McGranahan et al., 'The rising tide: assessing the risks of climate change and human settlements in low elevation coastal zones', *Environment and Urbanization* (April 2007), Volume 19, Issue 1.

Page 157 *tens or hundreds of millions of people exposed to coastal inundation* … McMichael et al., 'A review of estimating population exposure to sea-level rise and the relevance for migration', *Environmental Research Letters* (November 2020), Volume 15, Number 12.

Page 158 *hard coral numbers almost double on those reefs that are far from agricultural areas* … See, eg, 'Human Impact on the Great Barrier Reef', University of Michigan (April 2013). This is largely due to sediment runoff, which reduces the amount of light available for the algae within corals, and fertiliser runoff, which increases the amount of phytoplankton available to the larvae of coral predators such as crown-of-thorns starfish larvae.

Page 159 *ocean acidification has already increased by 30 per cent* … See UN Framework Convention on Climate Change, 'Rough Waters' (1 July 2022). This article quotes the Head of the United Nations Development Programme's Water and Ocean Governance Programme, who noted that '[t]he ocean has not acidified this fast or close to this fast for 55 million years'.

Page 159 *by 2100 the oceans of the world could be approximately 1.5 times more acidic* … See, eg, Liou, What Is Ocean Acidification? (June 2022), International Atomic Energy Agency.

Page 159 *these 'calcifying organisms' can exhibit slower growth rates* … See, eg, 'Effects of Ocean and Coastal Acidification on Marine Life', United States Environmental Protection Agency (November 2022).

Page 159 *the amount of dissolved oxygen in the Earth's oceans is decreasing* … See, eg, Aguirre, 'The Ocean Is Having Trouble Breathing', *Nautilus* (30 March 2022, https://nautil.us/the-ocean-is-having-trouble-breathing-15789/), who notes that '[g]iven what's already been emitted, and the secondary effects on the planet, the global deep oceans are already set to lose at least 10 percent of their oxygen'.

Page 159 *'risks of extirpation, extinction and ecosystem collapse' escalate rapidly* … IPCC AR6 WGII, Chapter 3.

Page 159 *The oceans of the world – which support more animal biomass than on land* … Ritchie, 'Oceans, land and deep subsurface: how is life distributed across environments?', *OWID* (26 April 2019). The author notes that 78 per cent of global animal biomass lives in marine environments, although, because almost all plant life is terrestrial, 86 per cent of living biomass exists on land.

CHAPTER 18: PLEASANT ISLAND

Page 164 *somewhere between a quarter and a third of the world's annual tuna supply* … When the Central Pacific Ocean fisheries are added to the Western Pacific Ocean fisheries that include Nauru, these fisheries together comprise almost 60 per cent of the global tuna yield (see Pacific Islands Forum Fisheries Agency, *The Western and Central Pacific Oceanic Fisheries management story* (2022)).

Page 164 *The Nauru Agreement Concerning Cooperation in the Management of Fisheries of Common Interest* … Member nations of The Nauru Agreement comprise Nauru, the Federated States of Micronesia, Kiribati, the Marshall Islands, Palau, Papua New Guinea, the Solomon Islands and Tuvalu.

Page 164 *one of the most effectively managed large-scale fisheries in the world* … Comment from the Head of the Water & Ocean Governance Programme, UNDP, in the Foreword to *The Western and Central Pacific Oceanic Fisheries management story* (2022).

Page 165 *Hardin's … article is one of the most-cited academic papers ever* … See, eg, Mildenberger, 'The Tragedy of the Tragedy of the Commons', *Scientific American* (23 April 2019), which notes that Hardin's essay has subsequently received around 40,000 academic citations.

Page 166 *when the capital development of a country becomes a by-product of the activities of a casino* ... Keynes, *The General Theory of Employment, Interest and Money*, Chapter 12.

Page 167 *the sector's share of GDP has tripled since 1950* ... Greenwood and Scharfstein, 'The growth of finance', *The Journal of Economic Perspectives* (Spring 2013), Volume 27, Number 2. The authors note that '[a]t its peak in 2006, the financial services sector contributed 8.3 percent to US GDP, compared to 4.9 percent in 1980 and 2.8 percent in 1950'. Similar trends are evident in other developed economies (see, eg, Haldane, 'The contribution of the financial sector – miracle or mirage?', speech to the Future of Finance conference, London (14 July 2010)).

Page 168 *Low-income countries, which on average depend on natural capital for almost half their total wealth* ... Lange et al., *The Changing Wealth of Nations 2018: Building a Sustainable Future*, World Bank (2018).

Page 168 *there is no simple answer to the problems of our capitalism* ... Minsky, *Stabilizing an Unstable Economy* (2008).

CHAPTER 19: SEA CHANGE

Page 169 *almost three-quarters of all global freshwater withdrawals flow to the agriculture sector* ... See FAO, *The state of the world's land and water resources for food and agriculture: Systems at breaking point* (2021), which notes that irrigation accounts for 72 per cent of all freshwater withdrawals.

Page 169 *irrigated land now provides 40 per cent of the global grain harvest* ... Although only representing around 20 per cent of total cultivated land, irrigated agriculture now provides around 40 per cent of the global grain harvest, and is therefore roughly twice as productive as rainfed agriculture (see 'Water in Agriculture', World Bank, https://www.worldbank.org/en/topic/water-in-agriculture).

Page 169 *only 2.5 per cent of all water in the world is fresh* ... 'The distribution of water on, in, and above the Earth', United States Geological Survey (25 October 2019).

Page 170 *freshwater withdrawals have more than tripled since the beginning of the Great Acceleration* ... See, eg, Ritchie and Roser, 'Water use and stress', *OWID* (July 2018), which notes that global freshwater withdrawals for agriculture, industry and domestic use has increased from 1.23 trillion cubic metres per year in 1950 to 3.99 trillion cubic metres per year in 2014.

Page 170 *It is estimated that over 2 billion people live in countries now suffering from 'water stress'* ... The UN notes that '2.3 billion people live in water-stressed countries, of which 733 million live in high and critically water-stressed countries' (see https://www.unwater.org/water-facts/water-scarcity).

Page 171 *within a decade its ancient aquifers were largely exhausted* ... In 2008 the Saudi leadership announced that, given the depletion of aquifers, the heavily subsidised wheat plantings would be reduced by an eighth each year, with wheat production expected to cease in 2016 (see Brown, 'The real threat to our future is peak water', *The Guardian* (6 July 2013)).

Page 171 *a quarter of all irrigated crop production relies on unsustainable groundwater extraction* ... World Wildlife Fund, 'Five facts you might not know about groundwater' (https://www.worldwildlife.org/stories/five-facts-you-might-not-know-about-groundwater).

Page 171 *estimated that over 20 million unregulated irrigation wells pump water from depleted groundwater sources* … Shiferaw, 'Addressing groundwater depletion: Lessons from India, the world's largest user of groundwater', World Bank (23 August 2021).

Page 172 *Freshwater fish as a proportion of the total piscatorial diet fell from 80 per cent* … Roberts, *The Ocean of Life*, Chapter 2.

Page 172 *global aquaculture production comprised less than 10 per cent of the total seafood catch until* … In 1980, global aquaculture production was an estimated 7.35 million tonnes and total wild caught seafood landed an estimated 68.26 million tonnes, compared to global aquaculture production of 106 million tonnes and total wild caught seafood landed an estimated 93.74 million tonnes in 2015 (see Ritchie, 'The world now produces more seafood from fish farms than wild catch', *OWID*, 13 September 2019).

Page 173 *[ITQs yield] only mixed results in terms of rebuilding fish biomass* … Garrity, 'Individual Transferable Quotas (ITQ), Rebuilding Fisheries and Short-Termism: How Biased Reasoning Impacts Management', *Systems* (March 2020), Volume 8, Number 1. The author notes that for rights-based fishery management 'the results are mixed and success varies by geographic region'.

Page 174 *if global fishing efforts were to be approximately halved then this would eventually double the fishable biomass* … See *The Sunken Billions Revisited: Progress and Challenges in Global Marine Fisheries*, World Bank (2017). The report notes that '[b]y implementing reform along a more moderate path, the attainable present value of net benefits would reach $1.2 trillion, or more than double the present value ($514 billion) of the current path'.

Page 174 *In a rare victory amid … the global extinction crisis* … See 'Tuna species recovering despite growing pressures on marine life – IUCN Red List', IUCN, 4 September 2021.

CHAPTER 20: THE WAR ON TERRA

Page 182 *worms have much bigger souls than anyone would suppose* … Letter from Charles Darwin to his son William (31 January 1881, https://www.darwinproject.ac.uk/letter/DCP-LETT-13034.xml).

Page 182 *responsible for almost all the calories consumed by humans* … See, eg, Kopittke et al., 'Soil and the intensification of agriculture for global food security' (2019), *Environment International*, Volume 132. The authors note that '[a]n estimated 98.8% of the daily calories consumed by humans come from soil'.

Page 183 *experience temperature levels that are intolerable to humans* … Pal and Eltahir, 'Future temperature in southwest Asia projected to exceed a threshold for human adaptability', *Nature Climate Change* (2016), Volume 6.

Page 183 *it is estimated that food production accounts for approximately 30 per cent of global energy consumption* … 'UN urges food sector to reduce fossil fuel use and shift to "energy-smart" agriculture', United Nations (30 November 2011, https://news.un.org/en/story/2011/11/396792-un-urges-food-sector-reduce-fossil-fuel-use-and-shift-energy-smart-agriculture).

Page 183 *intensive agriculture is the extraction of food from petroleum* … Quoted in Pilling, 'How oil affects the price of peas in China', *Financial Times* (13 January 2011).

Page 184 *the proportion of people in the world with not enough to eat has fallen* … See *The State of Food Security and Nutrition in the World 2022: Repurposing food and agricultural policies to make healthy diets more affordable*, FAO, IFAD, UNICEF, WFP and WHO (2022). The report notes that '[b]etween 702 and 828 million people were affected by hunger in 2021', and that '[p]rojections are that nearly 670 million people will still be facing hunger in 2030'.

Page 184 *In 1950 ... a quarter of West Germans were employed in farming-related occupations ...* see Coggan, *More: A History of the World Economy from the Iron Age to the Information Age*, Chapter 12.

Page 184 *the number of global citizens living in built-up urban areas has increased from 750 million ...* See, eg, '68% of the world population projected to live in urban areas by 2050, says UN', United Nations Department of Economic and Social Affairs (May 2018). Referencing the *Revision of World Urbanization Prospects* report, the article notes that the global urban population has increased from 751 million in 1950 to 4.2 billion in 2018, and that 55 per cent of the world's population lives in urban areas, with that proportion expected to increase to 68 per cent by 2050.

Page 184 *four-fifths of the planet's population now eat calories produced in another country ...* See, eg, 'The tables not yet turned', *The Economist* (9 May 2020), and Kinnunen et al., 'Local food crop production can fulfil demand for less than one-third of the population', *Nature Food* (2020), Volume 1.

Page 185 *the industrial food economy ...* Berry, *The Pleasures of Eating* (1989).

Page 185 *In Asia ... cereal production more than doubled between 1970 and 1995 ...* See, eg, Hazell, 'Think again: the Green Revolution', *Foreign Policy* (22 September 2009). The author notes this doubling of cereal production, from 310 million to 650 million tons per year, meant that '[a]lthough the population increased 60 percent over the same period, the rise in food production was so great that cereal and calorie availability per person actually increased nearly 30 percent, and wheat and rice became cheaper' and that this doubling of production was achieved with 'only a 4 percent increase in land use'.

Page 185 *households in the US and Britain ... now spend only around a tenth of their disposable income on food ...* The US Department of Agriculture, for example, noted that in 2021 American consumers spent an average of 10.3 per cent of their disposable personal income on food, with a consistent downward trajectory (other than a Covid-induced spike in 2020) in the share of disposable income spent on food since the early 1960s (see https://www.ers.usda.gov/data-products/ag-and-food-statistics-charting-the-essentials/food-prices-and-spending/). This trend conforms with 'Engel's law' – named after the German statistician Ernst Engel – which holds that as household income increases then the proportionate expenditure on food decreases.

Page 185 *just three types of grain ... now provide now provide over 40 per cent of the world's calories ...* FAO, 'Once neglected, these traditional crops are our new rising stars' (2018, https://www.fao.org/fao-stories/article/en/c/1154584/).

Page 185 *Global meat production has more than quadrupled since the early 1960s ...* Ritchie et al., 'Meat and dairy production', *OWID* (November 2019). The authors note that 'Europe's meat output has approximately doubled over this period, whilst North American output has increased 2.5-fold. Production increases in Asia, however, have been staggering: meat production has increased 15-fold since 1961'.

Page 186 *lifted his revolutionary idea from the overhead trolleys ferrying carcasses ...* See Ford and Crowther, *My Life and Work* (1922). Ford noted in this book that '[t]he idea came in a general way from the overhead trolley that the Chicago packers use in dressing beef'. Meatpacking was an early beneficiary of railroads and refrigeration technologies, which enabled the centralisation of livestock processing from the early 1860s.

Page 186 *porkmaking by machinery* ... Sinclair, *The Jungle*, Chapter 3 (1906).

Page 186 *it is estimated, for example, that just over 50 plants* ... Corkery and Bellany, 'The Food Chain's Weakest Link: Slaughterhouses', *The New York Times* (18 Apr 2020). Note that just under 50 years ago, the largest four beef-packing firms controlled around a quarter of the US market, compared to over 80 per cent today (see https://www.whitehouse. gov/briefing-room/blog/2021/09/08/addressing-concentration-in-the-meat-processing-industry-to-lower-food-prices-for-american-families/).

Page 186 *40 per cent of the world's commercial seed market is controlled by two firms* ... These companies being Bayer and Corteva (see *Food Barons 2022*, ETC Group (2022, https:// www.etcgroup.org/files/files/food-barons-2022-full_sectors-final_16_sept.pdf).

Page 186 *four companies account for more than 60 per cent of global pesticide sales* ... Syngenta, Bayer, BASF and Corteva together account for 62.3 per cent of all global pesticide revenues (see *Food Barons 2022*).

Page 186 *just four corporations comprise a third of global nitrogen fertiliser production* ... The Institute for Agriculture and Trade Policy, 'The Fertilizer Trap' (8 November 2022).

Page 186 *who together control around 90 per cent of the global grain trade* ... Comprising the 'ABCD' companies, Archer Daniels Midland, Bunge, Cargill and Louis Dreyfus (see, eg, Murphy et al., *Cereal Secrets: the world's largest grain traders and global agriculture*, Oxfam, August 2012).

Page 187 *probably carcinogenic to humans* ... see, eg, Kogevinas, 'Probable carcinogenicity of glyphosate', *BMJ* (8 April 2019).

Page 188 *two-fifths of farmland is classed as 'degraded' or 'seriously degraded'* ... See 'Chronic land degradation: UN offers stark warnings and practical remedies', United Nations Convention to Combat Desertification (26 April 2002).

Page 188 *Half of these additional two billion people will be born in sub-Saharan Africa and another 30 per cent in South Asia* ... See, eg, 'Population', United Nations (https://www. un.org/en/global-issues/population).

Page 189 *The green revolution has won a temporary success* ... Borlaug, 'The Green Revolution, Peace, and Humanity', Nobel Lecture (11 December 1970).

Page 189 *A 2020 paper in the journal* Science ... see Clark et al., 'Global food system emissions could preclude achieving the 1.5° and 2°C climate change targets', *Science* (2020), Volume 370, No. 6517.

CHAPTER 21: THE WORLD'S FARE

Page 191 *the US Secretary of Agriculture frankly admitted in the 1970s that 'food is a weapon'* ... Earl Butz, speaking at the World Food Conference in Rome (1974).

Page 191 *without the productivity boost provided by the Green Revolution this proportion would be materially higher* ... Ritchie, 'Yields vs land use: how the Green Revolution enabled us to feed a growing population', *OWID* (22 August 2017).

Page 191 *our planet would have lost four times more fertile forest land* ... Ritchie, 'Yields vs land use: how the Green Revolution enabled us to feed a growing population'.

Page 192 *livestock production accounts for over three-quarters of the world's agricultural land* ... Ritchie, 'How much of the world's land would we need in order to feed the global population with the average diet of a given country?', *OWID* (3 October 2017). Note that the UN Food and Agriculture Organization gives a slightly lower figure, estimating that 'livestock production accounts for 70 percent of all agricultural land and 30 percent of the land surface of the planet' (Steinfeld and Castel, *Livestock's Long Shadow: Environmental Issues and Options,* FAO, November 2006).

Page 192 *The average American eats well over 100 kilograms of meat each year* ... Ritchie et al., 'Meat and Dairy Production', *OWID* (November 2019). The global average consumption of meat is 43 kilograms per year.

Page 192 *Over three-quarters of the world's production of soy* ... Ritchie and Roser, 'Soy', *OWID* (https://ourworldindata.org/soy). The authors estimate that 77 per cent of global soy production is fed to livestock and only 7 per cent is directly consumed by humans, with the remainder used for biofuels, industry or vegetable oils.

Page 192 *more than 40 per cent of global grain production is fed to animals* ... Ritchie, 'If the world adopted a plant-based diet we would reduce global agricultural land use from 4 to 1 billion hectares', *OWID* (March 2021). Slightly under half (48 per cent) of global cereal consumption is consumed directly by humans, with 41 per cent used for animal feed, and the remaining 11 per cent used for biofuels.

Page 192 *animal production ... generates up to 60 times more greenhouse gases* ... See, eg, Ritchie, Rosado and Roser, 'Environmental impacts of food production', *OWID* (2022). The greenhouse gas emissions (measured in carbon dioxide equivalents) per kilogram of food product range are approximately 100 kilograms for beef, 40 kilograms for lamb and mutton, 12 kilograms for pigs, and 10 kilograms for poultry (although note that relative emission rates can vary significantly with differing methods of animal production). These rates compare to less than 2 kilograms for almost all fruit and vegetables, with cereals such as wheat recording an emissions rate of around 1.5 kilograms for each kilogram of final product.

Page 192 *how we eat determines, to a considerable extent* ... Berry, *The Pleasures of Eating.*

Page 193 *with the UN estimating that a third of all food produced globally is thrown away* ... The Economics of Ecosystems and Biodiversity, *TEEB for Agriculture & Food: an interim report,* United Nations Environment Programme (2015). The TEEB report estimated that approximately 1.3 billion tonnes of food produced for human consumption every year was lost or wasted, while more recent studies suggest the figure could be as high as 1.6 billion tonnes with an implied value of $1.2 trillion. In rich countries, the problem tends to be at the consumer end of the supply chain, whereas in poorer countries food loss occurs predominantly on farms and during storage.

Page 193 *You have just dined, and however scrupulously* ... Emerson, *The Conduct of Life* (1860).

Page 194 *The World Health Organization estimates that globally around 40 per cent of adults are overweight or obese* ... The *WHO Fact sheet – Obesity and overweight* (updated February 2018) states that '[g]lobally, 39% of adults aged 18 years and older were overweight or obese in 2016'. In the US, more than a third (36 per cent) of adults were classed as obese in 2016, compared to only 3.9 per cent in India (see Ritchie and Roser, 'Obesity', *OWID,* https://ourworldindata.org/obesity).

Page 194 *the share of children and adolescents ... at an unhealthy weight has more than quadrupled* ... The *WHO Fact sheet – Obesity and overweight* (updated February 2018) comments that 'the share of children and adolescents aged 5–19 who are overweight or obese has risen from 4% in 1975 to around 18% in 2016'. A 2017 study in the medical journal *The Lancet* noted that 'child and adolescent obesity is expected to surpass moderate and severe underweight by 2022' ('Worldwide trends in body-mass index, underweight, overweight, and obesity from 1975 to 2016', *The Lancet*, December 2017, Volume 390, Issue 10113).

Page 195 *it is thought that around three billion people still cannot afford a healthy diet* ... See, eg, FAO, *The State of Food Security and Nutrition in the World 2022*, Chapter 2, which states that '[a]lmost 3.1 billion people could not afford a healthy diet in 2020'.

Page 195 *More than two billion people suffer from 'hidden hunger'* ... Lowe, 'The global challenge of hidden hunger: perspectives from the field', *Proceedings of the Nutrition Society* (August 2021), Volume 80.

Page 195 *in the ant kingdom alone some scientists believe that at any given time there may be approximately 20 quintillion members* ... Schultheiss et al., 'The abundance, biomass, and distribution of ants on Earth', *Proceedings of the National Academy of Sciences* (September 2022), Volume 119.

Page 196 *three-quarters of farmed crops depend on pollinators to some extent* ... Ritchie, 'How much of the world's food production is dependent on pollinators?', *OWID* (August 2021).

Page 196 *pollination ... globally is worth somewhere between $235 billion and $577 billion each year* ... IPBES, *The assessment report on pollinators, pollination and food production* (2016).

Page 196 *the population of the world's terrestrial insects is decreasing by almost 10 per cent a decade* ... See, eg, van Klink et al., 'Meta-analysis reveals declines in terrestrial but increases in freshwater insect abundances', *Science* (April 2020), Volume 368, Issue 6489, which estimates 'an average decline of terrestrial insect abundance by ~9% per decade and an increase of freshwater insect abundance by ~11% per decade'.

Page 196 *This decadal decimation is due to* ... For bees, the insect usually indentured by humans to help fertilise crops, an additional stressor is a monotonous diet of pollen from monocrops.

Page 197 *Global pesticide use in the three decades from 1990 ... increased by approximately 80 per cent* ... *Pesticide Atlas: Facts and figures about toxic chemicals in agriculture* (October 2022, https://www.pan-europe.info/sites/pan-europe.info/files/public/resources/reports/PesticideAtlas2022_Web_20221010.pdf).

Page 197 *possibly the most significant threat that has been documented for climate change* ... See, eg, Myers et al., 'Increasing CO_2 threatens human nutrition', *Nature* (June 2014), Volume 510. One of the authors of this paper, Samuel Myers, made this comment in reference to the problem of nutrient deficiency due to global warming.

Page 197 *'You are what what you eat eats, too'* ... Pollan, *In Defense of Food: An Eater's Manifesto* (2008).

Page 197 *animals feeding on these less nourishing grains and plants produce less nourishing meat and milk* ... van Vliet et al., 'Health-promoting phytonutrients are higher in grass-fed meat and milk', *Frontiers in Sustainable Food Systems* (2021), Volume 4. The authors note that 'Grazing livestock on plant-species diverse pastures concentrates a wider variety and higher amounts of phytochemicals in meat and milk compared to grazing monoculture pastures, while phytochemicals are further reduced or absent in meat and milk of grain-fed animals'.

Page 197 *estimated that three-quarters of the food eaten by humans today comprise just 12 crops and five animal species* ... See, eg, 'What is happening to agrobiodiversity?', *FAO* (https://www.fao.org/3/y5609e/y5609e02.htm).

CHAPTER 22: LOSING THE PLOT

Page 199 *the economy shown by nature in her resources is striking* ... Darwin, *On the Various Contrivances by which British and Foreign Orchids are Fertilised by Insects, and on the Good Effects of Intercrossing* (1862), Chapter VI.

Page 200 *soils are the world's second-biggest carbon sink after the ocean* ... See, eg, Cho, 'Can soil help combat climate change?', Columbia Climate School (21 February 2018), who notes that '[t]he Earth's soils contain about 2,500 gigatons of carbon ... more than three times the amount of carbon in the atmosphere and four times the amount stored in all living plants and animals'.

Page 200 *topsoil contains more carbon than exists in terrestrial vegetation* ... FAO, 'World's most comprehensive map showing the amount of carbon stocks in the soil launched' (5 December 2017), which notes that 'the first 30 cm of soil contains around 680 billion tonnes of carbon – almost double the amount present in our atmosphere. This is a significant amount compared with the carbon stored in the whole vegetation (560 billion tonnes)'.

Page 201 *legislation empowering the 'annexation of any islands thought to be rich'* ... The *Guano Islands Act* was passed by the US Congress in 1856, permitting American citizens to take possession of unclaimed islands containing guano deposits.

Page 201 *causes the urban population to achieve an ever-growing preponderance* ... Marx, *Capital*, Volume 1.

Page 202 *all progress in capitalistic agriculture is a progress in the art ... of robbing the soil* ... Marx, *Capital*, Volume 1.

Page 203 *The amount of annual global 'throughput' ... has more than tripled since 1970* ... UNEP, 'Worldwide extraction of materials triples in four decades, intensifying climate change and air pollution' (20 July 2016). The related report, *Global Material Flows and Resource Productivity*, notes that '[t]he amount of primary materials extracted from the Earth rose from 22 billion tonnes in 1970 to a staggering 70 billion tonnes in 2010, with the richest countries consuming on average 10 times as many materials as the poorest countries and twice as much as the world average'. The report projects that by 2050 material throughput could rise to 180 billion tonnes per annum if present consumption trends are maintained.

Page 203 *The more a country starts its development on the foundation of modern industry* ... Marx, *Capital*, Volume 1, Chapter 15.

Page 204 *the Canadian scientist Vaclav Smil estimates that if average crop yields had remained* ... Smil, 'Nitrogen cycle and world food production' (https://www.vaclavsmil.com/wp-content/uploads/docs/smil-article-worldagriculture.pdf).

Page 205 *soil on cropping and intensively grazed lands estimated to be wearing away 100 to 1,000 times faster* ... FAO, Global Symposium on Soil Erosion (January 2019, https://www.fao.org/about/meetings/soil-erosion-symposium/key-messages/en/).

CHAPTER 23: ROOT PROBLEM

Page 207 *it is estimated that between half and two-thirds of the original carbon stored in cultivated soils has been released* ... Lal, 'Soil carbon sequestration to mitigate climate change', *Geoderma* (November 2004), Volume 123, Issues 1–2.

Page 207 *up to a third of excess historic carbon dioxide emissions are attributable to the degradation of soil organic matter* ... See, eg, Ontl et al., 'Soil Carbon Storage', *Nature Education Knowledge* (2012), Volume 3, Number 10.

Page 208 *warmer soils also produce greater amounts of carbon dioxide due to increased microbial activity* ... See, eg, Hicks et al., 'The whole-soil carbon flux in response to warming', *Science* (March 2017), Volume 233, Issue 6332, which notes that 4 degrees Celsius of additional warming could result in soils releasing as much as 37 per cent more carbon dioxide than normal.

Page 208 *the Arctic has warmed nearly four times faster than the rest of the world over the last 40 years* ... Rantanen et al., 'The Arctic has warmed nearly four times faster than the globe since 1979', *Communications Earth & Environment* (2022). At both ends of the globe, 'polar heatwaves' are becoming more frequent and severe – in 2022, for example, a research station on the Antarctic Plateau, previously declared 'the coldest place on Earth', recorded a temperature 40 degrees Celsius above the seasonal average.

Page 210 *mycorrhizal fungi can modify or withhold the export of minerals to plants* ... Whiteside et al., 'Mycorrhizal Fungi Respond to Resource Inequality by Moving Phosphorus from Rich to Poor Patches across Networks', *Current Biology* (June 2019), Volume 29, Issue 12. The authors found that in cases of high inequality of resources between organisms, '[f]ungi responded to high resource variation by (1) increasing the total amount of phosphorus distributed to host roots, (2) decreasing allocation to storage, and (3) differentially moving resources within the network from rich to poor patches'.

Page 211 *The incidence of 'evolutionary mismatch diseases' such as obesity and diabetes is increasing* ... See, eg, 'Obesity and disease tied to dramatic dietary changes', *Science Daily* (21 October 2020).

Page 213 *global glyphosate use has increased approximately 15-fold* ... Benbrook, 'Trends in glyphosate herbicide use in the United States and globally', *Environmental Sciences Europe* (February 2016), Volume 28, Number 3.

Page 213 *glyphosate may trigger epigenetic changes and other human health risks* ... See, eg, Bukowska et al., 'Glyphosate disturbs various epigenetic processes in vitro and in vivo – A mini review', *Science of The Total Environment* (December 2022), Volume 851, Part 2.

Page 213 *humans are increasingly viewed as 'holobionts'* ... See, eg, Gilbert et al., 'A Symbiotic View of Life: We Have Never Been Individuals', *The Quarterly Review of Biology* (December 2012), Volume 87, Number 4. The authors note that '[a]nimals cannot be considered individuals by anatomical or physiological criteria because a diversity of symbionts are both present and functional in completing metabolic pathways and serving other physiological functions', and conclude that '[f]or animals, as well as plants, there have never been individuals'.

Page 214 *Around 1.7 million undescribed viruses are estimated to reside in mammals and birds* ... Grange et al., 'Ranking the risk of animal-to-human spillover for newly discovered viruses', *Proceedings of the National Academy of Sciences* (April 2021), Volume 118, Number 15.

Page 214 *the first economic crisis of the Anthropocene* ... Tooze, 'We are living through the first crisis of the Anthropocene', *The Guardian* (7 May 2020).

Page 215 *reduced global output more than any event since the Great Depression* ... See, eg, 'COVID-19 to slash global economic output by $8.5 trillion over next two years', United Nations Department of Economic and Social Affairs (2020).

Page 215 *requiring primary producers to dispose of millions of 'slaughter-ready' animals* ... The US National Pork Producers Council estimated, for example, that in mid-2020 more than

10 million pigs exceeded the industry's processing capacity, resulting in these 'surplus hogs' subject to improvised slaughter methods – including what is called 'ventilation shutdown', in which animals are deprived of air, food and water and sealed chambers are heated (see Woodhouse, 'Pigs to the slaughter', *Tablet* magazine (21 December 2021)).

Page 215 *up to three-quarters of human viruses are zoonotic in origin* … See, eg, 'Zoonoses: a closer look at our relationship with animals', BMJ Case Reports (https://casereports.bmj.com/pages/zoonoses-a-closer-look-at-our-relationship-with-animals/).

Page 215 *causing the cross-species transmission of their associated viruses an estimated 4,000 times* … Carlson et al., 'Climate change increases cross-species viral transmission risk', *Nature* (April 2022), Volume 607, Issue 7919.

Page 216 *annual global spending in the range of $20 billion to $30 billion* … Dobson et al., 'Ecology and economics for pandemic prevention', *Science* (July 2020), Volume 369, Issue 6502. The authors estimate that preventive actions such as reducing deforestation and curbing wildlife trafficking would cost in the order of $22 billion to $31 billion per year.

CHAPTER 24: WOOD WIDE WEB

Page 217 *if the eye attempts to follow the flight* … Entry from Darwin's *Beagle* diary, 28 February 1832.

Page 217 *nothing more nor less than a view in the Arabian Nights* … Entry from Darwin's *Beagle* diary, 1 March 1832.

Page 218 *I cannot persuade myself that a beneficent and omnipotent God would have* … Letter from Darwin to the botanist Asa Gray, 22 May 1860.

Page 218 *the number of native Americans across both continents had declined by 90 per cent* … Koch et al., 'Earth system impacts of the European arrival and Great Dying in the Americas after 1492', *Quaternary Science Reviews* (March 2019), Volume 207.

Page 219 *Wherever the European has trod, death seems to pursue* … Darwin, *The Voyage of the Beagle* (1839), Chapter 19.

Page 219 *We should almost say that the European is to the other races* … Tocqueville, *Democracy in America* (1835), Volume I, Chapter XVIII.

Page 220 *contributing to a period of global cooling through to the nineteenth century* … Koch et al., 'Earth system impacts of the European arrival and Great Dying in the Americas after 1492', *Quaternary Science Reviews* (March 2019), Volume 207. The authors conclude that 'the Great Dying of the Indigenous Peoples of the Americas led to the abandonment of enough cleared land in the Americas that the resulting terrestrial carbon uptake had a detectable impact on both atmospheric CO_2 and global surface air temperatures in the two centuries prior to the Industrial Revolution'. This climate anomaly was likely also impacted by other global factors, such as reforestation in parts of the Old World still recovering from the bubonic scythe of the Black Death.

Page 220 *it is estimated that the world has lost a third of its forests since the Agricultural Revolution* … Ritchie & Roser, 'Deforestation and Forest Loss', *OWID* (2021, https://ourworldindata.org/deforestation).

Page 220 *approximately half of all global forest loss occurred in the period from the dawn of the Agricultural Revolution until 1900* … Ritchie & Roser, 'Deforestation and Forest Loss'.

Page 220 *when The Wealth of Nations was published … forest covered approximately half of all habitable land* … Ritchie & Roser, 'Deforestation and Forest Loss'.

Page 221 *the Amazonian rainforest ... is believed to have switched from a carbon sink to a carbon source* ... Gatti et al., 'Amazonia as a carbon source linked to deforestation and climate change', *Nature* (July 2021), Volume 595, Issue 7867.

Page 221 *net tropical forest loss in the period 2010 to 2020 estimated at around 50 million hectares* ... Ritchie & Roser, 'Deforestation and Forest Loss'. The authors note that over the decade to 2020, 53 million hectares of tropical forest was lost, but there was a net gain of 6 million hectares in temperate regions.

Page 222 *should present trends continue, up to 60 per cent of the Amazonian rainforest could disappear by 2050* ... See, eg, Castilla-Rubio, 'Nature-inspired design: how the Amazon can help us solve humanity's greatest challenges', World Economic Forum paper (25 June 2017). The author explains that 'Earth system models predict that up to 60% of the Amazon forests could vanish by 2050, with most of the forest replaced by dry savannas with far fewer species and much less carbon stored'.

Page 222 *high-latitude temperate and boreal regions have recorded a net gain in forest area since 1990* ... Ritchie and Roser, 'Deforestation and Forest Loss'.

Page 222 *Around 30 per cent of tropical deforestation is driven by the production of commodities that are then exported* ... See Ritchie and Roser, 'Deforestation and Forest Loss'. The authors note that 29 per cent of deforestation in the tropics is attributable to the production of goods that are internationally traded.

Page 223 *led to a flood that killed thousands* ... The flood resulted in 3,704 deaths and was estimated to have caused $24 billion in economic loss. The Yangtze, Asia's longest river, has been subject to periodic flooding which in the past has resulted in millions of deaths. The Three Gorges Dam on the Yangtze – the world's largest hydroelectric power station, completed in 2012 – was constructed primarily for electricity generation purposes, but a subsidiary function is also flood control.

Page 224 *over 600 million hectares ... already pledged for reforestation* ... Dooley et al., *The Land Gap Report 2022* (https://www.landgap.org/wp-content/uploads/2022/11/Land-Gap-Report_FINAL.pdf). The authors note that '[m]ore than half of the total land area pledged for carbon removal – 633 million hectares – involves reforestation' and that '[t]he total area of land needed to meet projected biological carbon removal in national climate pledges is almost 1.2 billion hectares – equivalent to current global cropland'.

Page 224 *their territories ... are thought to cover around a third of the Earth's terrestrial surface* ... Diaz et al., *The Global Assessment Report on Biodiversity and Ecosystem Services*, IPBES (2019). The authors note that indigenous communities hold or manage lands covering at least 32 per cent of the planet's terrestrial surface.

Page 224 *Recent research indicates that primary forests are in fact social networks built on reciprocity and nutrient exchange* ... See, eg, the work of Suzanne Simard, who argues that forests are social superorganisms that exchange resources and provide mutual support (https://longnow.org/ideas/mother-trees-and-social-forest/).

Page 225 *Studies show that traditional communities with secure land rights tend to outperform* ... See, eg, Diaz et al., *The Global Assessment Report on Biodiversity and Ecosystem Services*, IPBES (2019). The authors note that '[e]vidence to date shows that IPs [Indigenous Peoples] and LCs [Local Communities] with secure land rights vastly outperform both governments and private landholders on issues relating to deforestation, biodiversity conservation, sustainable food production and other land-use priorities'. They additionally note, however, that while indigenous communities 'exercise customary rights to at least half of the world's lands, less than 20 percent of this area is formally recognized as owned by or designated for communities, rendering them and their territories vulnerable to the surging global demand for land'.

Page 225 *The woodland is generally so open that a person on horseback* ... Darwin, *The Voyage of the Beagle* (1839), Chapter 19.

CHAPTER 25: GROUNDED

Page 227 *More than half of all seafood consumed* ... Ritchie, 'The world now produces more seafood from fish farms than wild catch', *OWID* (13 September 2019).

Page 227 *caged poultry comprises just over 70 per cent of all bird life* ... Bar-On et al., 'The biomass distribution on Earth', *Proceedings of the National Academy of Sciences* (2018), Volume 115, Number 25. The authors note that 'the biomass of domesticated poultry (≈0.005 Gt C, dominated by chickens) is about threefold higher than that of wild birds'.

Page 228 *The Food and Agriculture Organization projects that global food demand will rise* ... FAO, *Global agriculture towards 2050*, How to Feed the World Forum (12–13 October 2009).

Page 228 *more than 100 million tonnes of synthetic nitrogen fertiliser, around 50 million tonnes of phosphate and more than 40 million tonnes of potassium* ... FAO, *World fertilizer trends and outlook to 2022* (2019). The FAO estimates that in 2022 global demand for nitrogen fertiliser would be approximately 112,000 tonnes, phosphorus 49,000 tonnes, and potassium 40,000 tonnes.

Page 228 *phosphorus and potassium are locked in the Earth's crust in limited quantities* ... Because of its non-gaseous environmental cycle, there is no ready substitute for phosphorus. As Isaac Asimov noted, 'We may be able to substitute nuclear power for coal power, and plastics for wood ... but for phosphorus there is neither substitute nor replacement' (Asimov, *Life's Bottleneck* (1962)).

Page 228 *Almost 90 per cent of global phosphorus deposits are found in just five countries* ... An estimated 85 to 90 per cent of the world's phosphorus reserves are found in Morocco, China, South Africa, Jordan and the US.

Page 228 *Some studies predict that 'peak phosphorus'* ... Cordell et al., 'The story of phosphorus: global food security and food for thought', *Global Environmental Change* (May 2009), Volume 19, Issue 2. The authors note that 'phosphate rock ... is a non-renewable resource and current global reserves may be depleted in 50–100 years'.

Page 230 *global meat production has more than tripled* ... Ritchie et al., 'Meat and dairy production', *OWID* (November 2019). The authors note that global meat production in 1970 is estimated to have been 99.5 million tonnes, compared with an estimated 337.2 million tonnes in 2020.

Page 230 *Over three-quarters of the world's agricultural land is now used for* ... Ritchie, 'Half of the world's habitable land is used for agriculture', *OWID* (11 November 2019).

Page 230 *For grain-fed livestock, every 100 calories of grain provides* ... See 'The Future of Food', *National Geographic* (July 2019, https://www.nationalgeographic.com/foodfeatures/feeding-9-billion/).

Page 231 *if the world's human population did not consume animal products then* ... Ritchie, 'If the world adopted a plant-based diet we would reduce global agricultural land use from

4 to 1 billion hectares', *OWID* (4 March 2021). The author notes that '[i]n the hypothetical scenario in which the entire world adopted a vegan diet ... researchers estimate that our total agricultural land use would shrink from 4.1 billion hectares to 1 billion hectares ... That's equal to an area the size of North America and Brazil combined'.

Page 231 *a diet heavy in primary animal products and processed meats* ... See, eg, Mayo Clinic, 'Meatless meals: the benefits of eating less meat' (https://www.mayoclinic.org/healthy-lifestyle/nutrition-and-healthy-eating/in-depth/meatless-meals/art-20048193).

Page 231 *greenhouse gas emissions for some forms of beef production* ... Ritchie, 'The carbon footprint of foods: are differences explained by the impacts of methane?', *OWID* (10 March 2020). The author estimates that the global average emissions for 1 kilogram of beef from non-dairy beef herds is 100 kilograms of carbon dioxide equivalent, with around half of this comprising methane emissions. With the exception of rice, which emits an average 4.5 kilograms of carbon dioxide equivalent due to cultivation in waterlogged soils that produce methane, other plant-based foods produce less than 2 kilograms of carbon dioxide equivalent per kilogram of final product.

Page 231 *since the early 1960s the global cattle herd has increased almost two-thirds* ... Based on FAO estimates, the global cattle herd has increased from 942 million in 1961 to 1.53 billion in 2020 (see https://ourworldindata.org/grapher/cattle-livestock-count-heads?tab=chart).

Page 232 *Methane emitted by animals ... is recycled carbon* ... Methane is a 'flow gas' that is short-lived and removed from the atmosphere at a far quicker pace than carbon dioxide, which is a long-lived 'stock gas' that once emitted continues to accumulate in the atmosphere.

Page 232 *Prior to the arrival of Columbus* ... see, eg, Hristov, 'Historic, pre-European settlement, and present-day contribution of wild ruminants to enteric methane emissions in the United States', *Journal of Animal Science* (2012), Volume 90, Number 4, which estimates that ruminant animals in pre-contact America emitted almost as much methane each year as America's entire herd of farmed livestock (including approximately 90 million cattle) now releases annually.

Page 233 *the Earth's soils contain more than three times the amount of carbon in the atmosphere* ... Ontl et al., 'Soil Carbon Storage', *Nature Education Knowledge* (2012), Volume 3, Number 10. The authors note that '[t]he soil carbon pool is approximately 3.1 times larger than the atmospheric pool of 800 GT ... Only the ocean has a larger carbon pool, at about 38,400 GT of C, mostly in inorganic forms'.

Page 233 *up to 70 per cent of soil organic carbon has been lost from cultivated land* ... Zomer et al., 'Global sequestration potential of increased organic carbon in cropland soils', *Scientific Reports* (2017), Volume 7, Number 15554.

Page 235 *Civilization is not ... the enslavement of a stable and constant earth* ... Leopold, 'The Conservation Ethic', *Sand County Almanac*.

Page 235 *Studies suggest that regenerative farming practices* ... For example, a 30-year study by America's Rodale Institute found that – after an initial decline in yields during the first few years of transition from conventional high-input production methods – organically produced corn and soybeans 'rebounded to match or surpass the conventional system' (see Moss and Bittman, 'Bringing farming back to nature', *The New York Times* (26 June 2018)). Evidence also shows that on an acreage basis smaller-scale polyculture farms that 'stack' different forms of agriculture production can be more productive than large-scale monocultures (see, eg, Montgomery, *Dirt* (2007), Chapter 7).

Page 235 *regeneratively farmed crops and pasture-fed livestock raised on low-input grassland also tend to record higher levels of* ... See, eg, Montgomery et al., 'Soil health and nutrient density: preliminary comparison of regenerative and conventional farming', *PeerJ* (2022). The authors assert that regenerative farming practices produce crops with 'higher soil organic matter levels, soil health scores, and higher levels of certain vitamins, minerals, and phytochemicals'. In respect of livestock, other studies suggest that

> [i]n direct contrast to grain-fed and grain-finished meat from intensive systems, wholly pasture-fed meat is high in beta carotene, calcium, selenium, magnesium and potassium and vitamins E and B, and conjugated linoleic acid (CLA) – a powerful anti-carcinogen. It is also high in the long-chain omega-3 fatty acid DHA, which is vital for human brain development but extremely difficult for vegans to obtain.

(Tree, 'If you want to save the world, veganism isn't the answer', *The Guardian* (25 August 2018).)

CHAPTER 26: THE ILLTH OF NATIONS

Page 239 *marked the near-complete demise of the dinosaurs* ... This event, known as the Cretaceous–Paleogene extinction event, caused the extinction of all non-avian dinosaurs.

Page 239 *until very recently boasted a greater variety of organisms than at any other time in the planet's history* ... Ceballos et al., 'The Sixth Extinction Crisis Loss of Animal Populations and Species', *Journal of Cosmology* (June 2010), Volume 8. The authors note that:

> Currently, the number of species is thought to be the largest in the history of life; i.e. never before have so many different kinds of organisms coexisted ... Over the past few centuries, however, human actions such as habitat destruction, toxic pollutant release, overharvesting, and transport of invasive species have caused a massive decline in biodiversity ... and greenhouse gas emissions may make the problem even more acute.

Page 239 *a period that scientists say could last another 50,000 years* ... See, eg, Berger and Loutre, 'An exceptionally long interglacial ahead?', *Science* (August 2002), Volume 297, Issue 5585.

Page 240 *The real price of every thing* ... *is the toil and trouble of acquiring it* ... Smith, *The Wealth of Nations*, Book I, Chapter V.

Page 240 *fossil fuels have been a crucial contributor to the spectacular economic growth* ... See, eg, Ayres et al., 'The underestimated contribution of energy to economic growth', *Structural Change and Economic Dynamics* (December 2013), Volume 27.

Page 241 *the solar income budget constraint* ... Daly, *Steady-State Economics*, Chapter 2.

Page 241 *each barrel of oil* ... *provides the energy equivalent of* ... See, eg, Hagens, 'Economics for the future – Beyond the superorganism', *Ecological Economics* (March 2020), Volume 169, Number 106520. Estimates vary widely based on the assumptions made, but the author sets out his calculation as follows:

> One barrel of crude oil can perform about 1700 kW h of work. A human laborer can perform about 0.6 kW h in one workday ... Simple arithmetic reveals it takes over 11 years of human labor to do the same work potential in a barrel of oil. Even

if humans are 2.5x more efficient at converting energy to work, the energy in one barrel of oil substitutes approximately 4.5 years of physical human labor.

Page 242 *The world's first professional economist* ... In 1805 Malthus became the first Professor of Political Economy in Britain with his appointment to the East India Company College.

Page 242 *population growth would outstrip 'the power in the earth to produce subsistence for man'* ... Malthus, *An Essay on the Principle of Population* (1798), Chapter 1.

Page 242 *human populations increased in what he called 'a geometrical ratio'* ... Malthus, *An Essay on the Principle of Population*, Chapter 1. Malthus commented that:

> Population, when unchecked, increases in a geometrical ratio. Subsistence increases only in an arithmetical ratio. A slight acquaintance with numbers will shew the immensity of the first power in comparison of the second.

Page 243 *in 1798, the world contained around 1 billion people* ... The global population is believed to have reached 1 billion people in 1804. Since that time, the world population has increased in 1 billion increments in 1927, 1960, 1974, 1987, 1999, 2011 and 2022.

Page 243 *over the course of the Great Acceleration the quantity of calories available per person globally has increased by around a third* ... Roser et al., 'Food supply', *OWID* (https://ourworldindata.org/food-supply). The authors note that the average daily per capita energy supply from all foods has increased from an estimated 2,181 kilocalories in 1961 to 2,920 kilocalories in 2019, with Asia recording the largest increase in food supply, increasing by around 60 per cent from 1,808 kilocalories to 2,896 over the same period.

Page 243 *although the world population has more than tripled* ... Roser et al., 'World population growth', *OWID* (https://ourworldindata.org/world-population-growth). In 1950, the world population was estimated to be 2.5 billion people.

Page 243 *world output as measured by GDP ... has increased more than 10-fold* ... Roser, 'Economic growth', *OWID* (https://ourworldindata.org/economic-growth). The author notes that global GDP in 1950 was an estimated $9.25 trillion, compared to $108 trillion in 2015.

Page 243 *annual energy consumption and carbon dioxide emissions have increased more than six-fold* ... See Ritchie and Roser, 'CO$_2$ emissions' and 'Energy production and consumption', *OWID* (https://ourworldindata.org/co2-emissions and https://ourworldindata.org/energy-production-consumption, respectively). The authors note that in 1950 an estimated 6 billion tonnes of carbon dioxide was emitted, compared to the 2021 figure of 37 billion tonnes. In terms of global primary energy consumption, the estimated figures are 28,500 terawatt hours in 1950, compared to 176,400 terawatt hours in 2021.

Page 243 *annual freshwater withdrawals have more than tripled* ... Ritchie and Roser, 'Water use and stress', *OWID* (https://ourworldindata.org/water-use-stress). The authors estimate that global freshwater withdrawals for agriculture, industry and domestic uses was 1.23 trillion cubic metres in 1950, compared to approximately 4 trillion cubic metres today.

Page 243 *consumption of synthetic nitrogen has increased more than 30-fold* ... Smil, *Nitrogen cycle and world food production* (https://www.vaclavsmil.com/wp-content/uploads/docs/smil-article-worldagriculture.pdf). The author notes that nitrogen production from ammonia synthesis rose from an estimated 3.7 million tonnes in 1950 to approximately 133 million tonnes in 2010, with around three-quarters of the ammonia used as fertiliser.

Page 243 *the dry mass of the Earth's living organisms … is now less than the weight of human-made products* … Elhacham et al., 'Global human-made mass exceeds all living biomass', *Nature* (December 2020), Volume 588.

Page 245 *Distinctions must be kept in mind between quantity and quality of growth* … Kuznets, 'How to Judge Quality' in Croly (editor), *The New Republic* (1962), Volume 147.

Page 245 *GDP is more an index of the welfare of capitalism* … See Hickel, *Less Is More: How Degrowth Will Save the World* (2020).

Page 245 *Richard Easterlin published a paper* … Easterlin, 'Does economic growth improve the human lot? Some empirical evidence', in David and Reder, *Nations and Households in Economic Growth: Essays in Honor of Moses Abramovitz* (1974).

Page 246 *it takes all the running you can do* … Carroll, *Through the Looking-Glass* (1871), Chapter II. In a slightly different context, Joan Robinson, one of Keynes's students, illustrated this dynamic by citing the example of a crowd watching a parade, in which 'anyone can get a better view of the procession if he stands on a chair … [but] if they all get up on chairs no-one has a better view' (Robinson, *Collected Economic Papers* (1951), Volume 1).

Page 247 *on average three times more material now has to be gouged from the ground* … United Nations Environment Programme, & International Resource Panel. *Recycling Rates of Metals: A Status Report* (2011).

Page 247 *the 'Energy Return on Investment' … has fallen from around 100:1* … See, eg, Hall et al., 'EROI of different fuels and the implications for society', *Energy Policy* (January 2014), Volume 64.

Page 247 *certain cells of the body enhance their fitness at the expense of the organism as a whole* … Aktipis, 'Cooperation and cheating across systems: From human sharing to multicellularity' (Lecture, Department of Human Evolutionary Biology, Harvard University, 13 November 2014).

CHAPTER 27: EIGHT BILLION ASTRONAUTS

Page 248 *in reality nothing on this planet is an individual* … See, eg, Gilbert et al., 'A Symbiotic View of Life: We Have Never Been Individuals', *The Quarterly Review of Biology* (December 2012), Volume 87, Number 4. The authors note that '[a]nimals cannot be considered individuals by anatomical or physiological criteria because a diversity of symbionts are both present and functional in completing metabolic pathways and serving other physiological functions', and suggest that the 'holobiont' is a 'critically important unit of anatomy'.

Page 252 *New York City was confronted with a choice to either build a water filtration system* … Chiusano, 'The deal that keeps New York's water safe to drink', *amNY* (20 February 2018).

Page 252 *The things which have the greatest value in use have frequently little or no value in exchange* … Smith, *The Wealth of Nations*, Book I, Chapter IV.

Page 253 *the rate of material efficiency use … has in fact decreased over the last three decades* … 'Worldwide extraction of materials triples in four decades, intensifying climate change and air pollution', United Nations Environment Programme (July 2016).

Page 254 *The UN Environment Programme notes that a true decoupling of escalating material use* … UNEP, 'Worldwide extraction of materials triples in four decades, intensifying climate change' (20 July 2016).

Page 254 *The scientist Vaclav Smil notes that Project Apollo* … Smil, 'Decarbonization is our costliest challenge' (October 2022), *IEEE Spectrum* magazine.

Page 254 *The McKinsey Global Institute has conservatively estimated* ... Krishnan et al., *The net-zero transition*, McKinsey & Company (January 2022). Note, however, that net additional expenditure – that is, after taking account of existing infrastructure that would need to be replaced or upgraded in any case over this period – would be significantly lower (see, eg, 'Have economists led the world's environmental policy astray?', *The Economist*, 26 March 2022).

Page 255 *media coverage of the effects of global warming was around eight times higher* ... Legagneux et al., 'Our house is burning: discrepancy in climate change vs biodiversity coverage in the media as compared to scientific literature', *Frontiers in Ecology and Evolution* (January 2018), Volume 5, Article 175.

CHAPTER 28: GREENPRINT

Page 256 *He knew nothing of characters* ... Buchan, *Adam Smith and the Pursuit of Perfect Liberty*, Chapter 2.

Page 256 *The qualities most useful to ourselves are* ... *superior reason and understanding* ... Smith, *The Theory of Moral Sentiments*, Part IV, Chapter II.

Page 257 *complex biological systems rely on enforcement mechanisms to suppress selfish behaviour* ... See, eg, Ågren et al., 'Enforcement is central to the evolution of cooperation', *Nature Ecology & Evolution* (June 2019), Volume 3, Number 7.

Page 257 *a program for destroying collective structures which may impede pure market logic* ... Bourdieu, 'The essence of neoliberalism', *Le Monde Diplomatique* (1 December 1998).

Page 259 *a particular resource is almost always exhausted if extraction decisions are made individually* ... Hauser et al., 'Cooperating with the future', *Nature* (June 2014), Volume 511.

Page 261 *are unable, or not yet ready, to achieve the scale of removal* ... IPCC AR6, WGI, Chapter 6, FAQ 5.3.

Page 262 *less than 3 per cent of the Earth's land surface can be considered to be 'faunally intact'* ... Plumptre et al., 'Where might we find ecologically intact communities?', *Frontiers for Global Change* (April 2021), Volume 4. The authors estimate that 'no more than 2.9% of the land surface can be considered to be faunally intact'.

Page 262 *view ourselves* ... *with the eyes of other people* ... Smith, *The Theory of Moral Sentiments*, Part III, Chapter I.

Page 263 *research suggests that members of unequal societies devote a greater proportion of their resources to competitive consumption* ... See, eg, Walasek et al., 'Income inequality and status seeking: searching for positional goods in unequal US states', *Psychological Science* (March 2015), Volume 26, Issue 4.

Page 263 *if 'the great empire of China* ... *was suddenly swallowed up by an earthquake'* ... Smith, *The Theory of Moral Sentiments*, Part III, Chapter II.

CHAPTER 29: EVERY MAN FOR HIMSELF?

Page 264 *not 'able to make this story clear enough for the public'* ... Borenstein, 'James Hansen wishes he wasn't so right about global warming', *The Associated Press* (18 June 2018).

Page 267 *In 1992 a majority of Nobel science laureates sounded a 'Warning to Humanity'* ... Kendall et al., 'World Scientists' Warning to Humanity', The Union of Concerned Scientists (16 July 1992).

Page 267 *a group of scientists issued a '"code red" on planet Earth'* ... Ripple et al., 'World scientists' warning of a climate emergency 2022' (2022), *BioScience*, Volume 72, Issue 12.

Page 267 *William Nordhaus claimed with pinpoint precision that 87 per cent of the US economy would be 'negligibly affected by climate change'* ... Nordhaus, 'To slow or not to slow: The economics of the greenhouse effect', *The Economic Journal* (July 1991), Volume 101, Number 407. Nordhaus concluded that 'for the bulk of the economy ... it is difficult to find major direct impacts of the projected climate changes over the next 50 to 75 years'.

Page 267 *today many of his peers remain just as sanguine* ... See, eg, Warren et al., 'Global and regional aggregate damages associated with global warming of 1.5 to 4 °C above pre-industrial levels', *Climatic Change* (2021), Volume 168, Article 24. The authors estimated in this paper that global warming of 2 degrees Celsius above pre-industrial levels would result in additional damages equivalent to only 0.4 per cent of world GDP.

Page 267 *Food production ... comprises less than 1 per cent of GDP in many developed economies* ... In the US, for example, the 'Agriculture, forestry and fishing' sector category comprised 0.9 per cent of GDP in 2021, compared to the 'Finance and insurance' category, which comprised 8.4 per cent of GDP (see US Bureau of Economic Analysis; https://www.bea.gov). The agriculture sector's contribution to GDP varies among countries – generally ranging between 0.5 and 2 per cent in developed economies, while in low-income countries the proportion tends to be around 25 per cent.

Page 268 *would then set in motion changes that would be 'irreversible for millennia'* ... IPCC, *Special Report on the Ocean and Cryosphere in a Changing Climate*, Technical Summary (2019), Chapter 6.

Page 268 *economic damage from adverse weather events accelerate* ... See 'Natural disasters in past decade broke records for economic, insured losses', *Insurance Journal* (22 January 2020). The author notes that the insurer Aon estimated that damages from natural disasters grew from around $1.8 trillion in the first decade of the twenty-first century to almost $3 trillion over the second decade.

Page 269 *both the rate of increase in greenhouse gas emissions and the absolute magnitude of these gases are higher than at any other time over the last 800,000 years* ... See, eg, Bauska, 'Ice cores and climate change', British Antarctic Survey (30 June 2022). The author notes that '[t]he fastest natural increase [of carbon dioxide] measured in older ice cores is around 15ppm (parts per million) over about 200 years. For comparison, atmospheric CO_2 is now rising 15ppm every 6 years'.

Page 270 *the affluent citizens of the world are responsible for most environmental impacts* ... Wiedmann et al., 'Scientists' warning on affluence', *Nature Communications*, Volume 11, Article 3107.

Page 270 *The top 1 per cent of global emitters are estimated to have a carbon footprint more than 1,000 times greater than the bottom 1 per cent* ... Cozzi et al., 'The world's top 1% of emitters produce over 1000 times more CO_2 than the bottom 1%', IEA (22 February 2023).

Page 270 *the US and the European Union ... together ... account for just over half of all cumulative carbon dioxide emissions since 1750* ... Ritchie, 'Who has contributed most to global CO_2 emissions?', *OWID* (October 2019).

ACKNOWLEDGMENTS

While writing this book I have built up substantial debts of gratitude to many people, but there are three in particular I would like to thank for their early support.

The first is my indefatigable agent, Jeanne Ryckmans – hustler extraordinaire, a creative whirlwind in her own right, and a reliable source of both wisecracks and wise counsel. The second is Natasha Solomun, to whom I confided an outline of *Eating the Earth* a few years ago, and whose reaction persuaded me there might be something in the idea. And last but not least, Charlie Massy – a gentleman and a gentle man, although full of fire when it comes to protecting the good things on this planet – for his unwavering faith in this book.

My sincere thanks also to the team at University of Queensland Press for their professionalism, patience and encouragement – especially Madonna Duffy and the stellar editorial team of Felicity Dunning, Nikki Lusk and Ian See.

And finally, a shoutout to my kids. I'm tempted to lift PG Wodehouse's line that without them this book would have been finished in half the time – but the truth is that it was their enthusiasm and interest that sustained me, and that this book was written for them.